HOW LIFE IMITATES CHESS

Garry Kasparov is the greatest chess player of our time, world champion at the age of twenty-one and the number one ranked player in the world for two decades, longer by many years than any other player in the history of organised international competition. He made international front-page news when, in 1996, he accepted a challenge from IBM to play chess with their Big Blue computer, a match that was featured in the award-winning documentary *Game Over*.

Kasparov writes a column for the *Wall Street Journal* on world affairs and lectures widely to business and academic groups. He created the Kasparov Foundation to promote charitable activities, and is the leader of the united Civil Front and a founder of the opposition coalition group 'The Other Russia'. He also actively promotes the use of chess as a learning tool in schools through the Kasparov International Chess Academy. He lives in Moscow.

HOW LIFE
IMITATES CHESS

by

GARRY KASPAROV

with

MIG GREENGARD

arrow books

Published by Arrow Books 2008

10

Copyright © Garry Kasparov, 2007

Garry Kasparov has asserted his right under the Copyright, Designs and Patents Act,
1988 to be identified as the author of this work.

First published in Great Britain in 2007 by
William Heinemann
The Random House Group Limited
20 Vauxhall Bridge Road, London, SW1V 2SA

www.randomhouse.co.uk

Addresses for companies within The Random House Group Limited can be found at:
www.randomhouse.co.uk/offices.htm

The Random House Group Limited Reg. No. 954009

A CIP catalogue record for this book
is available from the British Library

ISBN 9780099489863

The Random House Group Limited supports The Forest Stewardship
Council® (FSC®), the leading international forest-certification organisation.
Our books carrying the FSC label are printed on FSC®-certified paper.
FSC is the only forest-certification scheme supported by the leading
environmental organisations, including Greenpeace. Our
paper procurement policy can be found at
www.randomhouse.co.uk/environment

MIX
Paper from
responsible sources
FSC
www.fsc.org   FSC® C016897

Printed and bound in Great Britain by Clays Ltd, St Ives plc

To my Mother, for a lifetime of inspiration and support

TABLE OF CONTENTS

INTRODUCTION

The secret of success

As a teenage chess star in the chess-mad Soviet Union I became used to interviews and public speaking at a very young age. Apart from occasional questions about hobbies and girls, these early interviews focused solely on my chess career. Then in 1985 I became world champion at the age of twenty-two, the youngest ever, and from then on the type of questions I received changed dramatically. Instead of wanting to know about games and tournaments, people wanted to know how I had achieved my unprecedented success. How did I come to work so hard? How many moves ahead did I see? What went on in my mind during a game? Did I have a photographic memory? What did I eat? What did I do every night before going to sleep? In short, what were the secrets of my success?

It didn't take long for me to realize that my audiences were disappointed with my answers. I worked hard because my mother taught me to. How many moves ahead I saw depended on the position. During a game I tried to recall my preparation and to calculate variations. My memory was good, but not photographic. I usually ate a heavy lunch of smoked salmon, steak and tonic water before each game. (Sadly, when I hit my late thirties my physical trainer mandated this 'diet' to become a thing of the past.) Every night before going to bed I brushed my teeth. Not exactly inspiring material.

Everyone seemed to be looking for a precise method, a universal recipe they could follow to achieve great results every time. Famous writers are asked about what type of paper and pen they use, as if their tools were responsible for their writing. Such questions of course miss the point that we are all one of a kind, the result of millions of elements and transformations running from our DNA to this afternoon. We each build our own unique formula for making decisions. Our goal is to make the best of this formula, to identify it, evaluate its performance and find ways to improve it.

This book describes how my own formula developed, both how I viewed the process at the time and now looking back with the benefit of hindsight. Along the way I will look back at the many people who contributed to that development, directly and indirectly. The inspirational games of Alexander Alekhine, my first chess hero, find a place alongside Sir Winston Churchill, whose words and books I still turn to regularly.

From these and other examples I hope you will gain insight into your own development as a decision-maker and into how to encourage further growth. This will require great honesty in your evaluation of yourself and of how well you have fulfilled your potential. There are no quick fixes and this is not a book of tips and tricks. This is a book about self-awareness and challenge, about how to challenge ourselves and others so we can learn how to make the best possible decisions.

The idea for this book came when I realized that instead of coming up with clever answers for the eternal 'What's going on in your head?' questions it would be more interesting for me to actually find out. But the life of a chess professional, with its rigorous calendar of travel, play and preparation, did not allow me much time for philosophical – as opposed to practical – introspection. When I retired from chess in March 2005 I finally gained the time and perspective to look back on my experiences and attempt to share them in a useful way.

This would be a very different book had I completed it before my dramatic career shift from chess to politics. First, I needed time to absorb the lessons my life in chess had taught me. Second, my new experiences are forcing me to look at who I am and what I am capable of. Being passionate about advocating for democracy isn't enough. To build coalitions and organize conferences requires me to apply my strategic vision and other chess skills in entirely new ways. After twenty-five years in a comfort zone of expertise I have to analyse my abilities in order to build and rebuild myself for these new challenges.

A map of the mind

On my sixth birthday I woke up to find the best present I have ever received. Next to my bed was an enormous globe – I had to rub my eyes to make sure it was real! I had always been fascinated by maps and geography, and my favourite childhood stories were those in which my father would recount the voyages of Marco Polo, Columbus and Magellan. It started with my father reading to me from Stefan Zweig's *Conqueror of the Seas: The Story of Magellan*. Now our favourite game became tracing the journeys of these great explorers across the globe.

It wasn't long before I knew the capitals of all the world's countries, their populations, and everything else I could find out. These real-life tales of adventure fascinated me more than any fairy tale could. While we didn't focus on the terrible hardships sea travel involved in the past, I knew it must have taken incredible courage to be the first to make such a journey. These stories fired my own sense of pioneer spirit. I wanted to blaze new trails, even if at that point in my life that meant little more than taking a new route on the walk home. And throughout my chess career I sought out new challenges, looking for things no one had done before.

The time of great explorers and emperors has passed, but there are still a few precious territories to discover. We can explore our own boundaries and the boundaries of our lives. We can also help others do the same, perhaps by giving a child a globe, or the digital age equivalent, for his birthday.

Having a personalized map is essential, and this book can only roughly chart the stages of observation and analysis that go into drawing that map. To exaggerate only slightly, the lowest common denominator is useless. No advantage, no improvement, can be found in what is obvious, or identical, for everyone. We must look higher and dig deeper, move beyond the basic and universal. In theory, anyone can learn to play chess in half an hour and the rules are of course the same for every man, woman and child. When we first step beyond the rules, however, leaving that initial level where we are concerned only with making legal moves, we begin to form the patterns that distinguish us from everyone else who has ever pushed a pawn.

Acquired patterns and the logic to employ them combine with our inherent qualities to create a unique decision-maker. Experience and knowledge are focused through the prism of talent, which itself can be pushed, pulled and cultivated. This mix is the source of intuition, an absolutely unique tool for each of us. Here we begin to see the influence of individual psychology and our emotional make-up expressed in our decisions – what we call style in a chess player. Chess is an ideal instrument for examining these influences because to excel at the game we are forced to analyse the decisions we make and how we arrived at those decisions. This is what my questioners really needed instead of information about my trivial habits: self-investigation.

We cannot pick and choose which style we would prefer for ourselves. It's not generic software we download and install. We must instead recognize what works best for us and then, through challenge and trial, develop our own method. What am I lacking? What are my strengths? What type of challenges do I tend to avoid and why? The method for success is a secret because it can only be discovered by analysing our own decisions. Better decision-making cannot be taught, but it can be self-taught.

There is what at first appears to be a contradiction in what I have described. We must become conscious of our decision-making processes and with practice they will improve our intuitive – unconscious – performance. This unnatural behaviour is required because as adults we have already formed our patterns, good and bad. To correct the bad and enhance the good we must take an active role in becoming more self-aware.

This book attempts to use anecdotes and analysis to open the doors to that awareness. Part I looks at the fundamental ingredients, the essential abilities and skills that go into making a decision. Strategy, calculation, preparation – we must understand these essentials and see them in ourselves. Part II is the evaluation and analysis phase. What changes are needed and why? Here we see the methods and benefits of our self-investigation. Part III examines the subtle ways we combine all of these things to improve our performance. Psychology and intuition affect every aspect of our decisions and our results. We must develop our ability to see the big picture and deal with, and learn from, crises.

Such decisive moments are turning points – every time we select a fork in the road knowing we won't be able to backtrack. We live for these moments and in turn they define our lives. We learn who we are and what truly matters to us. The 'secret' then is to pursue these challenges instead of avoiding them. This is the only way to discover and to exploit all our gifts. Developing our own personal blueprint allows us to make better decisions, to have the confidence to trust our instincts, and to know that no matter what the result, we will come out stronger. That, for each of us, is our unique secret of success.

PART I

PART 1

I

THE LESSON

Personal lessons from the world champion

When I first played for the chess world championship in 1984 I was playing the role of young challenger against a champion who had held the title for almost ten years. I was twenty-one years old and had risen to the top of the chess world with such speed that I couldn't imagine this last hurdle blocking my way. It was therefore quite a shock when I quickly found myself down four losses without a win, only two defeats away from a humiliating rout.

If ever there was a time for a change in strategy, this was it. Instead of giving in to my feelings of desperation, I forced myself to prepare for a long war of attrition. I switched to guerrilla warfare in game after game, reducing risk, waiting for my chance. My opponent, fellow Soviet Anatoly Karpov, fell in with my plan for his own purposes. He wanted to teach the upstart a lesson by scoring a perfect 6–0 score, so he also played cautiously instead of pressing his advantage and going in for the kill.

Karpov was also inspired by the shadow of his predecessor as champion, Bobby Fischer. En route to the title he claimed in 1972, the American had scored two perfect 6–0 wins against world-class opponents, both times without ceding even a draw. Karpov had it in mind to in some measure imitate this legendary feat when he altered his strategy against me. But adding Fischer's ghost to his opposition turned out to be a serious mistake.

An incredible seventeen games followed without a decisive result. These draws weren't without interest, but it appeared my new strategy was working. The match dragged on month after month, breaking every record for the duration of a world championship match. My team and I spent so much time thinking about how Karpov played, which strategies he would employ, that I uncannily felt as if I were becoming Karpov.

During the hundreds of hours of play and preparation I also got a very good look at my own play, and at my own mind. Up until that point in my career everything had come easily for me; winning had simply become the natural state of things. Now I had to focus on how I made my own decisions so I could fix whatever was going wrong. It was working, but when I lost game 27 to go down 0–5 it looked as though I wasn't learning fast enough to save the match. One more loss and it would be three long years before I could even hope for another shot at the title.

I stayed in my defensive crouch as the match entered its third month. The change in style had made things much tougher for Karpov. I felt I was getting closer to solving the puzzle while at the same time my opponent was becoming more frustrated and tired.

At last the dam broke. After surviving game 31, when Karpov failed to land a decisive blow, I won game 32 and went on the offensive. Another five weeks of drawn games followed, but the difference was that now I was creating more winning chances than my opponent. Meanwhile, the world began to wonder if the match would ever end. No championship match had ever gone beyond three months and here we were entering the fifth. Karpov looked exhausted and I started to press harder. After coming close to winning game 46 I won game 47 in crushing style. Could there be a miracle? Exactly at that moment the organizers decided the players needed a break and the next game was postponed for several days. Despite this unprecedented decision I also won the next game. Suddenly it was 3–5 and all the momentum was on my side.

Then, in a bizarre twist, on 15 February 1985, in Moscow, the president of the international chess federation (FIDE), Florencio Campomanes, responding to pressure from the Soviet sport authorities, called a press conference to declare that the match was cancelled. After five months, forty-eight games, and thousands of hours of play and study, the match was over without a winner. We would have to return six months later to do battle again, and next time there would be a limit of twenty-four games. Karpov was removed from immediate danger and could be content that he would hold on to his title a while longer. The official press release stated that Karpov 'accepted' the decision and Kasparov 'abided' it. A curious but accurate semantic distinction. (The Hotel Sport, where the infamous press conference took place, has since been demolished. Its totalitarian spirit, however, lives on in my memory and, increasingly, in Moscow itself.)

Along with this bitter insight into Soviet and chess politics, I had learned a huge amount during the match. The world champion had been my personal trainer for five gruelling months. Not only had I learnt the way he played, I was now deeply in touch with my own thought processes. I was increasingly able to identify my mistakes and why I made them and had learned how best to avoid them, how to improve the decision-making process itself. This was my first real experience at questioning myself instead of relying on my instincts.

When the second match got under way in Moscow I didn't have to wait months for my first win; I won the very first game. The match was still a very tough fight – I trailed for most of the early stages – but this time I wasn't the same innocent twenty-one-year-old. I had patched the holes Karpov had exploited so effectively at the start of the first match. Now a savvy veteran at twenty-two, I became world champion and went on to hold the title for fifteen years. When I retired in 2005 I was still the highest-rated player in the world, but for a chess player forty-one is old for remaining at the summit, when many of my opponents were in their teens.

Becoming aware of the process

It wouldn't have been possible for me to stay at the top for so long without the education Karpov gave me about my own game and my own weaknesses. Not just revealing to me the weaknesses, but the importance of finding them for myself. I didn't fully realize it at the time, but the notorious 'Marathon Match' showed me the key to success. It's not enough to be talented. It's not enough to work hard and to study late into the night. You must also become intimately aware of the methods you use to reach your decisions.

Self-awareness is essential to being able to combine your knowledge, experience and talent to reach your peak performance. Few people ever take the opportunity to perform this sort of analysis. Every decision stems from an internal process, whether at the chessboard, in the White House or the boardroom or at the kitchen table. The subject matter of those decisions will be different, but the process can be very similar.

With chess having been the focus of my life from such an early age it is no wonder that I tend to see the rest of the world in chess terms. I find that the game is usually accorded either too much or too little respect by those looking in on its sixty-four-square world from the outside. It is neither a trivial pursuit nor an exercise to be left only to geniuses and supercomputers. In order for us better to grasp our principal themes the next chapter will first take a quick look at some of the concepts and misconceptions of the 'Royal Game'.

Anatoly Yevgenyevich Karpov (1951 –), USSR/Russia

The adversary who shaped my life

The twelfth world chess champion – 1975–85. Born in Zlatoust, USSR. After rapidly rising through the ranks to challenge for the title, Karpov received the world championship crown in 1975 when American champion Bobby Fischer forfeited his title after protracted negotiations with the international chess federation. Karpov felt the need to prove his mettle after acceding to the title in this way and he won tournament after tournament. He still holds the most impressive tournament record of any player.

He successfully defended the title in 1978 and 1981, both times against Viktor Korchnoi. Karpov and I played five consecutive world championship matches: 1984, 1985, 1986, 1987, 1990, a total of 144 games. Our score after this marathon was remarkably balanced: twenty-one wins for me, nineteen for Karpov, and 104 draws!) These 'K-K' matches are widely considered one of the most intense head-to-head rivalries in sports history.

Karpov gained huge political support in the USSR as a result of the perceived necessity of regaining the title from the American Fischer. He was strongly connected with the Soviet power structure and by nature he has always tended to align with power. Our contrasting fire and ice chess styles also reflected our 'collaborator versus rebel' reputations away from the board.

His mastery of a circumspect manoeuvring style led to the introduction of the adjective 'Karpovian' to the chess vocabulary. It refers to the python-like strangulation of the opponent with methodical, quiet play.

On Karpov: 'Karpov's intentions become understandable to his opponents only when salvation is no longer possible.' – Mikhail Tal

In his own words: 'Let us say that a game may be continued in two ways: one of them is a beautiful tactical blow that gives rise to variations that don't yield to precise calculations; the other is clear positional pressure that leads to an endgame with microscopic chances of victory. I would choose the latter without thinking twice.'

2

LIFE IMITATES CHESS

Chess goes to Hollywood

It's difficult to think of a more paradoxical set of images than the reputation of the game of chess contrasted with that of the chess player. Chess is accepted as a universal symbol of intellect and complexity, sophistication and cunning. And yet there persists an image of the devoted chess player as eccentric, perhaps even psychotic.

In many Western nations the stereotype of the chess player is often synonymous with the underfed weakling or the brainy-but-misanthropic nerd. These perceptions about players linger even while positive images and associations of chess are regularly employed by Hollywood and Madison Avenue.

Who can forget the opening sequence of the James Bond film *From Russia With Love*, in which the villain Kronsteen goes directly from victory in a tournament chess game to plotting global mischief? Bond author Ian Fleming and the director paid careful attention to the game between Kronsteen and his opponent 'McAdams', basing it on a real game between two great Soviet players, tenth world champion Boris Spassky and one-time championship challenger David Bronstein. The story makes transparent use of chess as a metaphor, as when one of Bond's associates warns him, 'These Russians are great chess players. When they wish to execute a plot, they execute it brilliantly. The game is planned minutely, the gambits of the enemy are provided for.'

Dozens of other films have used chess in similar fashion to show braininess and strategic thinking on the part of the protagonist. The 1995 film *Assassins* portrays Sylvester Stallone and Antonio Banderas as professional killers trying to murder each other by day while playing online chess against each other by night. In Stanley Kubrick's 1968 film *2001*, the computer HAL

9000 easily defeats the character Frank Poole at chess, foreshadowing the fact that the machine will eventually kill him.

The stereotype of chess players also includes our being introverted creatures, bordering on the obsessive, even the autistic. Vladimir Nabokov was a chess enthusiast but he did the game no favours with his 1930 novel *The Defense* (later *The Luzhin Defense*) in which the main character is a lumbering savant of a Grandmaster, barely fit for human society beyond his ability to play chess. The 2000 film version attempted to draw a more pleasant picture, turning it into something of a romance.

The Austrian Stefan Zweig also populated his chess world with damaged and eccentric characters. The posthumously published novella *The Royal Game* is a psychological and political commentary on Nazism that centres around two games between a barely literate world chess champion and a doctor driven insane by playing chess against himself while imprisoned by the Gestapo. In the book, Zweig contributed this dazzling description of the game itself:

> But is it not an offensively narrow construction to call chess a game? Is it not a science, a technique, an art, that sways among these categories as Mahomet's coffin does between heaven and earth, at once a union of all contradictory concepts: primeval yet ever new; mechanical in operation yet effective only through the imagination; bounded in geometric space though boundless in its combinations . . . as proved by evidence, [chess is] more lasting in its being and presence than all books and achievements; the only game that belongs to all people and all ages; of which none knows the divinity that bestowed it on the world, to slay boredom, to sharpen the senses, to exhilarate the spirit . . . Children can learn its simple rules, duffers succumb to its temptation, yet within this immutable tight square it creates a particular species of master not to be compared with any other – persons destined for chess alone, specific geniuses in whom vision, patience and technique are operative through a distribution no less precisely ordained than in mathematicians, poets, composers, but merely united on a different level.

Non-fiction chess characters

Several prominent players of the past have indeed experienced psychiatric difficulties either during or after their careers. The German master Curt von Bardeleben committed suicide in 1924 in the same way Luzhin does in Nabokov's book, by throwing himself out of a window. The first official world champion, Wilhelm Steinitz, battled off and on with mental trouble in his final years. One of the most successful players of the first quarter of the twentieth century, Akiba Rubinstein, slowly fell victim to a pathological timidity. After making a move he would hide in the corner of the playing hall awaiting his opponent's reply.

The two greatest chess players ever produced by the United States both left the game in their prime and suffered bouts of mental instability. New Orleans's Paul Morphy demolished the world's best players in his 1858–9 European tour, only to leave the game a few years later to struggle in legal practice. He never played serious chess again and in his final years America's first chess hero suffered bouts of delusion that some in the press attributed to his prodigious mental feats.

In 1972, Robert (Bobby) Fischer wrested the world championship title away from Boris Spassky and the Soviet Union in a legendary match held in Reykjavik, Iceland. He then left the game for twenty years, refusing to defend his title in 1975 and then literally disappearing for over a decade. When Fischer was lured out to play a so-called championship rematch with Spassky in Yugoslavia – then under UN sanctions – in 1992, his predictably rusty chess was accompanied by vociferous anti-Semitic paranoia.

But exceptional cases like these in both fiction and non-fiction make it easy to ignore the vast majority of chess players who are entirely unexceptional apart from their capacity to play chess well.

The pedigree of the Royal Game

If the only chess you ever see is the diagram in the morning paper, it may be surprising to realize that the game has an extensive literature going back hundreds of years, even thousands if you include mythical variants of the game, which according to most popular accounts originated in India. One of the first books produced by Caxton's press in the fifteenth century was *The Game and Playe of the Chesse*. Five hundred years later, some of the earliest communications over what would become the internet contained the moves of a chess game between scientists in the test laboratories.

The technique of recording chess games with symbols ('chess notation') gives chess a detailed history, enabling millions of chess players through the ages to enjoy and learn from the games of the legendary players of the past.

Taking in the sweep of chess history as a single piece of cloth, we can observe the steady development of the game. Here I'm not referring to the rules, which were largely standardized towards the end of the eighteenth century. While the rules have remained unchanged, the style and central ideas of the game have changed dramatically in the past 150 years, albeit in small, evolutionary steps.

After I wrote a series of short newspaper articles on the world champions who had gone before me I became obsessed with the idea of analysing in depth how the game has changed over the decades and how its development has been pushed along by its greatest practitioners. I had in mind a biography of chess itself, told through the careful analysis of the greatest and most influential games. This project, which has taken up a large part of my life for the past three years, came to life as a series of books titled *My Great Predecessors*.

At the time of writing we are now well into Part 6; in the process I have learned a tremendous amount about the great players of the past. Each world champion had individual gifts and contributed immensely to the evolution of the game. Studying the twelve world champions who came before me and their greatest rivals made me wonder what enabled this 'great dozen' to succeed? What did the champions have that the challengers lacked?

It's natural for chess players to suggest that aptitude at chess signifies great intelligence, even genius. There is little to support this theory, unfortunately. Nor is there much truth in the common public perception of top chess players as human computers, capable of memorizing megabytes of data and calculating dozens of moves ahead.

In reality, as I have observed, there is little evidence that chess masters possess talents beyond the obvious one of playing chess.

This has led generations of researchers to try to figure out exactly why some people play chess well and others do not. There is no chess gene, no common pattern in infancy, and yet, as in music and mathematics, there are true prodigies in chess. Children as young as four have become stars, beating adults just a few months after learning the game simply by watching their elders play.

So we know that there is such a thing as chess talent, but this in itself isn't very helpful. Even if you are blessed with talent it may never be realized unless many other factors are present, and it is more worthwhile to focus on the factors we can better observe and influence.

Sport, art or science? Sport, art AND science

If you ask a Grandmaster, an artist and a computer scientist what makes a good chess player you will realize why the game is such an ideal laboratory for the decision-making process. The professional player is likely to agree with the second world champion, Emanuel Lasker of Germany, who observed: 'Chess is above all a struggle.' According to Lasker, no matter how you define it, the point is to win.

The artist Marcel Duchamp was a strong and devoted chess player. At one point he even gave up art for chess, saying the game 'has all the beauty of art – and much more'. Duchamp further affirmed this aspect of the game by saying 'I have come to the personal conclusion that while all artists are not chess players, all chess players are artists.' And it is true that we cannot ignore the creative element, even though we have to rationalize it against the primary objective of winning the game.

Then we come to the scientific aspect, the one most non-chess players tend to over-emphasize. Memorization, precise calculation, and the application of logic are essential. When chess-playing computers first came on the scene in the 1950s, most scientists assumed that the iron beasts would soon demolish any human player. And yet fifty years later the battle for supremacy between human and machine still continues.

The sixth world champion, Mikhail Botvinnik, my great teacher, dedicated his last thirty years to creating a computer chess player. That is, not just a computer that could play chess, which was relatively simple to achieve and already by then commonplace, but a program that generated its moves the way the human does, a true artificial player.

Botvinnik was an engineer and he discussed his ideas with many scientists, including the legendary American mathematician Claude Shannon, who had himself outlined the design of a chess machine in his spare time. Most chess programs essentially 'count beans', although they do it very quickly. They employ brute force to examine every possible move as deeply as possible in the allotted time. They evaluate each one with a score and then choose the move with the highest score. Botvinnik wanted to go beyond this, to design a program that employed logic to select moves instead of brute calculating force.

In short, his project was a failure. His years of position papers and theoretical models never produced a program that could play better than a human beginner. (Brute force programs were playing at a relatively competent level even in the 70s.) How could a computer emulate human creativity and intuition? Even today, thirty years later, when computers play at world championship level, they mainly rely on brute force methods.

However, chess programmers are starting to reach the limits of such methods. To improve their creations they are being forced to examine some of Botvinnik's concepts. His own project was a failure but many of the ideas behind it were both valuable and ahead of their time. Now that we are realizing that brute force cannot exhaust this ancient game we are beginning to return to Botvinnik's vision of teaching chess programs to think more like humans.

More than a metaphor

We know computers calculate better than we do, so where does our success come from? The answer is synthesis, the ability to combine creativity and calculation, art and science, into a whole that is much greater than the sum of its parts. Chess is a unique cognitive nexus, a place where art and science come together in the human mind and are then refined and improved by experience.

This is the way we improve at anything in our lives that involves thinking, which is to say, everything. A CEO must combine analysis and research with creative thinking to lead his company effectively. An army general has to apply his knowledge of human nature to predict and counter the strategies of the enemy.

It also helps that we have a common vocabulary to work with. If you overheard a discussion that referred to 'the opening phase', 'sector vulnerability', 'strategic planning', and 'tactical implementation' you might assume a corporate takeover was in the offing. But it could equally refer to any weekend chess tournament.

Of course the fields of the business and military worlds are limitless compared to the confined sixty-four squares of the chessboard. But it is due to its limited scope that chess provides such a versatile model for decision-making. There are strict standards of success and failure in chess. If your decisions are faulty your position deteriorates and the pendulum swings towards a loss; if they are good it swings towards a victory. Every single move reflects a decision and, with enough time, it can be analysed to scientific perfection whether or not each decision was the most effective.

This objectivity can provide a great deal of insight into the quality of our decision-making processes. The stock market and the battlefield aren't nearly as tidy, but success in these fields also depends on the quality of our decisions and these are subject to comparable methods of analysis.

What makes someone a better manager, a better writer, a better chess player? For there can be no doubt that not everyone performs at the same level or has the capacity to do so. What is critical is to find our own paths to reach our peaks, to develop our talents, improve our skills, and to seek out and conquer the challenges we need to push us to the highest level. And to do all this we first need a plan.

Mikhail Moiseyevich Botvinnik (1911–95), USSR/Russia
The uncompromising patriarch

The sixth world chess champion – 1948–57, 1958–60, 1961–3. Born in Kuokkala, Russia. When Alexander Alekhine died in 1946, still holding the world championship title, a tournament of the world's best players was organized to establish the new champion. This 1948 event was dominated by Botvinnik, who thereby became the first in a long line of Soviet world champions. He was also a practising engineer, though chess was always his first priority.

Along with his title as 'the patriarch of Soviet chess', Botvinnik could also be called the king of the rematch. Twice he was defeated in world championship matches only to come back a year later and demolish his victor. His ability to deeply investigate and prepare for the characteristics of his specific opponents established a new level of rigour and professionalism in chess. The ability to come back and win those rematches required more than tenacity. Botvinnik was able to objectively analyse his own play and repair the weaknesses his opponents had exploited the first time around.

His uncompromising nature persisted until the end of his life. In 1994 we asked him to honour us with his presence at a tournament of rapid chess in Moscow. Botvinnik, then eighty-three, declined, saying, 'Rapid chess is not serious!' We told him that rapid chess was the new fashion and that everyone was playing in this event, even his old rival Vassily Smyslov. He responded: 'I'm used to thinking with my own brain. Even should a hundred people think otherwise, I do not care!'

Botvinnik left professional chess in 1970 to concentrate on coaching and the new field of computer chess. The Botvinnik school invited the top junior chess talents from all over the country two or three times a year and it went on to produce several generations of champions. In the first output, in the early 60s, was the young Anatoly Karpov. In 1973, one of its students was the ten-year-old Garry Kasparov. By the time the young Vladimir Kramnik arrived in 1987 it had become the joint Botvinnik–Kasparov school – quite an impressive record of champions.

On Botvinnik: 'Where dangers threaten from every side and the slightest slackening of attention might be fatal; in a position which requires nerves of steel and intense concentration, Botvinnik is in his element.' – Max Euwe, the fifth world champion

In his own words: 'The difference between man and animal is that man is capable of establishing priorities!'

3
STRATEGY

'The man who knows how will always have a job. The
man who also knows why will always be his boss.'
– *Ralph Waldo Emerson*

Success at any speed

Football and, to a lesser extent, hockey were the spectator sports I
grew up with in the USSR. The 'beautiful game', as football is
widely known, is also one of the simplest games when it comes to
the rules. It doesn't take long to figure out how to play simply by
watching a few matches. A few friends have tried to explain
baseball and American football to me, an experience that makes
me wonder if the sheer simplicity of *real* football has been what has
made it unpopular in the US. (Though, as it is often observed, it is
perhaps more likely that it's because football offers too few
opportunities for commercial breaks.)

As simple as football is, the strategies of the game are deep
and complex. The obvious aim is to score goals while preventing
your opponent from doing the same. The best way to achieve this,
however, is endlessly debatable. The traditional strategy of the
Italian national team, for example, is defensive. If your opponent
never scores, so the logic goes, you can never lose. Others, like the
Brazilians, employ contrasting means to achieve the same end of
outscoring their opponents.

Imagine learning how to play chess from a primer missing a
few pages. It teaches you how to set up the board and how to move
and capture the enemy pieces, but gives nothing about checkmate,
nothing about the end of the game. Someone learning from such a
book could become competent at calculation and proficient at
manoeuvring, but would have no higher objectives. Without a goal
his play would be aimless.

The old chess saying, 'A bad plan is better than no plan at all',
is more clever than true. Every step, every reaction, every decision,

has to be made with its place in your planning clearly understood. Otherwise you can't make any but the most obvious decisions without knowing for sure if they are really to your benefit. This is even more important given the accelerated pace of the world today.

During my thirty years as a professional chess player we've gone from researching an opponent by digging through musty books and journals for days to being able to pull up every single game in his career in seconds on a PC. It used to take months for tournament games to be published in specialist magazines. Now anyone can watch the games on the internet in real time.

The implications of the information revolution go much deeper than matters of convenience. With more data becoming available more quickly, the ability to deal with this information must also move more quickly. When a game is played in Moscow it is instantly available for the entire world to analyse. An idea that took weeks to develop can be imitated by others the next day, so everyone must also immediately be aware of it and prepare for it.

This acceleration has also affected the game itself. In 1987 I played a six-game match of 'rapid chess' on the stage of the London Hippodrome against England's Nigel Short, who would challenge me for the world championship six years later. It was the first serious match of its kind, with a greatly accelerated rate of play. In these rapid games we had just twenty-five minutes each to make all our moves, a far cry from traditional chess where games can last up to seven hours.

I trained extensively with this new time limit and discovered that it was still possible to play deep concepts despite the impossibility of calculating deeply on each move. Instead of a profound study of a position we must rely more on instinct. It would be fair to assume that in rapid chess careful planning and strategic goals are secondary, or even ignored, in favour of quick calculation and intuition. And I would even say that for many players this is exactly the case. If you don't like planning during a seven-hour game you'll likely abandon it entirely in a rapid game. But the most successful players – at any speed – base their calculations firmly in strategic planning. Far from being mutually exclusive, the most effective analysis, and the fastest, is possible when there is a guiding strategy.

If you play without long-term goals your decisions will become purely reactive and you'll be playing your opponent's game, not your own. As you jump from one new thing to the next you will be pulled off course, caught up in what's right in front of you instead of what you need to achieve

Take the 1992 American presidential campaign, the one that took Bill Clinton to the White House. During the Democratic primaries it seemed as if every day brought a new scandal that was sure to destroy Clinton's candidacy. His campaign team reacted instantly to each new disaster, but they weren't only reacting. They made sure each press release also hammered home their candidate's message.

The general election against President Bush followed a similar pattern. Against each attack the Clinton team responded with a defence that also refocused the debate on their own message – the now famous 'It's the economy, stupid' – constantly reinforcing their own strategy. Four years earlier, by contrast, the Democratic candidate, Michael Dukakis, had become completely distracted by his opponent's aggressive tactics. People only heard him defending himself, not presenting his own message. The 1992 Clinton team knew that it wasn't only about how quickly they responded, but how well their responses fitted in with their overall strategy. Before you can follow a strategy, however, you have to develop one.

The future of the decisions you make in the present

The strategist starts with a goal in the distant future and works backwards to the present. A Grandmaster makes the best moves because they are based on what he wants the board to look like ten or twenty moves in the future. This doesn't require the calculation of countless twenty-move variations. He evaluates where his fortunes lie in the position and establishes objectives. Then he works out the step-by-step moves to accomplish those aims.

These intermediate objectives are essential. They are the ingredients necessary to create conditions favourable to our strategy. Without them we're trying to build a house starting with the roof. Too often we set a goal and head straight for it without considering all the steps that will be required to achieve it. What conditions must be true for our strategy to succeed? What sacrifices will be required? What must change and what can we do to induce or enable those changes?

My instincts or analysis tell me that in a given position there is potential for me to attack my opponent's king. Next, instead of throwing my forces at the king, I search for objectives I must achieve in order to do this successfully, for example, to weaken the protection around the opponent's king by exchanging a key defending piece. I first must understand which strategic objectives will help me accomplish my goal of attacking the king and only then do I begin to plan exactly how to achieve them and to look at the specific moves that will lead to successful implementation. Failing to do this leads to simplistic, single-minded plans with little hope of success.

In the second round of the 2001 Corus tournament in the Netherlands I faced one of the tournament underdogs, Alexei Fedorov of Belarus. This was the strongest tournament he had ever played in, and the first time we had met at the board. He quickly made it clear that he did not intend to show too much respect for the august surroundings, or for his opponent.

Fedorov quickly abandoned standard opening play. If what he played against me had a name it might be called the 'Kitchen Sink Attack'. Ignoring the rest of the board he launched all his available pawns and pieces at my king right from the start. I knew that such a wild, ill-prepared attack could only succeed if I blundered. I kept an eye on my king and countered on the other side, or wing, and in the centre of the board, a critical area where he had completely ignored his development. It was soon apparent that his attack was entirely superficial and he resigned the game after only twenty-five moves.

I admit I didn't have to do anything special to score this easy victory. My opponent had played without a sound strategy and eventually reached a dead end. What Fedorov failed to do was to ask himself early on what conditions would need to be fulfilled for his attack to succeed. He decided he wanted to cross the river and walked right into the water instead of looking for a bridge. It's also worth noting that relying on the competition to make a serious mistake is not a viable strategy.

Consistency doesn't contradict adaptability

Having a goal and objectives is the first step; sticking with them and staying on course is the next. Military history is full of examples of commanders who have got carried away by the action on the battlefield and forgotten about strategy. As the historical record, and William Shakespeare tell us, the French forces were routed by the English at Agincourt in 1415 when the French cavalry allowed a long-distance volley of arrows to provoke them into a disorderly charge. When your opponent complicates things there is a strong temptation to look for a refutation of his idea, to pick up the gauntlet, to rise to the challenge. Of course this is exactly what he wants and why such distractions must be resisted. If you have already decided on a good strategy, why drop it for something that suits your opponent? This requires strong self-control, as pressure to switch can be both internal and external. Your ego wants to prove you can beat him at his own game as well as to quiet your critics – actual or potential.

Before the start of my 1993 world championship match against England's Nigel Short, my team and I had decided the best strategy was to take on the impetuous Englishman in manoeuvring positions. He was a dangerous attacker who was well prepared in many sharp lines of play, and while this was also my strong suit, we felt I would have a considerable advantage in slower games. Our analysis revealed how uncomfortable Short was playing without activity.

White has the first move in chess, and this confers a slight advantage that is comparable, if less marked, to having the serve in tennis. With the first move you can better control the tempo and direction of the game. In my preparation for the Short match we designed my opening repertoire with white to steer clear of the double-edged variations he preferred. To this end I selected the slower-developing lines of the venerable Ruy Lopez opening, well known for positional manoeuvring. It takes its name from a sixteenth-century chess-playing Spanish priest and its grinding effectiveness has given the opening the nickname 'the Spanish Torture'.

I started out with three wins in the first four games to take a commanding lead in the match, scheduled for twenty-four games. I had won both my games with white using this slow manoeuvring style, and many wondered whether I would switch to more aggressive variations to try to knock out my opponent while he was against the ropes. Short was reeling – maybe this would be a good time to switch gears to keep him off guard, was how this line of thought went.

I did make a change, but not of strategy. I opened with a completely different system, another unhurried, methodical opening designed to limit his counterplay. I used my lead to probe his defences, looking for weaknesses. I soon scored two more wins by sticking to my strategy of opening quietly with the white pieces.

Sticking with a plan when you are winning sounds simple, but it's easy to become over-confident and to get caught up in events. Long-term success is impossible if you let reactions trump planning.

Play your own game

Two strong chess players can have very different strategies in the same position and they might be equally effective – leaving aside those positions in which a single forced winning line is available. Each player has his own style, his own way of solving problems and making decisions. A key to developing successful strategies is to be aware of your own strengths and weaknesses, to know what you do well.

Two leading lights of opposing schools of chess thought have become world champions. Mikhail Botvinnik trusted in immense self-discipline, hard work and scientific rigour. His rival Mikhail Tal fed his own wild creativity and fantasy and cared little either for his health or methodical preparation. Thomas Edison famously claimed that 'success is one per cent inspiration, ninety-nine per cent perspiration'. This formula certainly worked for Edison and Botvinnik but would never have worked for Tal – or indeed for Alexander Pushkin, the founder of modern Russian literature. Pushkin's love of the fast life, of gambling and romance, were all part of his ability to create some of the greatest works in the Russian language.

Tigran Petrosian, another former world champion, perfected the art of what we call 'prophylaxis' in chess. Prophylaxis is the art of preventative play, strengthening your position and eliminating threats before they are even threats. Petrosian defended so well that his opponent's attack was over before it started, perhaps even before he'd thought of it himself. Instead of attacking, Petrosian would set up perfect defences, leaving his opponents frustrated and prone to making errors. He was alert to every small opportunity and exploited these mistakes with ruthless precision.

I like to refer to him as a true chess 'inaction hero'. He developed a policy of 'vigilant inaction' that showed how to win without going directly on the offensive. To generalize, Petrosian's strategy was to look first for his opponent's opportunities and eliminate them. Only when his own position was invulnerable did he begin to look for his own chances. This strategy of being an immovable object proved very effective for him, but few players could imitate his patient, defensive style.

When I played Petrosian in the Netherlands in 1981 I was eighteen and Petrosian was fifty-two. I was eager to avenge losing to him earlier in the year in Moscow, where I had developed an impressive attacking position that exploded in my face. At the time I thought it was an accident, but then it happened again. Every time it looked like my offensive was crashing through he would calmly make a little adjustment. All my pieces were swarming around his king and I was sure it was only a matter of time before I would land the decisive blow. But where was it? I started to feel like a bull chasing a toreador around the bullring. Exhausted and frustrated, I made one mistake, then another, and went on to lose the game. In football something similar occurred a year later at the World Cup in Spain. The defensive *catenaccio* style of the Italians triumphed over the attacking *jogo bonito* of the Brazilians. Sometimes the best defence is the best defence.

Over the next two years I equalized our career score by twice beating Petrosian with a quiet positional style, almost the style of Petrosian himself. I credit my successful change of approach to advice given to me by the man who took the world title from Petrosian in 1969, Boris Spassky. Before I played Petrosian again, less than a year after the defeats described above, I spoke with Spassky, who was playing in the same tournament in Yugoslavia. He counselled me that the key was to apply pressure, but just a little, steadily. 'Squeeze his balls,' Spassky told me unforgettably, 'but just squeeze one, not both!'

Spassky's own experiences against Petrosian had followed a pattern similar to mine. He first fought Petrosian for the world championship in 1966 and was turned back in a tight contest. He went into their match believing – wrongly – that Petrosian didn't play sharp, attacking chess because he lacked the skills to do so. Spassky complicated at all costs only to find his attacks brilliantly repelled by the wily world champion.

Three years later, Spassky demonstrated that he had learned his lesson by showing much more respect for Petrosian's skill. In their 1969 match he played a more balanced game and went on to triumph. My first two losses had given me both a deep respect for Petrosian's abilities and for the art of defence in chess. But I also realized that such a style wasn't for me. I always wanted to be on the attacking side and my game strategies reflected that. You must be aware of your limitations and also of your best qualities.

My aggressive, dynamic style of play fits my strengths and my personality. Even when I am forced on the defensive I am constantly looking for a chance to turn the tables and counter-attack. And when I'm on the offensive I'm not content to seek modest gains. I prefer sharp, energetic chess with pieces flying all over the board and where the player who makes the first mistake loses. Other players, including the man I defeated for the world championship, Anatoly Karpov, specialize in the accumulation of small advantages. They risk little and are content to slowly improve their position until their opponent cracks. But all these strategies – defensive, dynamic, manoeuvring – can be highly effective in the hands of someone who understands them well.

Nor is there a single best type of strategy in business. Risk-takers coexist with conservative managers at the top of Fortune 500 companies. Perhaps 50 per cent of a CEO's decisions would be made in identical fashion by any competent businessperson, just as there are many chess moves that are obvious to any strong player regardless of his style. It's that other 50 per cent, or even the most complicated 10 per cent, where the difference is made. The best leaders appreciate the particular imbalances and key factors of each situation and can devise a strategy informed by that understanding.

Nokia CEO Jorma Ollila turned the Finnish company into the mobile phone leader with an unorthodox, even chaotic style that turned convention on its head at every turn. Top managers were asked to swap jobs, research and development staff met directly with customers, and the company's chief phone designer once compared its management to the way a jazz band improvises as it plays together.

Such a loose and dynamic style might not be so successful in another industry, or another country, or with another CEO. For decades IBM built its business on a conservative, even stodgy, reputation. In the world of office machinery that stood for reliability, which was far more important to IBM's business customers than style. New mobile phone models come out every month, while IBM was selling and servicing machines over five-year and even ten-year periods. In the eyes of their customers this very conservatism was a virtue.

You cannot always determine the battlefield

You do not become a world champion without being able to play in different styles when necessary. Sometimes you are forced to fight on unfamiliar terrain; you can't run away when conditions aren't to your liking. The ability to adapt is critical to success.

Occasionally you can even switch styles by design to catch your competitor off guard, although this always contains the risk of the trapper being trapped. I was rewarded for employing this technique in my 1995 world championship match against Indian star Viswanathan (Vishy) Anand in New York. Halfway through the match, with the score tied at one win apiece, I abandoned my favourite lines for the fearsomely named Dragon Sicilian, a defence I had never played before in a serious game.

It wasn't change for the sake of it; other factors contributed to my selection of the Dragon. It leads to an uncompromising game, one in which you must choose the most aggressive continuation to have any chance of gaining the advantage. Anand was faced with the surprise of seeing it and the knowledge that I would have prepared it extensively. In addition, our research showed that Anand had little previous experience with the Dragon and felt less comfortable against it than against other sharp opening lines. If he went for the risky main variations he could be sure I'd have something nasty waiting for him. Instead, unable to adjust, he played tamely and lost twice.

The ability to adapt on demand served Napoleon Bonaparte well for most of his legendary career. He was famous for maintaining the element of surprise on the battlefield, particularly by pressing on with an attack that had apparently stalled. But he was not above using his own reputation for aggression to entrap his enemies.

Napoleon prepared for the 1805 battle of Austerlitz by retreating his forces from an excellent outpost, intentionally allowing the Russian Tsar's forces to move in and see the thin French lines in retreat. Young Tsar Alexander decided that this was his chance for glory and prepared an all-out attack, exactly what Napoleon wanted. He had quietly brought up reinforcements to the area he had made the Russians believe to be weak, and the Tsar's forces were routed in a single day.

This wasn't only a case of a clever trick working to perfection. First, Napoleon realized that he was outnumbered and that direct methods wouldn't suffice. He knew his opponent was young and impulsive and eager for glory. He also knew that no one would believe the great Napoleon would retreat from a commanding position voluntarily. Napoleon's strategy combined all these factors into a brilliant victory. The one-eyed Russian General Mikhail Kutuzov was the lone voice of caution, but his warnings to the Tsar went unheeded. Even a tsar can learn from his mistakes, however. Seven years later Napoleon's Grande Armée marched on Moscow in what we Russians call the Patriotic War of 1812. This time Alexander listened to Kutuzov and followed his strategy of harassing the French troops and playing a waiting game. Moscow was burned to the ground but Napoleon was eventually forced – disastrously – to retreat.

I was forced to adapt during my advance on the road to the world championship in 1983. I was a twenty-year-old upstart taking on the fifty-two-year-old Viktor Korchnoi, a two-time world championship finalist who is still playing strong chess today at the age of seventy-five. Unsurprisingly, the veteran controlled the tempo in the early stages of our twelve-game qualification match. He won the first game and consistently prevented me from getting into the sort of open attacking positions I enjoyed.

Instead of continuing to be frustrated in my attempts to change the character of the games, I decided my best chance was to go with the flow. Instead of making sharp moves that I thought were more in my style, I played the best solid moves available even if they led to quiet positions. It freed me from the psychological difficulty of trying to force the issue in each game and I could just play chess. Korchnoi forced me to fight on his terrain, but once I was conscious of it I was able to adapt, fight and win.

I had won games 6 and 7 to take the lead when Korchnoi decided to try and turn the tables. In game 9 he switched to a tactical style, trying to surprise me with aggressive play. But having lost the battle on his territory he wasn't able to make a successful transition to fighting on mine and he suffered a devastating loss. This experience of adapting under fire was most helpful when I had to do the same under even less favourable conditions against Karpov in our world championship match a year later.

As any reader of Darwin knows, the failure to adapt almost always brings dire consequences. A classic example comes from American history, in 1755, when George Washington was a volunteer aide-de-camp fighting in the British army against French and Indian forces. The British made almost no effort to adapt to the frontier warfare practised by their enemies. Their General Edward Braddock was a tragically typical case. He would line up his British redcoats in orderly rows out in the open, to fire well-organized volleys into the forest as the French and Indian snipers picked them off from cover. Only when Braddock himself was finally killed in a disastrous battle could his few remaining men retreat, led by none other than Washington.

Less calamitous is the story of the *Encyclopaedia Britannica* as it encountered the computer age. Perhaps the best-known brand name in reference books, its first blunder was coming very late to releasing its products on CD-ROM. After all, who would want to replace all those beautiful books with a computerized version? Everybody, as we now know. This allowed Microsoft's Encarta and others to take a huge market share as sales of printed encyclopedias dropped to a tiny fraction of the reference market.

Next came the internet and its promise of almost unlimited customers around the world. *Britannica* charged for access at a time when everyone else was giving content away for free and business was predictably poor. A few years later the dot-com boom was busting – something I remember only too well from my first-hand experience with my own chess portal. The online advertising market collapsed entirely just as *Britannica* finally decided to give away their content for free. No matter what they did they were on the wrong side of change.

What was responsible for *Britannica*'s series of debacles? They were clearly well behind the curve when it came to moving from print to digital media. The failure of their internet strategies is more complex. Being too far ahead of your environment can be just as bad as lagging behind your competitors. Instead of relying on their huge brand advantage they tried to out-think a new and unpredictable market and ended up fighting on a losing battlefield each time.

A frequently changed strategy is the same as no strategy

Change can be essential, but it should only be made with careful consideration and just cause. Losing can persuade you to change what doesn't need to be changed and winning can convince you everything is fine even if you are on the brink of disaster. If you are quick to blame faulty strategy and change it all the time, you really don't have any strategy at all. Only when the environment shifts radically should you consider a change in fundamentals.

We must walk a fine line between flexibility and consistency. A strategist must have faith in his strategy and the courage to follow it through and still be open-minded enough to realize when a change of course is required. Changes must be considered carefully, and when they come they must be made decisively. Success is seldom analysed as closely as failure and we are always quick to attribute our victories to superiority, rather than circumstance. When things are going well it is even more important to question. Over-confidence leads to mistakes, a feeling that anything is good enough.

One of the tensest games of my life saw my opponent fail to have faith in his own plans. In 1985 I was locked in yet another battle with my long-time foe, Anatoly Karpov. It was the final game of our second world championship match and I was in the lead by a single point. He had the advantage of the white pieces and if he won he would draw the match and retain the title for three more years.

He played aggressively right from the start and built up an impressive attacking position against my king. Then came the critical decision, whether to completely commit to his attack by pushing his pawn forward against my kingside or to continue with more circumspect preparations. I think we both knew that this was the critical moment in the game.

Karpov decided against the push and the opportunity was gone. After spending the first twenty moves of the game preparing a direct assault, he got cold feet and missed his chance. Suddenly I was in my element, counter-attacking instead of defending. The game entered complications on my terms, not my opponent's, and I brought home the victory that made me world champion.

When it came time to play for the kill, Karpov played a move that fitted his prudent style but not the win-at-all-costs situation.

His personal style was in conflict with the required game strategy and he veered off course.

In an illuminating postscript to the critical game that cost him the world championship, Karpov subsequently almost entirely stopped opening with his king's pawn. He recognized that at key moments his style wouldn't fit the sharp positions it created. He learned and adapted and stayed near the top for many, many years because he was quick to recognize that he needed to change.

We must know what questions to ask and ask them frequently. Have conditions changed in a way that necessitates a change in strategy, or is a small adjustment all that is required? Have fundamental goals changed for some reason? Avoid change for the sake of change.

We must also avoid being distracted away from our strategic path by the competition. If you are employing a powerful and successful strategy, whether gaining space on the chessboard or a market share in global commerce, the competition will try to trip you up by getting you to abandon it. If your plans are sound and your tactical awareness is good, he can only succeed with your help.

Against solid strategy, diversionary tactics will either be insufficient or flawed. If they are insufficient you can and should ignore them, continuing along your path. If they are radical enough to force you from your path they are likely flawed in some way unless you have blundered. Often an opponent is so eager to get you to change your course that he fatally weakens his own position in the attempt.

An interesting side-effect of my years of success was that some of my opponents chose to employ unorthodox variations to take our games into original channels. Here, they felt, my long experience would be nullified and they would be better prepared for the unusual positions. The problem, as many of these players discovered, is that most of these concepts were rare for good reason. The virtue of innovation only rarely compensates for the vice of inadequacy.

Don't watch the competition more than you watch yourself

Even if the competition isn't interfering directly we can divert ourselves. When I'm playing in a head-to-head event like a world championship match I only have one guy to watch and he's sitting right across the board from me. It's a zero-sum situation: I win, he loses, or vice versa. But in a tournament with a dozen players what goes on in the other games can have an impact on my own success. It's like any business with multiple partners and competitors; Continental has to pay attention if United and American start talks.

In 2000 I was playing in a very strong tournament in Sarajevo. Entering the final round I was in the lead by the slimmest of margins, a half-point. (Wins are worth a point, draws half a point, losses no points.) Two of the world's top players, Alexei Shirov and Michael Adams, were right behind me. It would have been nice to face one of them for all the marbles in the final round, but we were all playing different opponents. If I drew my game and Adams or Shirov won they would tie with me for first place. If I lost I could drop as far as third.

So before my game I had to decide whether to play cautiously or to go all out for a win. It would be heroic to enter every battle with 'Victory or death' on our lips, but few situations in chess or life are as dire as when those words were written from the Alamo.

First off, I had the disadvantage of the black pieces. Next there was my opponent, an outsider in this elite event. Sergei Movsesian, representing the Czech Republic, had done poorly in the tournament but had defeated two of the highest-rated participants in the previous two rounds. I should also mention that there was a minor personal element in our contest. I had once, in 1999, dismissed Movsesian and a few other players as 'tourists' and he had taken his strong objections to this designation to the press. Now this tourist surely wanted my scalp as a souvenir.

Then I had to consider the day's other match-ups. Shirov's opponent, the Frenchman Etienne Bacrot, had already lost five games and was at the bottom of the standings. I couldn't count on him gaining a draw when his opponent had everything to play for.

Incorporating that information into my game strategy, I went on the attack from the start against Movsesian. The game was turning my way when I got up to check on my pursuers. I knew that if I won my game how they did would be irrelevant, but it was hard not to watch. If they both drew or lost it would be folly for me to take undue risks in my own game. In that case, I could draw and still win the tournament. Admittedly, thoughts like that made it hard to focus on my own game. There is a precarious balance between knowing what your competition is up to and becoming distracted from the factors you control directly.

Thus it was almost a relief to see that both Shirov and Adams were on the way to victory. I knew for sure that I had to ignore them and focus on my own game and that it was now a matter of winning at all costs. Any cautious strategies were tossed out of the window as soon as I got back to my chair. In the end all three of us won so I kept my slim lead and took first place. We can't spend so much time worrying about the other guy that we lose sight of our own goals and our own performance.

'Why?' turns tacticians into strategists

In his book on Japanese business, Kenichi Ohmae summed up the role of the strategist this way: 'The strategist's method is to challenge the prevailing assumptions with a single question: Why?'

'Why?' is the question that separates functionaries from visionaries, mere tacticians from great strategists. You must ask this question constantly if you are to understand and develop and follow your strategy. When I watch novice students play chess I'll see a terrible move and ask the student why he played it. Very often he'll have no answer at all. Obviously something in his brain pushed that move forward as the best choice, but it goes without saying that it wasn't part of a deeper plan with strategic goals in mind. Everyone would benefit greatly from stopping before each move, each decision, and asking, 'Why this move? What am I trying to achieve and how does this move help me achieve it?'

Chess shows us the power of 'why' in a very clear manner. Every move has a consequence; every move either fits into your strategy or it doesn't. If you aren't questioning your moves consistently you will lose to the player who is playing with a coherent plan.

Imagine doing that regularly at work, or even in your private activities. We all have hundreds of personal and professional objectives, but they are usually vague, unformed wish lists instead of goals that can form the basis of a strategy. 'I want to make more money' is like saying 'I want to find true love' or 'I want to win this game.' A wish isn't a goal.

To take a practical example, the desire to find a better job is one almost everyone experiences at some point. Only when you have a thorough understanding of why you want to change should you begin. Maybe it's not just the job, maybe you need an entirely new career. Or perhaps there are changes you can make at your current workplace. You won't know what you are looking for until you are aware what conditions will satisfy you.

When you do begin your search, your guide is that list of intermediate objectives that add up to your goal of 'better job'. For example, if money isn't your biggest issue in your current position you shouldn't be tempted by a job that offers more cash but won't change the things that are really driving you crazy where you are now.

Once you have a strategy, employing it is a matter of desire

Finally we come to the hardest part of developing and employing strategic thinking: the confidence to use it and the ability to stick to it consistently. Once you have your strategy down on paper the real work begins. How do you stay on track, and how do you know when you have slipped away from thinking strategically?

We must have faith in our analysis, the courage of our convictions. We must constantly monitor the conditions that will make our strategy succeed or fail. We stay on track with rigorous questioning of our results, both good and bad, and our ongoing decisions. During a game I question my moves and after the game I question how accurate my evaluations were in the heat of battle. Were my decisions good ones? Was my strategy sound? If I won, was it due to luck or skill? When this system fails, or fails to operate quickly enough, disaster can strike.

In 2000 I met a former pupil of mine, Vladimir Kramnik, in a sixteen-game match for the world chess championship, my sixth title defence. I had won the title back in 1985 and had been playing some of the best chess of my life headed into the match. In other words, I was ripe for defeat.

Years of success had made it difficult for me to imagine I could lose. Going into that match I had won seven consecutive grand slam tournaments in a row and I wasn't aware of my own weaknesses. I felt I was in great form and unbeatable. After all, hadn't I beaten everyone else? With each success the ability to change is reduced. My longtime friend and coach, Grandmaster

Yuri Dokhoian, aptly compared it to being dipped in bronze. Each victory added another coat.

When he played black in our match, Kramnik shrewdly chose a defence – the Berlin variation of the Ruy Lopez – in which the powerful queens quickly came off the board. The game became one of long-range manoeuvring rather than dynamic, hand-to-hand combat. Kramnik had evaluated my style and had rightly assessed that I would find this kind of tranquil play boring and would unwittingly let down my guard. I had prepared intensely and was ready to fight on perhaps 90 per cent of the chess battleground, but he forced me to play on the 10 per cent that he knew better and that he knew I would least prefer. It was a brilliant strategy that worked to perfection.

Instead of trying to wrest the games back to positions where I would be more comfortable I took up his challenge and tried to beat him at his own game. This played right into Kramnik's hands. I was unable to adapt, unable to make the necessary strategic changes quickly enough, and I lost the match and my title. Sometimes the teacher must learn from the student.

In the long run I learned that I needed to be more flexible about the kinds of chess positions I enjoy. But this painful lesson could have been avoided with a greater sense of vigilance, by working harder to find and repair my weaknesses before Kramnik could exploit them.

Every leader in every field, every successful company or individual, has got to the top by working harder and focusing better than someone else. The top achievers believe in themselves and their plans and they work constantly to ensure those plans are worthy of their belief. It becomes a positive cycle, work reinforcing desire that spurs more work. Questioning yourself must become a habit, one strong enough to surmount the obstacles of over-confidence and dejection. It is a muscle that can be developed only with constant practice.

There's a business saying that goes: 'Planning without action is futile, action without planning is fatal.' This echoes Sun Tzu, who centuries ago wrote, 'Strategy without tactics is the slowest route to victory. Tactics without strategy is the noise before defeat.'

Strategic battle plan – 1985 world championship match – Moscow, USSR

My difficulties in my first world championship match with Anatoly Karpov were not only at the board. Heading into that match I was also lacking in experience in preparing a plan for the entire event. I went in thinking that extensive opening preparation and energy would be enough. We had no plan beyond showing up for each game and playing hard and this was quickly shown to be inadequate. I came to the second match better prepared and as a result felt much more comfortable even when I experienced setbacks in the first half. Here was my team's battle plan for that second match.

Goal: To win the match. I needed to score 12.5 points from the twenty-four games to win. It was important to remember that it wasn't necessary to wipe Karpov out, as much as I would have liked to. I needed only to win one game more than he did over the course of twenty-four games. (A drawn match would leave him with the title.) It wasn't necessary to win every game or to win spectacularly. When I fell behind in the match after the fifth game I didn't panic, instead continuing to play my game and follow the battle plan. Sticking to this plan, with minor adjustments along the way, allowed me to take the initiative and push Karpov against the ropes.

Advantages and disadvantages: Karpov's style and experience gave him an advantage in technical positions where dynamic imbalances were not so important. One of my intermediate goals, then, was to seek out complicated positions that fitted my strengths of accurate calculation and evaluating the initiative. We also felt my youthful energy would be used to advantage in these sharp, complex games, in which it was necessary to maintain peak concentration for long periods. If the position was simplified, Karpov's relentless technique could grind me down.

Specific preparation: After playing so many games against Karpov in the first match we had a good idea of what sort of positions he didn't like to play. We designed my opening repertoire for the match around reaching these types of positions, not just their objective value. For example, we might discard a position we evaluated as objectively equal but that suited Karpov's style well.

We developed a very risky gambit variation with the black pieces. We knew it was objectively a little shaky, but it was exactly the sort of dynamic position I enjoy and that Karpov despised. I first used it in game 12 and Karpov agreed to a short draw, mostly due to the shock value of this new idea. It was assumed I wouldn't risk the gambit again since Karpov's team would now be ready for it. But in game 16 I brought it back and scored one of my greatest victories. (A counter to this gambit was later found by Karpov against another opponent.)

Result: A 13–11 match win. Karpov only rarely achieved positions he enjoyed and in game eleven he committed one of the worst blunders of his career. To his credit, Karpov absorbed the same lessons we had about his strengths and weaknesses. After this match he completely changed his opening repertoire with white to be more in line with his natural style.

4
STRATEGY AND TACTICS

'Tactics is knowing what to do when there is something
to do; strategy is knowing what to do when there is
nothing to do.' – *Savielly Grigoryevich Tartakower*

To make the right moves we have to know what we're looking for,
what we are after. No quantity of analysis can give us the answer
to this question. As we have observed, chess has a relatively simple
objective: to win the game. To achieve victory we establish game
strategies and decide on the right course of action to accomplish
them. The words 'strategy' and 'tactics' are routinely used
interchangeably, a waste of many valuable distinctions.

While strategy is abstract and based on long-term goals,
tactics are concrete and based on finding the best move right now.
Tactics are conditional and opportunistic, all about threat and
defence. If you don't immediately exploit a tactical opportunity the
game will almost certainly turn against you. Here we can also
introduce the concept of the 'only move', where everything else
loses. We even have a special symbol in chess literature to mark a
move that was absolutely essential. Not good or bad, or difficult
or easy, but simply required to avoid disaster.

When your opponent has blundered, a winning tactic can
appear suddenly and serve as both means and end. Imagine a
football game where the coaches have spent months training their
players in complex strategies and set plays. But if the opposing
goalkeeper slips on the grass you toss strategy to the side and shoot
for goal without hesitation, a purely tactical reaction.

A tactician feels at home reacting to threats and seizing
opportunities on the battlefield. His problem is how to make
progress when there are no obvious moves, when action is
required, not reaction. The great Polish chess master and wit
Savielly Tartakower half-joking called this the 'nothing to do'
phase of the game. In reality, it is what separates pretenders
from contenders.

In chess we have the obligation to move; there is no option to skip a turn if you can't identify anything to do. This obligation can be a burden to a player without strategic vision. Unable to form a plan when there isn't an immediate crisis, he is likely to try to precipitate a crisis himself, usually succeeding only in damaging his own position. We learned from Tigran Petrosian that vigilant inaction is a viable strategy in chess, but the art of useful waiting takes consummate skill. What exactly do you do when there is nothing to do?

We call these phases 'positional play' because our goal is to improve our position. We must avoid creating weaknesses, find small ways to improve our pieces, and think small but never stop thinking. There is a tendency to get lazy in quiet positions, which is why positional masters like Karpov and Petrosian were so deadly. They were always alert and were happy to go long stretches without any real action on the board if it meant gaining one tiny advantage, and then another. Eventually their opponents would find themselves without any good moves at all, as if they were standing on quicksand.

In life there is no such obligation to move. If you can't find a useful plan you can watch television, stick with business as usual, and believe that no news is good news. Human beings are brilliantly creative at finding ways to pass time in unconstructive ways. It's at these times that a true strategist shines by finding means to make progress, strengthen his position and prepare for the inevitable conflict. And conflict, we cannot forget, IS inevitable.

Europe was largely at peace entering the twentieth century, and pacifist movements were making political inroads in European parliaments. Germany, meanwhile, was preparing for war, and its naval build-up was matched, even provoked in some cases, by Britain's. The responsibility for this lay with one man, Admiral John (Jackie) Fisher.

Britain had quite literally ruled the waves for over a century and in 1900 the British politicians and military leaders took this superiority entirely for granted. But Admiral Fisher insisted on modernizing the Royal Navy, building the first giant dreadnoughts and encouraging the development of submarines, which others in the Admiralty saw as sneaky and, worst of all, 'un-English'.

Fisher, whose belligerent personality was ill-suited to affairs of state, had to push relentlessly to achieve his programme of peacetime modernization. In 1910 he retired, exhausted by political battles rather than by sea battles. He was recalled by Winston Churchill at the outbreak of the First World War in 1914, and although their disagreement over the Dardanelles campaign caused Fisher to resign less than a year later, his years of reforming the Royal Navy soon proved their worth.

Jackie Fisher is now recognized by historians as one of Britain's greatest admirals, and many of his most important contributions took place without firing a shot. Here was a strategist who knew that not having anything to do didn't mean doing nothing.

Tactics must be guided by strategy

Every time we make a move we must consider our opponent's response, our answer to that response, and so on. A tactic ignites an explosive chain reaction, a forcing sequence of moves that carries the players along on a wild ride. You analyse the position as deeply as you can, computing the dozens of variations, the hundreds of positions. One slip and you are wiped out.

We can compare this to a trader who must decide 'Buy or sell?' a dozen times a day. He looks at the numbers, analyses as much as he can, and makes the best decision possible in the limited time available. The more time he spends, the better his decision will be, but while he is thinking the opportunity to make the decision is passing.

Tactics involve calculations that are very hard for the human brain, but when you boil them down they are the simplest part of chess and almost trivial compared to strategy. They are forced, planned responses, basically a series of 'if – then' statements that would make a computer programmer feel quite at home. 'If he captures my pawn I will play my knight to e5. Then if he attacks my knight I'll sacrifice my bishop. Then if . . .' Of course, by the time you get to the fifth or sixth 'if' your calculations have become incredibly complex because of the sheer number of possible moves. The chance of making a mistake increases the further ahead you look.

We all make our decisions based on a combination of analysis and experience. The goal is to be conscious of that process and to be able to improve it. In order to do that we have to be able to take a wider view so that we can evaluate the deeper consequences of our tactical decisions. In other words, we need strategy to keep our tactics on course.

An ever-expanding example

Not long after the hundredth anniversary of the Wright brothers' famous first flight at Kitty Hawk, North Carolina, in March 2004, I gave a lecture titled 'Achieving Your Potential' to an audience of executives in Interlaken, the Swiss mountain resort. As an example illustrating the danger of a lack of strategic vision, I chose the Wright brothers and their famous invention. Hundreds of engineers had died attempting to invent a flying machine and Orville and Wilbur succeeded, going down – or up – in history for all time.

And yet they never believed the aeroplane would amount to much beyond novelty and sport. This idea was shared by the American scientific community, a mentality that soon left the USA well behind in the aircraft business. The Wright brothers failed to envision the potential of their creation and it was left to others to exploit the power of flight for commercial and military purposes. To this cautionary tale I added a punchline, pointing out that we don't fly in Wright aeroplanes today. America needed someone who combined entrepreneurial vision with engineering prowess and that man was William Boeing. The familiar name received an approving laugh from the audience, but later I discovered that his example was more illuminating than I had imagined. More than just a strategist, Boeing was also a creative tactician.

In 1910, the magazine *Scientific American* wrote that to affirm that the plane could revolutionize the world 'is to be guilty of the wildest exaggeration'. Back then, William Boeing didn't even know how to fly and was living in Seattle, Washington, far from the East Coast, where most aeronautic research was going on. Boeing, who dropped out of engineering classes at Yale, didn't have the technical knowledge of the Wright brothers. What he had was a vision of the potential of flight and the ability to develop a strategy to achieve it.

Boeing saw the potential before the market and understood that technological excellence was the required foundation for a company in this new field. In order to fulfil his concept of a successful commercial aircraft company, several technical obstacles had to be overcome. Boeing bet his life savings that technology would catch up with his vision before he went broke. He didn't just wait around for this to happen. Strategy: better technology. Tactic: he had a wind tunnel built at a local university so that it could produce the engineers he needed.

In 1917 the American military was getting ready to enter the First World War. They needed planes and Boeing had a new design he thought they could use. The problem was that the Navy was testing new planes 3,000 miles away in Florida, too far to fly the little planes. Boeing knew that this was a crucial opportunity and had his planes taken apart, boxed up like pizzas and shipped across the country, a brilliant tactical manoeuvre.

That modest success allowed Boeing to continue for a few more years, during which time his struggling aeroplane factory also produced boats and, believe it or not, furniture. He continued to hire the most talented engineers and invest in research. When mail delivery and passenger travel, plus Charles Lindbergh's sensational New York to Paris flight, created a real boom, Boeing and his superior technology were ready and waiting to dominate the industry.

Later that year I spoke at two business expos in Brazil and was able to add another chapter to this story. Brazil has its own 'father of flight', the inventor Alberto Santos-Dumont, who was flying heavier-than-air craft in public before the Wright Brothers. His daring exploits and flamboyant personality made him perhaps the most famous individual on earth in 1900, although he is largely forgotten in much of the world today. For Brazilian audiences the faded fame of their hero Santos-Dumont made an ideal comparison to the renown of Boeing. Beyond a utopian dream of world peace brought about by global travel, Santos-Dumont had little interest in the implications of his inventions. He was horrified by the wartime use of aircraft, which allegedly contributed to the motive for his suicide in 1932.

If strategy represents the ends, tactics are the means. Boeing employed countless clever tactics and manoeuvres in the service of his long-term plan. Once we have a clear set of goals and intermediate objectives, we can measure potential tactics and combinations against them. The more we do this the easier it becomes; our strategic goals become incorporated into our tactical thinking. Our reactions will be faster and at the same time more accurate, and speed is always of the essence.

The vicious circle of time trouble

The worst enemy of the strategist is the clock. Time trouble, as we call it in chess, reduces us all to pure reflex and reaction, tactical play. Emotion and instinct cloud our strategic vision when there is no time for proper evaluation. Even the most honed intuition can't entirely do without accurate calculations. A game of chess can suddenly seem a lot like a game of chance.

It was 4 March 2004, and my clock was ticking down in a critical game at the Linares tournament in Spain. The most important tournament of the year was coming to a close and I was sitting in second place. If I won this game I would move into a tie for first. There were ten minutes left on my clock and a storm was brewing on the board. I had a double-edged position against Bulgarian star Veselin Topalov, the current FIDE world champion. I amassed a giant army against his king, and, confident of my over-whelming power on that side of the board, launched an attack.

I saw a promising continuation but I couldn't find anything concrete in my calculations; there were too many possibilities for both sides. Eight minutes. It looked good, my intuition said it must be good. I went for it. Now it was Topalov's turn to sweat, but he proved up to the task. He defended well, setting me new problems that I had to solve in my very limited time. We both played quickly, on instinct, with our hands as much as our brains. Four minutes.

Wait, was his last move a mistake? True to his combative nature, Topalov had lashed out instead of defending. To keep my attack going I sacrificed a piece, creating a serious material disadvantage. If my attack failed I would lose the game, so there was no way back. My heart leapt and adrenaline flooded my system. I sensed the decisive blow was close at hand. With a leap of my knight I could discover an attack by my rook against his king. It looked devastating. Where to move the knight? The e4 square or the e6 square? Forward or backward? Two minutes.

My brain was crunching through the alternatives at top speed, trying to find the best moves for both sides through the mind-bending variations. I visualized how I would counter his possible defences, if here, then there, if this, then that. Four moves ahead, five moves, six moves . . . There was no time to analyse deeply enough to be sure of everything. One minute.

Wait, it looked as if the backwards move was a losing option! Unnerved, I pushed my knight to the forward square, already sensing that the opportunity was gone. Topalov reacted quickly, his king running for cover. With seconds left I could only force his king back and forth; there was no way to administer a *coup de grâce*. The game ended in a draw by repetition, no win, no loss. I felt deflated in my chair; had I missed a win? After such a thrilling hunt my quarry had eluded me. I finished the tournament in a bitter tie for second place and I was just as concerned about how my intuition had betrayed me at a critical moment.

As it turned out I had moved my knight to the wrong square. Analysis showed that moving it backwards to e4, the 'wrong' direction, away from the enemy king, would have given me an overpowering attack. I had looked at that move during my calculations but had seen that his queen could check my king, coming back to defend. When the game ended, Topalov suggested the alternative knight leap to e4 as winning and I replied, 'Yes, but what about the queen check on c1?' He looked puzzled, and just from the look on his face I suddenly realized that this move would have been illegal, the queen could not reach c1 at all. A total hallucination. Ironically, or perhaps just cruelly, the winning move would have removed a key defensive piece, just the sort of strategic objective I would have naturally pursued had I had enough time to back it up with calculation.

The most disturbing thing about this miss at the time was that one of the strongest parts of my game had always been fast and deep calculation – tactics. I was always confident of my ability to analyse complications better than my opponents. When it came time for me to deliver the killer blow my adversary rarely escaped.

I left Linares with my self-confidence shaken. Of course nobody scores 100 per cent on every exam, but this was still troubling. At forty I was considerably older than most of my competitors, who were usually in their twenties and occasionally in their teens. If age was creeping up on me and my tactics were getting shaky, how much longer could I stay on top? I would have to take a close look at my game, especially my tactical abilities, before I got back on the stage.

In hindsight, the real problem was not my mistake during time trouble. As later positive results would show, my faculties were still in fine working order. The culprit was letting myself get into such a time crunch. I hadn't been playing often and my rustiness had led to a lack of decisiveness, a lack of faith in my calculations. I had spent precious minutes double-checking things that I should have played quickly. The best plans and the most devious tactics can still fail without confidence.

Good strategy can fail with bad tactics

Winston Churchill's books are among my favourites. His tenacity – some called it stubbornness – pervaded every aspect of his character. His proposal of a military campaign in the Dardanelles during the First World War – the very one that led to the resignation of Admiral Fisher – turned into one of the worst military disasters in British history. And yet twenty-five years later he had the insight to realize that his essential idea had been correct, and the courage to try again to implement the plan.

In 1915 Churchill, then First Lord of Admiralty, convinced the cabinet and Britain's allies to attack Gallipoli, at the heart of the Ottoman Empire, in order to create a supply line to Russia and to force the Germans to open a new front. Ships and troops were diverted from the Mediterranean – this is what angered Fisher – and sent to the Dardanelles Strait, a strategic point that divides the Asian and European parts of Turkey.

Initial naval attacks went well, but that was the end of the good news for the British. When troops were brought in they were put under the command of Sir Ian Hamilton, who knew little of the situation on the ground. He was paired with two other commanders with no one in overall charge of the operation. One tactical blunder followed another as the British troops suffered heavy casualties against the inspired defence of the Turks, whose eventual victory led to the rise of Colonel Mustafa Kemal – later known as Ataturk – who after the war would go on to found the Turkish Republic.

The British finally retreated after losing 200,000 men and three battleships. This humiliating disaster cost Churchill his job at the Admiralty, although he was called back right after the start of the Second World War. In 1941, when Nazi Germany attacked the Soviet Union, Churchill realized that the Allies were facing a problem similar to that of 1915. The Soviets were very low on supplies, much as Russia had been at the start of the First World War. One of the first British–Soviet actions, in July 1941, was to occupy Iran to ensure overland supply lines and communication with the Soviets. (The northern sea lines would be unsafe and insufficient in a long war.)

In October the Allies began to supply the Soviets, much in the way Churchill had imagined in 1915. In 1943 this proved to be vital to the USSR's war effort, with over 300,000 tons of food, ammunition and other essential supplies coming in per month. Churchill had recognized that the failure of the Gallipoli campaign didn't mean the reasoning behind it was faulty. No matter how good, or bad, the results, our analysis into the causes must be rigorous.

In chess we see many cases of good strategy failing due to bad tactics and vice-versa. A single oversight can undo the most brilliant concepts. Even more dangerous in the long run are cases of bad strategy succeeding due to good tactics, or due to sheer good fortune. This may work once, but rarely twice. This is why it is so important to question success as vigorously as you question failure.

Pablo Picasso nailed it in a typically elliptical way when he said that 'Computers are useless. They can only give you answers.' Questions are what matter. Questions, and discovering the right ones, are the key to staying on course. Are our tactics, our day-to-day decisions, based on our long-term goals? The wave of information threatens to obscure strategy, to drown it in details and numbers, calculation and analysis, reaction and tactics. To have strong tactics we must have strong strategy on one side and accurate calculation on the other. Both require seeing into the future.

Paul Morphy (1837–84), USA
Wilhelm Steinitz (1836–1900), Austria-Hungary
The founding fathers

The edifice of modern chess stands on twin pillars, Morphy and Steinitz. The first blazed a trail with unprecedented brilliance, the second documented how it had been done and codified the method into a system others could learn from. The play of Morphy and the games and writings of Steinitz moved chess from the turbulent romantic period into the modern era of logical principles.

It seems preposterous to suggest that a single player could have a serious impact on such an ancient game in as short a time as a year. And yet in 1857–8, America's Paul Morphy created a legacy that altered the chess landscape forever. The wealthy young man from New Orleans entered the chess world only because he was not yet of age to practise as a lawyer when he finished his studies. He quickly proved himself a class above the best players in the United States, but the real competition was across the Atlantic.

Morphy's trip to Europe can be compared with the greatest tales of conquest. Reversing the path of the conquistadors, the twenty-one-year-old demolished the greatest players of the day one after the other. Even the renowned German Adolf Anderssen was soundly defeated. Anderssen's prowess as an attacker was such that two of his greatest games acquired names of their own. Players today are still astonished by the beauty of the 'The Immortal Game' and 'The Evergreen Game' when they first come across them. And yet he was unable to muster much of anything against Morphy's sound play. (The aging English great, Howard Staunton, prudently avoided meeting Morphy at the board.)

Morphy returned to the States as a hero. Little wonder, as he was the first American to achieve such global pre-eminence. While the official title of world champion wouldn't be recognized for another thirty years, there is no question that Paul Morphy was the king of chess.

Tragically, he had a very short reign. Morphy had never considered chess to be a proper profession for a Southern gentleman and after his return from Europe he never again played chess seriously. He was distracted by the game and disenchanted with the law and never made much of a career in either discipline. These anxieties were exacerbated by his ambivalence during the Civil War and Morphy suffered a steady mental decline in his final years. With good reason the great Morphy is called 'the pride and sorrow of chess'.

How did he do it? How could such a young man with no adequate competition in his native land so easily humiliate the best players in the world? Morphy's secret, and it's unlikely he was aware of it himself, was his understanding of positional play. Instead of flying directly into an attack, as was the rule in those days, Morphy first made sure everything was ready. He understood that a winning attack should only be launched from a strong position and that a position with no weaknesses could not be overwhelmed.

Unfortunately, he left no map behind, few writings that could explain his method. Morphy was so far ahead of his time that after he left the scene the Romantics again dominated, as if they had learned nothing. It took another quarter-century for these fundamental principles of development and attack to be rediscovered and formulated.

This rediscovery was the achievement of Wilhelm Steinitz. Born in Prague, then part of the Austrian empire, Steinitz's early chess career was one of a steady rise and his play was similar in style to his contemporaries. That is, he played speculatively and sacrificially with little consideration of defence or soundness. He achieved prominence as a player for his daring attacks, acquiring the nickname 'the Austrian Morphy'.

It was after Steinitz moved to England, where he spent twenty years before becoming an American citizen, that he slowly transformed his thinking and his play. The long breaks between tournaments allowed him to contemplate and study while writing his popular chess column and giving exhibitions. By 1870 Steinitz had begun to develop his theories of defence, weaknesses, and strategic play. This is what divides the chess timeline into 'pre-Steinitz' and 'post-Steinitz' periods.

Although Steinitz's immortality would have been assured by his theoretical contributions, he was also successful in implementing them on the board. In 1886 he battled Johann Zukertort, a romantic attacker of the old school, in what is now remembered as the first official world championship match. Despite losing four of the first five games, Steinitz and his principles triumphed in the end. He took the measure of his opponent, adjusted, and scored nine wins to just one further loss. Zukertort could not comprehend how Steinitz could win without brilliant attacks. After all, wasn't that how games were supposed to be won?

By the time Steinitz handed the crown to Emanuel Lasker in 1894 a new generation of players had absorbed Steinitz's teachings thoroughly. All the champions have acknowledged our debt to his theories and principles. The evolution of the game has continued, but it was Steinitz, inspired by Morphy, who first brought the game out of the sea on to dry land.

On Morphy: 'To this day Morphy is an unsurpassed master of the open game. Just how great was his significance is evident from the fact that after Morphy nothing substantially new has been created in this field. Every player – from beginner to master – should in his praxis return again and again to the games of the American genius.' – Mikhail Botvinnik

Morphy in his own words: 'Unlike other games in which lucre is the end and aim, [chess] recommends itself to the wise by the fact that its mimic battles are fought for no prize but honour. It is eminently and emphatically the philosopher's game. Let the chessboard supersede the card-table, and a great improvement will be visible in the morals of the community.'

On Steinitz: 'The significance of Steinitz's teaching is that he showed that in principle chess has a strictly defined, logical nature.' – Tigran Petrosian

Steinitz in his own words: 'Chess is difficult, it demands work, serious reflection and zealous research. Only honest, impartial criticism leads to the goal.'

5

CALCULATION

'I see only one move ahead, but it is always the correct one.' – *José Raúl Capablanca, third world chess champion*

Perhaps the question I have most often been asked over the years is 'how many moves ahead do you see?' It is a question at once both profound and ignorant, aiming at the heart of the game of chess while at the same time being impossible to answer. It's like asking a painter how many brushstrokes he uses in a painting, as if that had anything to do with its quality.

Like most such questions, the honest answer is, 'It depends,' but that hasn't stopped people asking or generations of chess players concocting pithy replies. 'As far as needed,' is one, or 'One move further than my opponent.' There is no concrete figure, no maximum or minimum. Calculation in chess is not one plus one but more like figuring out a route on a map that keeps changing before your eyes.

The first reason it is impossible to reduce chess to arithmetic is simply because the numbers involved are so huge. For every move there might be four or five possible responses, then four responses to each of those moves, and so on. The branching of the decision tree grows geometrically. After just five moves from the starting position there are millions of possible positions. The total number of positions in a game of chess is greater than the number of atoms in the universe. True, the majority of these are not realistic game positions, but the vast scope of chess should manage to keep humans occupied for another few hundred years.

Like a weatherman's forecasts, the further ahead you look the less accurate your calculations will be. Uncertainty and randomness intrude as the number of possibilities grows too large to track. The law of diminishing returns comes into effect at the point at which it takes ever more work and time to produce results that are increasingly unclear.

We often hear just any type of mistake referred to as a miscalculation. It's more useful to think of this as a specific type of error, one in which the factors were known but the conclusion reached was incorrect. In chess both players know all the factors, but this is of course impossible in politics. It is still impressive how many political blunders derive from 'obvious' assumptions.

Via war and clever diplomacy, Otto von Bismarck created a German empire in the second half of the nineteenth century. After unifying Germany he managed to isolate France and cut off Russia while he allied with Austria and Italy. He was sure that France and Russia would never ally themselves because an absolute monarch like the Russian Tsar would never 'take off his hat and listen to the Marseillaise', the anthem that had led to so many royals being led to the guillotine.

In 1894, four years after Kaiser Wilhelm II had replaced Bismarck as Chancellor, the French signed a military alliance with Russia. And when a fleet of French ships visited Russia, the Tsar not only listened to the Marseillaise but indeed took off his hat. Bismarck had had all the information he needed but he came to the wrong conclusion and underestimated the growing Russian economy's need for French credit. Most of all he assumed royal pride would outweigh fiscal necessity; his miscalculation had repercussions that lasted into the First World War. Bismarck was a great tactician and strategist but in this case he failed to credit others with the same qualities. He committed the blunder of counting on his opponents to make a mistake he would never have made himself.

Calculation must be focused and disciplined

You might imagine that a game limited to a board with sixty-four squares would be easily dominated by the calculating power of today's computer technology. The refutation of this hypothesis is the second key to accurate decision-making: the ability to evaluate both static (permanent) and fluid factors. Deep calculation isn't what distinguishes the champions. The Dutch psychologist Adriaan de Groot, from whom we'll hear more later, performed studies showing that elite players don't in fact look ahead that much further than considerably weaker players while solving chess problems. They can, on occasion, but neither the ability to do so nor the doing can define their superior chess strength. Even a computer looking at millions of moves per second must have a way to evaluate why one move is better than another, and this evaluation capacity is where humans excel and where computers falter. It doesn't matter how far ahead you see if you don't understand what you are looking at.

When I contemplate my move I don't start out by immediately running down the decision tree. First I must consider all the elements in the position so that I can establish a strategy and develop intermediate objectives. I must keep all of those factors in mind when I finally begin to calculate variations so I know which results are favourable. Experience and intuition can guide this process, but a rigorous foundation of calculation is still required.

No matter how much practice you have and how much you trust your gut instincts, analysis is essential. As Ronald Reagan put it in a different context, 'Trust, but verify'. There are always exceptions to rules, and counter-intuitive scenarios abound in any discipline. Even relatively simple maths can be surprising. I recently attended a dinner party of around twenty-five people. During conversation it turned out that two pairs of guests shared the same birthday, and they were delighted by this extraordinary coincidence. But what were the chances of such a thing happening? As another guest pointed out, and as many people are aware, there is a 50 per cent chance of two people in a group of twenty-three sharing the same birthday, and having two such pairs in our group was roughly a one in four possibility. He went on to tell us that the percentage chance of a group containing two people with the same birthday rises to 99 per cent with only fifty-five people. The mathematics behind this aren't that complicated but the results are certainly counter-intuitive. No matter how sure you are of your conclusions, you must back it up with analysis.

That analysis process must be ordered to be effective. Anyone who has ever written down a list of errands understands that tasks can be done more effectively when prioritized and performed in optimal order. My experience guides me to select two or three candidate moves to focus on. Usually one can be discarded relatively quickly as inferior, and often another comes into consideration to take its place. Then I begin to expand the tree one move at a time, looking at the likely responses and my answering moves.

In a complicated game this tree of analysis usually stays within a depth of four or five moves – that is, four or five moves for each player, or eight to ten total moves. (We call these 'half moves', or what computer chess programmers call a 'ply'. One move for white and one for black equals one move.) Unless there are special circumstances, such as a particularly dangerous position or a moment you evaluate to be a key one in the game, that's a safe, practical amount of calculation.

The decision tree must be constantly pruned to be effective. Mental discipline is required to move from one variation to the next, discarding the less promising moves and following up the better ones. If you jump around too much you'll waste precious time and risk confusing yourself. You must also have a sense of when to stop. This can come either when you have reached a satisfactory conclusion – a path that is clearly the best, or essential – or when further analysis won't return enough value for the time spent.

Imagination, calculation and my greatest game

Invoking imagination here is not in contradiction of the need for discipline. Creativity and order must reign together to guide calculation. Circumstances and instinct inform us when it is necessary to break the routine. The best move might be so obvious that it's not necessary to spend time working out the details, especially if time is of the essence. This is rare, however, and it is often when we assume something is obvious and react hastily that we make a mistake. More often we should break routine by doing more analysis, not less. These are the moments when your instincts tell you that there is something lurking below the surface, or that a critical juncture has been reached and a deeper look is required.

In order to detect these key moments you must be sensitive to trends and patterns in your analysis. If one of the branches in your analysis starts to show surprising results, good or bad, it's worth investing the time to find out what is going on. Sometimes it's hard to explain exactly what makes those bells go off in your head telling you there is more to be found. The important thing is to listen to them when they ring. One of my best games came about thanks to this sixth sense. The scene was the strong traditional 'supertournament' at Wijk aan Zee, in the Netherlands, and my co-actor was again the 'Battling Bulgarian', Veselin Topalov.

Topalov also deserves marquee billing because it takes both players to create a truly beautiful chess game. Unless your opponent fights hard and puts up a good defence, you hardly have a chance to show your skill. Topalov's stern resistance pushed me to the limit of my calculation abilities in this game, in which I played the deepest combination of my career. The main branch of analysis reached fifteen moves, an almost ridiculous number. There was no way to come close to calculating all the possibilities, but miraculously I did visualize the final blow that occurred in the game.

An entire booklet dedicated to this one game was later published in Greece, and I admit that 90 per cent of its analysis didn't enter my mind during the game. Once I had registered a few of the exciting possibilities for chasing black's king across the board, I focused in and concentrated on his most likely attempts at defence. At a certain point in my calculations I realized that it would be like walking a tightrope, and one slip would be fatal. I had sacrificed half my pieces to flush his king out into the open. I kept pushing deeper into my mental image of the position, sure that there must be something, until finally I saw the final winning position, fifteen moves away.

It was a feat of calculation, but there is no way your mind can go that far without help from your imagination. The combination would never have occurred to me had I taken a purely deductive approach to the position. It was not the product of logical analysis showing a mathematically perfect conclusion. As proof I can only point out that on at least one point I missed the strongest move, found in later analysis by other Grandmasters.

As an aside, although it turned out well for me, my missing the very best move illustrates one of the perils of becoming fixated on a distant goal. I was so entranced by my vision of the gold at the end of this rainbow that I stopped looking around as I approached it. I'd managed to convince myself that such a pretty finish must be scientifically correct, too – a potentially dangerous delusion.

Man plus machine is stronger than either

We aren't computers, and our calculations will never be absolutely perfect. But if they are tied to goals and guided by our experience and instincts, our analysis will usually be on the money. In business we also have the advantage of working with computers instead of against them. Human strategy and evaluation skills combined with computers as calculation tools have reinvented many professions, from accounting and investing to managing inventory. With so much progress in just about every walk of life, I began to wonder why it wasn't possible to have the silicon beasts on my side in chess competition as well.

Chess software excels in the area of calculation, precisely the area that humans find most difficult. Your pocket calculator has no trouble with calculating 89 × 97, and chess programs like Fritz and Junior are just as quick to produce the solutions to complicated tactical positions. They trawl through all the possibilities looking for the path that leaves them with the most material. It's a brute force system that isn't particularly elegant, but in complex positions it's undeniably effective. Where they get into trouble is in the long-term planning and manoeuvring phases, where there is no clear path. In 1998 I had an idea. What if instead of human versus machine we played as partners?

My brainchild saw the light of day in a match in León, in Spain, and we called it 'Advanced Chess'. Each player had a PC at hand running the chess software of his choice during the game. Just like a CEO inspecting a spreadsheet, the humans would handle the strategy and we'd leave the number-crunching to the computers. The idea was to create the highest level of chess ever played, a synthesis of the best of man and machine.

That first experiment – yet again I faced Topalov – had a few glitches, mostly in not allowing enough time for the players to access the computers, but it showed promise. It was quite a feeling to harness the machine in combat, rather like wearing a suit of armour. I could concentrate on planning and identifying weaknesses instead of worrying over blunders.

Other Advanced Chess events were held and the games were often of strikingly high quality. There have even been tournaments in which teams of players using multiple computers do battle, no holds barred. Of course I'm still a believer in human chess, but even such an ancient game can benefit from a fresh approach now and then.

Computers may be reaching world championship level in chess, but humans aren't in any danger of being replaced by machines in most other areas. Human business dealings, all our personal interactions, are based on human feelings and reactions.

A manager doesn't manage computers, he manages people. Only a human can understand human weaknesses and tendencies, which is why computers still aren't very good at games like poker where there is a large human element.

A machine can play the odds perfectly, remembering every card on the table with no effort at all. But how can you teach a computer to bluff? That means doing something against the odds, betting more money when you have poor cards. Whether we are negotiating with a Fortune 500 CEO or with a ten-year-old child, experience and intuition are going to be just as important as our ability to analyse the facts.

As with all skills, calculation and the imagination that guides it must be used regularly and pushed to their limits if they are to improve. Many chess players shy away from complex positions because they are unsure of their calculation skills. This becomes a destructive, self-perpetuating cycle. If we avoid concrete analysis, relying only on our instincts, those instincts will never be properly trained. It's good to follow our intuition, as long as we make sure we aren't avoiding the work that's required to know whether or not our judgement is correct.

Siegbert Tarrasch (1862–1934), Germany
Emanuel Lasker (1868–1941), Germany
A rivalry of great minds that didn't think alike

The beginning of the twentieth century saw one of the great rivalries in the game of chess, between Emanuel Lasker and Siegbert Tarrasch. This rivalry extended beyond the chessboard, however. Germany's two greatest players had fundamentally conflicting ideas about the nature of chess, and indeed about life as well. A classic anecdote, probably apocryphal, tells of an attempt to bring peace between them before the start of the first game of their world championship match in Düsseldorf in 1908. Tarrasch entered the room, walked up to Lasker, and said, 'For you, Mr Lasker, I have only three words: "Check and mate!"' Unfortunately for Tarrasch and his supporters he didn't have many opportunities to use this phrase after the match began. Lasker won handily, eight wins to three.

Emanuel Lasker held the world championship crown longer than anyone, from 1894 to 1921. He defeated Wilhelm Steinitz in a title match, although the chess world wasn't really convinced at the time by the young German's play since Steinitz, then fifty-eight, was clearly not in his prime. Over the next five years Lasker removed any doubts about his strength, winning every event in which he participated in crushing style.

Lasker had a great gift for mathematics and made several lasting contributions in the field. He also had a keen interest in philosophy and sociology. A gracious foreword to his (posthumous) biography was written by Albert Einstein, who knew Lasker well. '[T]here are few men who have had a warm interest in all the great human problems and at the same time kept their personality so uniquely independent.' Remarkably, it also included a rebuttal to an essay Lasker had written on the theory of relativity.

For Lasker, chess was primarily a psychological battle between two human wills. As we like to say, he played the man, not the board. He realized that mistakes were inevitable and that victory would go to the player who applied the most pressure, and best resisted it. He was accused by his opponents of intentionally choosing inferior moves that he knew would disturb them. This is an exaggeration, but his games show that he was adept at changing his style to one that would most unsettle his opponent.

The addition of this profound psychological understanding to his many chess gifts allowed Lasker to play at a very high level into his sixties. Although he lost the title to the Cuban genius José Raúl Capablanca in 1921, Lasker took first place in one of the greatest tournaments of all time, New York, 1924, ahead of the champion Capablanca and future champion Alexander Alekhine.

Siegbert Tarrasch is best known for his classic books and droll sayings, but the good doctor was also a peer of the first two world champions, Steinitz and Lasker, and a close rival to both. It is also fair to say that he rivalled them in significance in the game's evolution and its teaching. His books and articles brought the game to a generation of players, and his dogmatic style of instruction was appreciated more then than it would be now.

Much like Steinitz, whose teachings he expounded, Tarrasch tried to bring order to the chaos of the board. In his writing he carefully set out strict guidelines for how the game should be played, and his pen was quick to punish anyone who dared break these rules. In his notes to one game he wrote, 'It is easier to find an excuse for blundering a piece than it is for not understanding the spirit of the game.' This condemnation of the strong English master J. H. Blackburne was delivered as early as move eight! A few moves later, prior to some weak play of his own, Tarrasch commented, 'The following weak moves can only be explained by my confusion caused by Blackburne's poor game.'

It is something of a paradox that someone with such a dogmatic mind had the soul of an innovator. His own play could be sparkling, and while keeping up his career as a general practitioner he also managed to remain one of the three or four leading players in the world for almost twenty years. Such a long stay near the top would have been impossible without the ability to adapt.

On Lasker: 'None of the great players has been so incomprehensible to the majority of amateurs and even masters, as Emanuel Lasker.' – José Raúl Capablanca

Lasker in his own words: 'On the chess board lies and hypocrisy do not survive long. The creative combination lays bare the presumption of a lie; the merciless fact, culminating in a checkmate, contradicts the hypocrite.'

On Tarrasch: 'Razor-sharp, he always followed his own rules. In spite of devotion to his own supposedly scientific method, his play was often witty and bright.' – Bobby Fischer

Tarrasch in his own words: 'Chess, like love, like music, has the power to make men happy.'

'Tarrasch teaches knowledge, Lasker teaches wisdom.' – Fred Reinfeld

6

TALENT

'When I was eleven, I just got good.'
– Bobby Fischer, the eleventh world chess champion

The designation of chess Grandmaster used to be reserved for only the very best players in the world. The Russian Tsar Nicholas II invented the title for the five finalists of the great 1914 tournament he sponsored in St Petersburg. From that legendary five the title was later adopted by the international chess federation (FIDE), which set up qualification guidelines. Inevitably the title proliferated until it reached the total of roughly 1,000 Grandmasters in the world today. There are so many 'GMs' now that unofficial titles like 'super Grandmaster' are used to distinguish the top players from the rest.

I'm often asked what separates an elite chess player, one in the top ten in the world, from the many strong players who never crack the top twenty, or the top hundred. Unfortunately there are as many reasons for failure as there are for success; it is impossible to make broad generalizations. Each player has his or her own reasons for success or failure. The most debated among these is that most elusive quarry, talent.

There are so many definitions and aspects of talent that it's little wonder we have trouble deciding who has it and who doesn't. Prodigies make this easy, but we can do little more than marvel at the likes of Mozart, who composed symphonies at the age of five, and Pascal, who was creating original geometric theorems on the walls of his childhood home at twelve.

Chess, along with music and mathematics, is one of the few pursuits in which superior ability and originality can manifest at a very young age. In 1918 Polish-born Samuel (Sammy) Reshevsky was trotted out in a sailor suit to give exhibitions at the age of seven, defeating entire rooms full of adult players across Europe. José Raúl Capablanca reputedly learned the game at the age of four just by watching his father play and soon proved a match for accomplished players. Reshevsky was poked and prodded by every type of psychologist in a search for the source of his miraculous abilities. How could mere children master a game synonymous with complexity and difficulty?

We are all familiar with tales of such precocity and in general are willing to accept that these individuals are born with special gifts. Still, even their extraordinary talents require the opportunity to display them. The nature versus nurture debate cannot be so easily resolved. Had his father been a painter instead of a music teacher, would we know of Mozart today?

My own early development certainly owed a great deal to external factors. My natural aptitude for chess was quickly discovered by my family. My father, Kim, then struggling with leukaemia, made the decision to send me for chess schooling at the age of seven and my mother enthusiastically supported his decision. Nowadays she likes to remind me how her efforts were often directed at controlling my wilfulness, rather than promoting it. She tells the story of a phone call from my second-grade teacher, who had chastised me for challenging her in class. When told I shouldn't do this because it would make everyone think I believed I was the cleverest, I had replied, 'But isn't that true?' I do not envy my former teachers.

Just about every young star in any field can give credit to a determined parent giving talent a push. As for internal factors, it is clear to me that I would not have achieved such success at anything other than chess. The game came to me naturally, its requirements fitting my talents like a glove.

Not everyone is so lucky, but we can do a great deal to make our own luck when it comes to matching our abilities and our careers. The problem is that as we get older we rarely test our resources and without such testing it is impossible to discover our gifts. If opportunity wasn't provided at a young age, it can be created in adulthood. We can look for ways to experiment and to push the boundaries of our capacity in different areas.

Recognizing the patterns in our lives

Experimentation is critical, because few activities require talent in only one area. A concert pianist needs physical dexterity as well as a good ear and a sense of rhythm. Most things can be broken down into such skill sets. Think about what it takes to be a good manager, a good general, a good parent. Chess is no exception to this rule, and to excel at it requires a synthesis of developed talent and acquired knowledge. As the most important innate qualities I would cite memory and fantasy.

Memory is often discussed as if it is something you either possess or do not possess, like height or blue eyes. Many try to categorize it, saying they have a good memory for faces or a bad memory for names. We have the stereotypes like the absentminded professor who has memorized the complete works of Chaucer but can never remember where he has parked his car.

We know that the brain stores long-term and short-term memories in different places. There are individuals with photographic memories, capable of effortlessly reciting entire phone books. People often believe that elite chess players must possess such faculties, but this is far from the truth.

It is correct to say that to be a great chess player you must have a good memory, but it is much harder to explain what, exactly, we are remembering. Patterns? Numbers? Mental pictures of the board and pieces? The answer, which both intrigues and annoys psychologists, seems to be 'all of the above'.

The practice of 'blindfold chess' has fascinated the world for centuries. In 1783 the great French player François André Danican Philidor played two games simultaneously without sight of the boards and was acclaimed as a genius without parallel. One newspaper account described it as 'a phenomenon in the history of man and so should be hoarded among the best samples of human memory, till memory shall be no more'.

Nearly 200 years later, the Polish Grandmaster Miguel Najdorf was stranded in Argentina at the outbreak of the Second World War. When the war ended Najdorf had the idea of trying to communicate word of his survival to his family in Poland by staging the largest exhibition of blindfold chess ever attempted, forty-five boards simultaneously. That's 1,280 pieces to keep track of, and the event lasted so long that some of his exhausted opponents had to find substitutes mid-game. After nearly twenty-four hours of play, Najdorf scored thirty-nine wins, four draws, and just two losses against his opponents, who, of course, each had full sight of the board.

This is not to say that Najdorf had a perfect, photographic memory; he did not. What he had was a remarkable 'chess memory', the ability to retain the patterns and movements of pieces on a sixty-four-square board, which is as essential to a player when he can see the board as when he cannot. This capacity for recall and visualization makes our calculations quick and accurate and means we don't have to rely on calculating every position from scratch. If you are familiar with a similar position and can remember what worked or didn't work before, you have a big advantage over someone seeing it for the first time.

A Grandmaster will retain tens of thousands of fragments and patterns of chess data and add to them constantly through frequent practice. My ability to recall so many games and positions doesn't mean I have an easier time remembering names, dates, or anything else. Adriaan De Groot illustrated this in an elegant fashion in his 1946 study of chess players. He tested players of every level, from former world champions to beginners, seeking to unlock the secrets of master chess.

De Groot gave the players a set of positions from games to memorize and then recorded how well they could reproduce them. Predictably, the stronger the player, the better he scored. The elite players scored 93 per cent, the experts 72 per cent, the average players just 51 per cent. Deeper insight into why this was the case came thirty years later in a similar study with a twist.

In 1973, researchers W. G. Chase and H. A. Simon replicated de Groot's experiment but added a key second set of test positions. For the second set they placed the pieces on the boards randomly, not following the rules of the game or any pattern at all. As in de Groot's study, the stronger players scored better on the positions taken from actual games. But with the random positions all levels of players scored approximately the same. Without being able to utilize patterns, or what psychologists call 'chunks', the masters didn't display superior memory prowess.

The same processes are at work in every human endeavour. Rote memorization is far less important than the ability to recognize meaningful patterns. When we tackle a problem we never start from scratch; we instinctively, even unconsciously, look for a past parallel. We work out the authenticity of the parallels and see if we can work out a similar recipe from these slightly different ingredients.

Usually this process goes on behind the scenes in the mind, but occasionally, even famously, it comes to the surface. A dazzling game played in St Petersburg in 1914 between two of the leading players of the day, Aaron Nimzowitsch and Siegbert

Tarrasch, was only given the second 'brilliancy prize', because Tarrasch's spectacular sacrificial attack was plainly similar to one from a game played twenty-five years earlier by Emanuel Lasker. The judges felt they couldn't give the first brilliancy prize to a game that appeared derivative.

Traders see trends in the graphs of a stock, parents observe patterns of behaviour in their children, an experienced courtroom lawyer can intuit the most effective way to handle a witness. All derive from a combination of experience and consciously observed memory. And while practice alone can make you competent, to excel requires actively examining what you are retaining.

How often do we review our performance at the end of the day? What did we see, what did we learn? Did we observe or experience something new we should take note of? Would we recognize that situation, that opportunity, that pattern, should it occur again? Elite performers like Olympic athletes must be this critical, this self-aware, to succeed.

The benefits of such rigorous behaviour aren't so obvious if you work in an office, but they are there just the same. Even people in leadership roles are too often content to just get through the day. Most people talk about unwinding after work or school, putting the day behind them so they can relax. How much more effective would they become if, at the end of each day, they asked themselves what lessons they had taken away for tomorrow?

The power of fantasy

'Tal doesn't move the pieces by hand; he uses a magic wand.'
– GM Viacheslav Ragozin, trainer of world champion
Mikhail Botvinnik

I'm not sure exactly when the phrase 'thinking outside the box' became so popular. Almost overnight it was as if it were a sin to think logically, deductively, conventionally. It was almost as if these former virtues had been tossed out and as if suddenly everyone had to be unorthodox or be considered a dinosaur. The dot-com bubble was built on this delusion, the belief that inductive reasoning and creativity could replace – instead of complement – fundamentals and logic.

The French novelist Anatole France wrote that 'to accomplish great things, we must dream as well as act'. In chess we have a name for the sort of imagination required to break out of the usual patterns and startle our opponents; we call it fantasy. This is where we let our mind drift away from the calculation of variations to imagine hidden possibilities in the position. Occasionally we can find a paradoxical idea that all but breaks the rules, but wins thanks to a unique confluence of factors on the board at that exact instant.

Ironically, chess computers are very good at producing moves that strike humans as full of tactical fantasy. Computers don't rely on patterns and hold no prejudices against moves that are ugly or appear illogical or absurd. They simply count the beans and play the best move they find. It's much harder for a human being, a creature of habit, to be so brutally objective.

My own tendency to over-dependence on convention was brought home to me after the publication of the first volume of *My Great Predecessors*. I was going over the analysis of an important game from the 1910 world championship match between Emanuel Lasker and Carl Schlechter. Many strong players, including the match participants themselves, had written commentary on this game, since it was Lasker's only defeat in the match. Towards the end of the game, Lasker, and later his successor as world champion, José Raúl Capablanca, published analysis showing that Lasker could have defended by sacrificing his queen.

I looked at their analysis and had to agree with them. The queen sacrifice was an ingenious defence that could have saved the game and I wrote as much in my book. It hadn't been on the shelves for long when the letters started arriving. Nowadays every chess aficionado has powerful chess software on his PC, and in no time at all this army of silicon-aided fans blew holes in my analysis. In this case, the point was that white was not forced to win the queen. The machine doesn't care that the queen is the strongest piece, it only cares about its evaluation score. Five generations of humans, myself included, had captured the queen and only then started analysing. The computer ignored the queen and showed that there was an easy way to win.

I would like to believe that had I been immersed in the position, playing the game myself, I would have found the winning manoeuvre. As we will discuss later, the focus of intuition in the heat of the moment is often more accurate than thorough analysis done from a distance.

Fantasy can cut through fog

Keeping an open mind is very difficult in a game where so much depends on patterns and logic. For inspiration we can look to those great players who consistently found original ways to shock their opponents, and none did this better than the eighth world champion, Mikhail Tal. The 'Magician of Riga' rose to become champion in 1960 at the age of twenty-three and was already famous for his aggressive, volatile play. He would sacrifice pawns and pieces in ways that went completely against the grain of the modern, scientific era of the game established by Botvinnik. Tal reinvented the romantic form of chess, the way it was played back in the mid-nineteenth century, when defence was considered cowardly.

How did he do it? How could it be that Tal's knights seemed more agile, his bishops faster, than those of other Grandmasters? He was a tremendous calculator, but that was only a small part of his gift. He had the ability to realize when calculation alone wasn't going to solve the problem, as he described in a classic interview. He was discussing his thoughts during a complicated game against the Soviet GM Vasiukov, when he was contemplating the correctness of a knight sacrifice.

Ideas piled up one after another. I would transport a subtle reply to my opponent, which worked in one case, to another situation where it would naturally prove quite useless. As a result, my head became filled with a completely chaotic pile of all sorts of moves, and the famous 'tree of variations', from which the trainers recommend that you cut off the small branches, in this case spread with unbelievable rapidity.

And then suddenly, for some reason, I remembered the classic couplet by [well-known Soviet children's poet] Korney Chukovsky:

Oh, what a difficult job it was
To drag out of the marsh the hippopotamus.

I don't know from what associations the hippopotamus got on to the chess board, but although the spectators were convinced that I was continuing to study the position, I was trying at this time to work out: Just how would you drag a hippopotamus out of the marsh? I remember how jacks figured in my thoughts, as well as levers, helicopters, even a rope ladder. After a lengthy consideration, I admitted defeat as an engineer, and thought spitefully, 'Well, let it drown!' And suddenly the hippopotamus disappeared. Went off from the chess board just as he had come on. Of his own accord. And straightaway the position did not appear to be so complicated. Now I somehow realized that it was not possible to calculate all the variations, and that the knight sacrifice was, by its very nature, purely intuitive. And since it promised an interesting game, I could not refrain from making it.

And the following day, it was with pleasure that I read in the paper how Mikhail Tal, after carefully thinking over the position for forty minutes, made an accurately calculated piece sacrifice . . .

That's a typical example of Tal's wit as well as his insight into problem-solving. He realized that he was wrong to attempt to fix with a wrench something that required a hammer. Even his imaginative mind occasionally required a push to shift into a different gear.

Developing the habit of imagination

Fantasy isn't something you can turn on with the flip of a switch. The key is to indulge it as often as you can to encourage the habit, to allow your unconventional side to flourish. Everyone develops his own device for prompting his muse. The goal is for it to become continuous and unconscious, so your fantasy is always active. It's not about being an inventor, with an occasional flash of creativity, but about being innovative in your decision-making process all the time.

When corporations and business expos first started approaching me to speak, I wanted to be able to better speak their language. As a contributing editor to the *Wall Street Journal* and a cable news addict, I considered myself reasonably well informed when it came to world news, including the business headlines. The problem is that the news does a relatively poor job of putting things into useful, insightful context. Surely we have much to learn from how the greats became great, or about why some companies succeeded where others failed.

This led me on a quest to discover how some of today's household names got that way. The story of William Boeing was one of these finds. Some were less inspirational, less useful for my audiences, but quite a few others were undeservedly unknown.

While the name Joseph Wilson might not ring a bell, the company he led, Xerox, certainly will. Wilson was himself an inventor, but the creative attitude he brought to the company, originally named the Haloid Company, was more important than anything Wilson created in a laboratory. He used to tell new employees, 'We do not want to do things in the same old way. Therefore, as you come here, I hope that you come with an attitude that change will be a way of life for you. You will not do things tomorrow the way you are doing them today.'

I confess to being a creature of habit myself, so it takes considerable effort for me to take this advice. At the board I always tried to let my mind wander, to occasionally ignore the fog of variations and take a mental stab in the dark. In a competitive situation such moves – outside the box if not outside the board – have the added benefit of often coming as a complete surprise to your opponent. The time he has spent thinking on your move has mostly been wasted and the landscape of the game has changed. It's more than playing a good move, an objectively strong move. Moves with an extra charge of fantasy can startle your competition into making mistakes.

Asking 'What if . . .?'

In 1997 I was playing in a tournament in Tilburg, in the Netherlands, and in the fifth round I had the black pieces against one of the world's leading 'fantasy players', the Latvian-born Alexei Shirov, who now plays for Spain. The creative Shirov was even trained in his early years by Mikhail Tal himself, a pedigree without peer when it comes to exotic attacking play.

This time, however, I was able to give him a taste of his own medicine. In a complicated position with chances for both sides,

Shirov moved his rook up the board, preparing to attack my queen on the next move. It was obvious that I had to get my queen out of the way and I sat looking at the few possible retreats. All the options would leave the position dynamically balanced, but I was disappointed there wasn't the opportunity for more.

Before I resigned myself to the inevitable queen move I took a deep breath and took in the rest of the board. As with so many fantasy moves, this one started with a mental 'wouldn't it be nice if . . .' If you daydream a little about what you would like to see happen, sometimes you find that it is really possible. What if I ignored his threat to my queen? He would have extra material, but my pieces, while technically outgunned by his queen, would be very active and he'd be under pressure.

So instead of picking up my queen, my hand lifted my king and moved it a single square towards the centre of the board. The paradox was satisfying, ignoring all the action and threats and playing an innocuous-looking move with the weakest piece on the board. Of course I was also sure that it was a strong move on its objective merits. Fantasy must be backed up by sober evaluation and calculation or you spend your life making beautiful blunders.

Shirov didn't adapt well to the new situation. A born attacker, he was suddenly on the defensive. The position was objectively about even, but he quickly made a serious mistake and it didn't take long to wrap up the game after that. I had the pleasure of sacrificing even more material at the very end to finish things off with a flourish. I didn't put much thought into it at the time, but thinking back on the game now I credit the idea with an attitude of not settling for routine solutions.

Too often we quickly discard apparently outlandish ideas and solutions, especially in areas where the known methods have been in place for a long time. The failure to think creatively is as much self-imposed as it is imposed by the parameters of our jobs and of our lives. 'What if?' often leads to 'Why not?' and at that point we must summon our courage and find out.

Be aware of your routines, then break them

There are as many ways to engage your fantasy as there are decisions you make during the day. You won't find new ways of solving problems unless you look for new ways and have the nerve to try them when you find them. They won't all work as expected, of course. The more you experiment, the more successful your experiments will be. Break your routines, even to the point of changing ones you are happy with, to see if you can find new and better methods.

If we're going to get the most out of the talent we're born with we have to be prepared to analyse ourselves critically and improve our weakest points. The easiest thing is to rely on talent and focus only on what we do well. It's true that you want to play to your strengths, but if there is too much of an imbalance growth is limited. The fastest way to improve overall is to work on your weak spots.

It's important not to listen to the stereotypes we have of ourselves when embarking on this project. Our own opinions of our abilities are often wildly inaccurate, driven by one or two incidents or comparisons. People who constantly tell others, and themselves, that they are forgetful or indecisive create a negative reinforcement loop that becomes hard to break. How do you know your memory is any worse than your spouse's, or mine? It's much better to be a little over-confident than the opposite. As Churchill wrote, 'Attitude is a little thing that makes a big difference.' If we trust in our abilities they will repay us.

José Raúl Capablanca (1888–1942), Cuba
Alexander Alexandrovich Alekhine (1892–1946), Russia/USSR/France
Geniuses who live on as opposing icons

World champions have often come in pairs. It is difficult to think of the great Cuban champion José Raúl Capablanca without thinking of Alexander Alekhine at the same time. Capablanca became the third world champion in 1921, convincingly defeating the ageing Emanuel Lasker in their Havana match. 'Capa' seemed invincible, at one point going ten years with the loss of only a single game.

And yet he held the crown for a mere six years, losing it to Alekhine in 1927 in Buenos Aires. The immovable object had been moved by the irresistible force of the Russian's unorthodox brilliance and iron resolve. Capablanca spent the next decade in vain pursuit of a rematch with Alekhine, who was in no hurry to face the Cuban again. Meanwhile Alekhine fended off the lesser challenge of Efin Boguljubow (a Russian émigré like Alekhine) before suffering an 'accident' against the Dutchman Max Euwe that cost him the title for two years. In 1946, his period as the world's best player already well over, he became the only champion ever to take the title to the grave.

Both players now exist as the ultimate symbols of the chess styles they epitomized. A smooth positional player is always said to 'play like Capablanca', while a sharp attacker is inevitably 'another Alekhine'.

Capablanca is justly remembered as the greatest natural genius the game of chess has ever seen. His lightning-quick understanding of a position was almost infallible. His lucid and methodical play drew the humble admiration of both his peers and the generations that followed. He was clearly strong enough to challenge for the title much earlier, but the First World War and financial considerations postponed his inevitable triumph.

Away from the board Capablanca was famous for his charm and good looks. He was made a diplomatic attaché by his country, an honorary post that allowed him to travel freely and enjoy life, a mission he embraced to the full.

Alekhine could be considered Capablanca's opposite in many ways, which makes their pairing in history an obvious and irresistible one. His games were wild and often baroquely difficult, infused with a spirit of complexity that has never been equalled. One of the first chess books I ever owned was a set of Alekhine's greatest games. I could play them over and over again and be amazed each time, always finding something new. His swashbuckling style overwhelmed his terrified opponents. This was the sort of chess I wanted to play!

Alekhine thought little about anything other than chess. (Even his cat was named Chess.) When he wasn't playing he was writing, and study took up the rest of his time. He was hardly considered charming, not that he cared. Alekhine's over-indulgence in alcohol damaged his health and his career – many credit his shocking (and brief) loss of the title to Max Euwe in 1935 with having as much to do with this as with his Dutch challenger's strong play and deep preparation. No longer under-estimating his opponent, and on a strict regimen of milk, Alekhine reclaimed the title two years later.

On Capablanca: 'I have known many chess players, but among them there has been only one genius – Capablanca!' – Emanuel Lasker

Capablanca in his own words: 'I always play carefully and try to avoid unnecessary risks. I consider my method to be right as any superfluous 'daring' runs counter to the essential character of chess, which is not a gamble but a purely intellectual combat conducted in accordance with the exact rules of logic.'

On Alekhine: 'Alekhine is dear to the chess world, mainly as an artist. Typical of him are deep plans, far-sighted calculation and inexhaustible imagination.' – Mikhail Botvinnik

Alekhine in his own words: 'Chess for me is not a game, but an art. Yes, and I take upon myself all those responsibilities which an art imposes on its adherents.'

7

PREPARATION

'If a man has a talent and cannot use it, he has failed.'
– *Thomas Wolfe*

Like the proverbial tree falling in the forest with no one around to hear, talent undiscovered may as well not exist. That being the case, we can hardly lament its loss. We can, however, mourn the talent that goes undeveloped, talent that is found and then squandered. In contrast, we often reserve the highest praise for those who over-achieved with limited natural abilities, those who outworked and outperformed rivals who possessed greater genetic gifts.

That last tendency has always struck me as unfair. Why isn't the capacity for hard work considered a natural gift? In my eyes it's not much of a compliment to say that someone 'did more with less', even though it is intended as one. If a football player who is short and can't run very fast practises more than everyone else and becomes the superior player, has he overcome a talent deficit or simply exploited his surplus of talent in another area?

It is true that the greatest achievements are reached by those who add a talent for hard work to other great natural abilities. Staying with sports, and a basketball player even I have heard of, Michael Jordan was famous for his athleticism and high-flying dunks. Yet he was also the first to arrive at practice and the last to leave. In interviews, Jordan's team-mates and coaches all talk about his extreme discipline, not his leaping ability. One veteran NBA manager said of Jordan's talent, 'Without the ceaseless work ethic, Jordan is merely another talented athlete gliding through an admirable career, but nothing historic.'

I agree with the sentiment, but again this comment makes it sound as if Jordan's discipline and capacity for work were not intrinsic parts of his talent. The ability to push yourself to the limit day after day, and to do so effectively, isn't as visible as physical skills, but it was something Jordan was born with and something he cultivated.

Results are what matter

Throughout my career I heard backhanded compliments about the depth and breadth of my chess preparation. In the 1920s, Alexander Alekhine worked harder than anyone before him, changing the culture of a gentleman's game. For his efforts he was often branded 'obsessed' by those he defeated. In the 1940s Mikhail Botvinnik's rigorous mind and habits transformed the game into a full-time profession. In the 1970s Bobby Fischer's fantastic dedication forced every other player to spend more time studying or be left behind.

My upbringing and timing made me the leader of the next wave of change in the 1980s. My work ethic was a product of the disciplined environment created by my mother and by my teacher Botvinnik. I had a ceaseless appetite for opening preparation, which is a combination of research, creativity and memorization. I studied all the latest games from the leading players and carefully noted their innovations, and I would then analyse them and try to improve on them. To me the opening systems were an avenue for creativity, not simply a matter of imitation.

Knowledge of the openings was always seen as a sign of maturity, but I was just a teenager. It wasn't long after my entry into the international chess world that I started to hear whispers crediting much of my success to deep study with a Soviet team. In the years that followed this developed into a full-scale legend. 'Kasparov has a team of Grandmasters churning out opening novelties day and night!' 'He has a supercomputer!' After a while it started to grate to hear these things repeated to me in interviews, although I tried to take them as compliments. As with most urban legends, however, these stories have a grain of truth.

It has long been common for top players to work with analytical assistants – called seconds, as in days of duels – especially during world championship matches. When I had the resources to do so, I began to work with a trainer full-time and not just right before and during big events. As for my computer, I was the first player to incorporate machine analysis into my preparation and to systematize the use of playing programs and databases. And while it was the best my techie cousin Eugeni could put together, the type of PC I used was never beyond the reach of anyone with a good computer store nearby.

Instead of listening to what people said about how I achieved them, I focused on the results. The methods I used wouldn't work for everyone but they worked very well for me. If critics and competitors can't match your results they will often denigrate the way you achieve them. Fast, intuitive types are called lazy. Dedicated burners of midnight oil are called obsessed. And while it is obviously not a bad idea to hear the opinions of others, we should be suspicious when these criticisms emerge right on the heels of success.

Inspiration versus perspiration

Everyone, at any age, has talents that aren't fully developed. Even those who reach the top of their professions aren't immune. The Cuban José Raúl Capablanca was considered an invincible chess machine. There was some truth to this reputation, as he once went eight years without a defeat. Capablanca, if not as lazy as his own statements and legend would have it, detested study. A bon vivant whose expenses were covered by a sinecure with the Cuban diplomatic office, he rarely prepared for his opponents and liked to brag that he had never studied seriously. His talent was so great that he was confident he could escape from any trap he fell into, and he was usually right.

When Capablanca took the crown from Emanuel Lasker in 1921 it was considered an overdue coronation for a reign that could last decades. 'Capa' made chess look easy, and for him it was. But he relied too much on his native ability and his grip on the title lasted only six years. Fittingly, his conqueror, the Russian Alekhine, was one of the most fanatically dedicated players the game has ever seen.

In an age where the gentleman chess player was still common and chess as a profession was considered questionable, Alekhine made chess his life as no one had before. An anecdote has a patron inviting Capablanca and Alekhine to the theatre and reporting afterwards: 'Capablanca never took his eyes off the chorus; Alekhine never looked up from his pocket chess set!'

Of course Alekhine had his own fiery brand of genius at the board, and by combining that with his intense dedication he was more than a match for the raw talent of Capablanca. He had made a careful study of all Capablanca's games, although he found few specific weaknesses to exploit. What he did find were occasional errors that gave the lie to the myth of Capablanca's invincibility. This gave Alekhine confidence but, critically, not over-confidence.

Even Alekhine considered Capablanca the favourite going into their 1927 match in Buenos Aires. He had never before defeated the mighty Cuban and had finished a distant second behind Capablanca at the New York tournament earlier that year. And yet that easy victory was part of Capablanca's undoing. As Alekhine later wrote of their match, 'I did not believe I was superior to him. Perhaps the chief reason for his defeat was the overestimation of his own powers arising out of his overwhelming victory in New York, 1927, and his underestimation of mine.'

Capablanca lost the first game in Buenos Aires, and although he came back to briefly take the lead he must have been surprised to find himself in such a bitter fight. The match became a test of wills, and here Alekhine, who once said, 'What I do is not play, but struggle,' was in his element. The drive that led him to prepare eight hours a day 'on principle' (his words) would not let him lose. Capablanca was unused to such strenuous effort and finally went down to defeat after thirty-four games (a record that would stand until my 1984–5 match with Karpov lasted forty-eight games.)

Preparation pays off in many ways

We can't all have the single-minded dedication of an Alekhine. Few lives and few endeavours permit such devotion. It's not a matter of becoming a 24/7 fanatic who counts every minute and second. The keys are self-awareness and consistency. Steady effort pays off, even if not always in an immediate, tangible way.

One interesting, and humbling, thing I've noticed while analysing my own games for publication is how poor some of the ideas I prepared really were. From the safety of retirement I can look back at the huge amount of analysis I did in preparation for my tournaments and world championship matches. Only a fraction of these ideas ever saw the light of day, having been avoided by my opponents or abandoned in favour of other variations. Now I see that in many cases that was not a bad thing. Under the microscope of strong computer programs it turns out that instead of wielding King Arthur's Excalibur, in many cases I was preparing to go into battle with a rusty pocketknife.

But while I was taken aback by the quality of some of my analyses, an overall positive pattern was clear. These periods of intense preparation were rewarded with good results even when I hadn't used the fruits of my labour. There was an almost mystical correlation between work and achievement with no direct tie between them. Perhaps I was benefiting from the chess equivalent of the placebo effect. Going into battle with what I believed were lethal weapons gave me confidence, even though they largely went unused and likely wouldn't have been very effective.

There is also a practical side of such 'wasted' effort, since there is such a great degree of overlap in most undertakings. The research a lawyer does preparing for a case that never goes to trial still contributes to his understanding and makes him better at his job. Work leads to knowledge and knowledge is never wasted. Even if our weapons remain sheathed, our opponents might be cowed by a reputation for nasty surprises.

This ethic has been followed by many people known to history as great geniuses. We cannot doubt the brain power of Thomas Edison, but his true genius lay in his capacity for endless experimentation. His electric light bulb was the result of persistence, not a single flash of inspiration. He tested thousands of substances looking for a filament that wouldn't burn out, even working with rare plant fibres sent from around the world. Edison aptly summarized his thoughts on invention when he said, 'Opportunity is missed by most because it is dressed in overalls and looks like work.' This was an echo of another great thinker and worker, Thomas Jefferson, who wrote, 'I'm a great believer in luck and I find the harder I work, the more I have of it.'

The worst of it is that we are usually aware of our own deficiencies in this area. We criticize ourselves harshly after spending an hour at work surfing the web or for leaving the gym bag by the door while we watch television. This self-flagellation produces as much benefit as those New Year's resolutions that rarely outlast the winter.

Turning a game into a science

If Alekhine brought a new level of dedication, yes, even obsession, to the game of chess, the man who succeeded him on the throne professionalized and codified this devotion. The first of the seven

Soviet champions, Mikhail Botvinnik sought to demystify the game through his writing and teaching. I was his favourite pupil at the chess academy and I owe a great deal to him for adding focus and discipline to my natural aptitude. He taught me to avoid complexity for complexity's sake, saying, 'You will never become an Alekhine if the variations control you and not the other way around.'

Botvinnik's most lasting contributions to chess culture were in the area of preparation. Ever the engineer, he established detailed training regimens. These encompassed not only specific chess research, but also physical and psychological preparation. These methods are so commonplace now that it is hard to imagine a time when every player didn't do these things, but at the time Botvinnik was a true innovator. His system involved researching the opening phase of the game, studying his opponents' styles, and rigorous analysis of his own games, which were published so that they could be criticized by others. To give just one example of the extremes he would go to: when preparing for a tournament Botvinnik would have distracting music playing in the background and even requested that one of his trainers, Viacheslav Ragozin, blow smoke in his face during their training sessions.

Botvinnik laid out the ideal tournament regime, establishing a strict timetable for meals, rest and brisk walks, a system I myself followed during my entire career. Botvinnik had no patience for people who complained they didn't have enough time. And forget about telling the great teacher you were tired that day! Sleep and rest were to be as carefully scheduled as training, and it was simply inexcusable to get insufficient rest.

I was lucky in that I had been well prepared for Botvinnik by my mother, Klara. She had inherited a strong sense of the importance of order and routine from her own family. For me it was simply the way things were and I always felt comfortable with it. Sleep, meals, school, study time, recreation time, all were part of a schedule.

It was easier thirty years ago when I was growing up. There were fewer distractions available, fewer acceptable activities for a child, especially in the USSR. Today potential distractions are virtually unlimited and the computerized world makes instant entertainment available to everyone. Mobile phones, video games and gadgets allow us to waste time in a dozen different ways that often don't add up to anything at all, certainly nothing deep and strategic for our development.

With so much activity in their lives, parents have few opportunities to teach, let alone demonstrate, rules and regimen. Parents are themselves living more hectic lives and find it hard to present good examples. I could observe the way my mother programmed her life and my activities and I had no doubt it was all for the best.

As I grew older and moved into the serious chess world as a young teenager, I continued to be surrounded by hardworking coaches and mentors. Botvinnik's words and example strengthened what I had already learned. He provided the details, adding them to the general ethic.

Now, though retired from professional chess, I stick with my routine. My new activities are adapted into the programme so I can maintain the patterns that have proven successful. All the key elements have been preserved and my comfort level and productivity along with them. Where there used to be chess preparation there is now politics. Where before I would analyse my opponents, I now analyse old games for my books and articles. My afternoon nap is still sacrosanct.

Targeting ourselves for efficiency

Alekhine and Botvinnik, and later Fischer, manifested a talent for maintaining an effective work rate. They could keep pouring more energy in and getting positive results back out. We can all work longer hours, study more, watch less TV, but the ability to remain effective under increasing strain varies from person to person. Everyone has a unique level of efficiency in their ratio of work to results. A Capablanca might be very creative for an hour but burn out after two. An Alekhine might need four hours to get those same results, but be capable of working for eight hours without a drop in productivity.

It is critical to know what motivates you, to find out how to push yourself that extra mile. For me it's sticking to a regimen. As long as I don't make exceptions to my programme I feel motivated. I also know that I need new challenges to stay engaged. The minute I begin to feel something has become repetitive or easy I know it's time to quickly find a new target for my energy.

Others use different devices, such as competition, setting goals or using incentives. Anatoly Karpov was not by nature a hard worker, but in his preparation for his match with Boris

Spassky in 1974 he spent ten to twelve hours a day preparing. Karpov is tremendously competitive, and his will to win spurred him to new levels of effort. It paid off and he beat Spassky convincingly.

If discipline sounds dull, or even impossible in today's fast-paced world, we should take a moment to consider what areas of our lives we can successfully programme and target for efficiency. Having a good work ethic doesn't mean being a fanatic, it means being aware and then taking action. How did we spend each of our waking hours today? How will we spend them tomorrow?

PART II

8

MATERIAL, TIME, QUALITY

Evaluation trumps calculation

This isn't a cookbook; we all need to create our own successful combinations with the ingredients we have. There are guidelines for what works, but each person has to discover what works for him through practice and observation. This cannot happen rapidly, if at all, of its own accord. We must take an active role in our education.

We know it's much harder to learn a second language later in life. Even if immersed in it daily, we can never recapture the effortless way we learned our native language as children. For adults a new language is an almost physical thing that must be wrestled with verb by verb. Children pick it up unconsciously, while adults have to study it consciously (often self-consciously).

Most of us don't know much about the mechanics of our native language but that doesn't prevent us from speaking it fluently. Yet millions of books on more effective writing are sold every year to native speakers who recognize the value of communicating with greater precision.

Improving our decision-making process is like studying our native language. It requires conscious thought about something we do unconsciously in order to improve something we've been doing all our lives. Every day since we first started to crawl we have been making countless choices. We have developed systems and tendencies that we employ instantly, constantly, without being the least conscious of them for the most part.

We aren't going to overturn a lifetime of experience, nor would we want to. We need to start out by becoming aware of the process and then move on to improving it step by step. What bad habits have we picked up in our decision-making? Which steps do we skip and which do we over-emphasize? Do our poor decisions tend to stem from bad information, poor evaluation, incorrect calculation, or a combination?

Material, the fundamental element

Few of us will ever direct a multinational corporation or a national election, but even routine daily decisions benefit from an improved process. What can we do to improve the quality of our own decisions? The ability to correctly assess a situation has to go beyond 'What do I do next?' By becoming more aware of all the elements, all the factors in play, we train ourselves to think strategically, or what we call 'positionally' in chess.

It was a curious experience when I first tried to think seriously about what exactly goes through my mind when I look at a chess position. After a lifetime of living and breathing the game, I can only compare it to trying to understand what happens in your brain as you read this book. For me, chess is a language, and if it's not my native tongue it is one I learned via the immersion method at a very young age. Like a native English speaker trying to explain the difference between 'that' and 'which', such familiarity makes it somewhat difficult for me to consider my approach to the game objectively. Now that I'm removed from the heat of battle and tournament play I can look back at my games and performances with greater introspection.

Evaluating a position goes well beyond looking for the best move. The move is only the output, the product of an equation that must first be developed and understood. It comes down to determining the relevant factors, measuring them and, most critically, determining the optimal balance between them. Before we can begin our search for the keys to a position we have to perform basic due diligence.

The fundamental building block of evaluation is material. Assets, stock, cash, goods, pieces and pawns, it's all material. We look at the board and the first thing we do is count the pieces. How many pawns, how many knights and rooks? Do I have more or less material than my opponent? Each piece has a standard value that allows us to quickly add up who's ahead in the arms race.

Our standard of measurement, our currency, is the pawn. Each player starts with eight of these foot soldiers, the most limited and least valuable members of the army. Even the word 'pawn' has come to mean weak and expendable. In other languages the pawns are often called peons, or farmers. We even say 'pawns and pieces', not including them in the same class as bishops, knights and rooks.

Pawns provide a useful system of equivalent value. Knights and bishops are said to be worth three pawns. Rooks are five pawns while the queen is worth nine. (The king, whose inevitable capture ends the game, is weak but priceless.) So informed, a beginner can go into battle knowing that he shouldn't give up a knight for a pawn, or a rook for a knight.

When we first learn the game we are all terrible materialists. We capture as many enemy pieces as we can without paying much attention to other factors. A game between two beginners can look more like Pac-Man than chess as they gobble up the pieces. This is a normal and healthy way to start out. Being told the values is one thing, but only experience teaches them to you.

In other areas too, most of our objective measurements of success and failure come down to material. It doesn't get any more basic than food, water and shelter. In primitive times things were worth exactly the good they did you. As society evolved we developed currency – gold, coins, paper – and representative value replaced, or joined, utility in our material consciousness. Now many of our assets are electronic in the form of shares of stock or funds in banks. In warfare it's which side has more soldiers, more guns, more ships. In business it's factories, employees, stock, cash on hand.

It doesn't take long in chess or elsewhere to realize that there is much more to life than material. It's a valuable lesson the first time you are checkmated despite having a big material advantage. The ultimate value of the king trumps everything else on the board and your value system begins to adjust. Material isn't everything.

Before moving to the next evaluation element, we should note an additional factor regarding material. We often form personal attachments to assets that have little to do with their objective value. These sentimental attachments can distort our evaluation ability considerably, if not always in a harmful way.

When I was a child my favourite piece was the bishop, for no reason I can remember today. Once I even played a curious match against an older teammate from the local Pioneer Palace in which I had only bishops and he had only knights. Even in my earliest games I was a great believer in the power of the bishop and avoided their exchange, a habit that could be detrimental. Other beginners might be attracted to the unusual leaping ability of the knight, or, alternatively, develop a fear of this most unpredictable piece.

A significant part of Mikhail Botvinnik's intensive research of his opponents was dedicated to discovering such biases in their play. He would comb through their games looking for errors and try to categorize those errors in a way he might be able to exploit. In his teachings he made it clear to us that the worst type of mistake was a mistake that made you predictable.

It is usually the case that our friends, colleagues and family know much more about our bad habits than we do. Hearing about these psychological tics can be as surprising as being told by our spouse that we snore. Prejudices and preferences in our decisions are unlikely to be harmful as long as we are aware of them and actively work to iron them out. Awareness can be the difference between a harmless affectation and a bias that leads to a dangerous loss of objectivity.

Time is money

Anyone who has ever worked for an hourly wage knows time has value, in the simplest possible terms. Material – money – is exchanged for labour as measured by hours and minutes. The amount depends on the utility you produce in that time span as judged by your employer. This is 'clock time', universally measured in the same way and readily understood. It is also quite different from what we'll call 'board time', which is the number of steps it takes to accomplish an objective.

Chess players are used to thinking of both types of time during a game. Your clock is ticking and you have a limited amount of time to make all your moves. (You may be familiar with the double clocks used in chess and other timed board games. You make your move and press your clock's button, which stops your clock and puts your opponent's in motion.) Then you have the game itself, where time is divided neatly into moves, alternating between you and your opponent, one at a time. How many moves does it take to get from point A to point B? How long will it take for my attack to arrive? Can I reach my objective before my opponent reaches his?

Chess is turn-based, not real-time. In theory, everything on the board can be analysed out to a definite number of moves but in reality this is only possible in the simplest of positions when there are only a handful of pieces on the board. Our calculations have to take our opponent's moves into account. It's easy enough to figure out how many moves it will take for certain pieces to reach certain squares. The problem is that your opponent gets to move too and he is unlikely to let you do exactly as you like.

The easiest demonstration of the time factor in chess is the difference between playing white and black. White goes first, putting him a single move ahead at the start, giving him an advantage in board time. It is a matter of long and fruitless historical debate whether or not the advantage of the first move should prove enough to force a win for white if both sides play perfectly. We are so far from perfection that this will never be proven one way or another. We do know that it is a significant advantage to have the white pieces, especially at the top level. Amateurs are more likely to make errors and wasteful moves, so the narrow advantage of that single move at the start is rarely a decisive factor.

Among professionals being one move ahead is a very tangible plus. With precise play, that single move allows white to apply pressure and make threats against the black position. White is acting, black is reacting. Statistics bear out the value of the first move quite clearly. At the Grandmaster level white wins 29 per cent of the time, black 18 per cent, and 53 per cent of games are drawn. As impressive as that may seem, time is a dynamic factor that can come and go fluidly. A time advantage can disappear with a single wasted move, one squandered opportunity.

A military commander is used to thinking of time in the same way as a chess player, but in the real world things are much more dynamic. There is practically no limit to the number of 'moves' you and your enemies can make at the same time. Multiple attacks and counter-attacks can take place concurrently around the battlefield, or around the world.

Time is not gained just by moving faster or by taking short-cuts. Time can often be bought, swapped for material assets. In combat, a light, fast-moving force can outmanoeuvre and outfight a numerically superior force. An outnumbered army can triumph by crashing through on the opponent's weak flank. Time for material is the first of the trade-offs in our evaluation system.

If both players are happy, can both be right?

I went from admiring the top players to facing them so quickly that I had very little time for hero worship. Still, there was nothing quite like the time I first saw Mikhail Tal in person. I was ten years old and there he was in flesh and blood. Although his year as world champion had come two years before I was born, his thrilling games were the favourite of every schoolboy. I quickly had to overcome my excitement at meeting this living legend because he was standing across from me in a 'Grandmasters versus Pioneers' event in Moscow as part of a simultaneous match against my team from Baku. The Grandmaster coach of each team of seven kids played the students on the other teams (all at the same time) and the team with the best combined score of coach and students was the winner. I faced many great players in these events, including my future world championship rival, Anatoly Karpov. Tal didn't require his famous glare to beat me that day, alas. But the inspiration he provided ensured that I would later follow his example by participating as a coach in such exhibitions after I had made a name for myself.

Tal was the ultimate 'time player'. When his attacking genius was in full flight his pieces seemed to move faster than his opponents'. How was this possible? The young Tal cared much less for material than most players and would happily give up almost any number of pawns and pieces in exchange for more time to bring his other forces into action against the enemy king. His opponents were constantly pushed on the defensive, leading to errors and disaster. This sounds simple, but few have been able to imitate Tal's tremendous success. He had a unique gift for knowing just how far he could go, how much material he could give up.

When attacking, being a move ahead is more important than material, but how much material for how much time? A bishop is worth roughly three pawns, but how much is a move worth, or two moves? There is no simple value chart for time, only case-by-case evaluation. Ask a general if he would rather have another company of men or an extra few days. During peacetime he'd rather have the men, while in a sharp combat situation the extra time could be much more valuable.

In chess we talk about open positions and closed positions. If things are open, that means open lines for your pieces, dynamic play, attack and counter-attack. A closed position usually means a slow, strategic manoeuvring game; consider it the chess equivalent of trench warfare. In an open game the value of a move is much greater than in a closed game because it can do much more damage. If the position is blocked and there is little activity overall, there is less need for speed.

Take a company working on a new product line. They know a

competitor is working on a similar project and is at around the same stage in development. Should Company A rush their products to market to beat Company B? Or should they spend more money on development to try to ensure their product is superior to Company B's? Of course hypothetical As and Bs eventually fall apart because the answers depend on real-world factors. What industry are they in? What type of product is it? Time is always a factor, but putting a new heart medicine on the market isn't the same as trying to get the latest gadget out in time for Christmas shoppers.

Recognizing what sort of situation we are in is a crucial part of the evaluation process. Before you start considering trade-offs, take a good look around. Is time really of the essence or are we just being impatient? On a trivial level we make decisions like this all the time. Do you pay extra for express delivery of your Amazon order? You can get your purchases within four days for the normal delivery charge, or next day if you pay extra. If either time or money isn't an issue for you, the choice is easy. In most cases they both matter to some degree and managing that balance is where the challenge lies.

My third world championship match with Anatoly Karpov contained an unusually clear example of this constant battle between time and material. It was the eighth game of our 1986 match, which was split between London and Leningrad, as St Petersburg was still known at the time. I was searching for an advantage and offered Karpov a pawn for attacking chances, judging that the two moves I would gain against his king were worth the price of a pawn on the other side of the board.

Karpov had done the same maths and his evaluation was evidently in favour of the pawn, because he took it. My attack quickly built up steam until it was Karpov's turn to offer material in order to organize a defence of his king. He would allow me to capture his rook with my bishop, which would give me a slight material advantage but at the cost of giving up my attack and allowing him to consolidate his position. This was a classic example of the fluidity of our Material, Time, Quality factors. I gave up material for attacking time and Karpov later offered the material back to gain time for his defence.

I felt compelled to decline the offer, not wanting to go from lender to borrower so quickly. It's worth noting that Karpov would have certainly taken the material had our positions been reversed. Taking the rook guaranteed a small advantage with no risk, exactly the sort of position Karpov enjoyed. I ignored the rook and instead continued on down a pawn, looking for a way to break through. A few moves later I even gave up another pawn to keep my attack alive, even though this meant a loss was likely if my attack didn't succeed. As so often happens, an advantage in board time – pressure and threats that force your opponent to react – resulted in an advantage in clock time. Karpov had to burn a lot of time finding his way through all the dangers to his king move after move. With ten moves still to go until we got more time added to our clocks, Karpov lost on time, a nearly unprecedented event in his long career. By that point I was also winning on the board, so I didn't feel at all guilty about winning the game by time forfeit.

The game serves as a testament to my philosophy of preferring time over material, favouring dynamic factors over static factors. These evaluation preferences are part of one's style and aren't necessarily superior or inferior to those of others, only different. Karpov lost that game; does that mean he was wrong in his evaluation of the position? I was right, he was wrong, he erred and I won? Not at all. He was true to his style and his evaluation, and his position was not objectively lost until the end, when time trouble contributed to his downfall.

Long-term versus dynamic factors

Much more goes into the evaluation of a position than counting the pieces and the moves. The piece values fluctuate depending on the position and can change after every turn. The same is true about the value of a move, unless we believe Tal's knights really were faster. Material is the fundamental reference point; time is movement and action. To be correctly understood and utilized they must be governed by a third element: quality.

Generations of platitudes teach us that there is good money and bad, and even 'quality time'. In chess we might talk about a weak knight or a particularly strong pawn, as if their value changed depending on their placement and on other factors, which is exactly the case. A knight located in the centre of the board – where it controls more territory and can join the fight in any region of the board – is almost always more valuable than one near the edge, a concept immortalized in the old chess maxim, 'A knight on the rim is dim.'

On the real field of battle all terrain is not valued equally. Throughout the history of warfare combatants have sought the highest ground available. From the heights your archers, later your artillery, can shoot further and your commanders can see the battle develop. Satellites and air power have changed these ancient equations in many ways, but it will always be true that where your forces are placed can be as important as their strength in numbers. Placement provides, or limits, utility, which is truly what we are seeking.

Even placement depends on other factors, such as the nature of the troops themselves. For this example I'll step away from my game and move to my son's, the computer game *Warcraft*. In this popular game you are put in command of a vast army and each unit has distinct characteristics. Your troops can be elves or trolls, mages or goblins, all with relative advantages and disadvantages. *Warcraft* is a real-time game, not turn-based like chess. There is a true element of time the player has to balance against his material forces. (In the new online version there are over 4 million *Warcraft* players.)

Also, unlike chess, you create your forces and therefore control the characteristics of your army. Do you want long-distance archers or heavily armoured knights? Once you take command of your forces you have to match your capabilities with the terrain to emphasize your strengths. If you don't have any long-distance weaponry and your opponent does, taking the high ground makes much less sense than staying under cover in a forest valley.

Warcraft is a distillation of the MTQ concept. You collect basic resources of wood and gold to build up your empire and its armies. This investment gives you faster and higher-quality troops. It's as much a game of resource management as of strategy and tactics. Your evaluation becomes increasingly multidimensional as you move from the individual soldier to the battalion and on up to the whole battlefield and the entire conflict.

Putting the elements into action

Only in extreme cases can material be completely inert and worthless. A knight that is trapped in the corner may some day escape and play a critical role in the fight. One of the difficulties programmers have in improving computer chess programs is the 'concept of never' and how it relates to the value of material. Even a weak human player can see that a piece has been permanently trapped and is therefore worthless. But to a computer that piece still has the same numeric value in its calculations as before it was trapped. Perhaps some points are deducted for loss of mobility, but there is no good way to teach a computer that a bishop on square X is worth three pawns but on square Y it's only worth one.

This gives us different classes of material: long-term and dynamic. Investment portfolios work much the same way. Depending on personal style and needs, your portfolio might be full of dynamic (liquid) assets in need of constant attention and calculation. Or it might be built for a retirement that is still decades off. My play in the aforementioned game with Karpov showed my preference for dynamism and his for the long-term. I sacrificed pawns to make my remaining material more valuable in the short run. Had my attack failed, his investment in long-term material advantages would have won the day.

This was a typical theme of many of my games against Karpov, thanks to our different natures regarding time and material. In our first world championship match my skills were not so well developed, and Karpov would take the material and then deflect my attacks. His evaluations were superior. Just over a year and a half later, at the London match, it was a different story. I had learned to be less rash with giving away material and this was reflected in the different result.

Material is only as valuable as what it can be used for. Time for action is only important if it helps us make our material more useful. Having an extra hour in the day would be welcomed by most anyone, but not the man in a jail cell. We must use time to improve our material, not just acquire more of it. Material for its own sake and time wasted are equally useless in reaching our goals.

Useful material and well-spent time lead to winning in a chess game. In the corporate world they mean higher revenues. In war and politics they lead to victory. In day-to-day life 'victory' can be simplistically, perhaps a little romantically, defined as happiness. Money can't buy it, after all. It must be cultivated by proper management of time. By using our time wisely we can create utility and our true goal of quality.

What makes a bad bishop bad?

We often talk about having a 'good bishop' or a 'bad bishop', and this jargon provides insight into the qualitative differences of material things. My childhood favourite, the bishop – called an elephant in Russian and a fool in French – is easily categorized this way because of the way its movement is limited. The bishop can travel as many squares as it likes in any diagonal direction, but on only one colour of the board. This gives it great range but makes it predictable. If many of the squares of the bishop's colour are occupied, its mobility is extremely limited.

Such a bishop is called 'bad', but its intrinsic nature is no different from when the game started. Its quality has been diminished by the circumstances around it. From a practical standpoint, that of utility, it is inferior and should be considered as such. This finds practical expression in how the game is played. If I have a bad bishop I would be glad to trade it off for another piece, for example. They might have nominally equal values but if the board conditions make my piece inferior that's the value I have to work with.

The CEO and the general have to be alert to bad pieces in their worlds as well. When Jack Welch took over the General Electric behemoth in 1981 one of the first things he did was to make a list of all the divisions in the company that weren't performing up to his standards. The directors of those operations were told they had to improve or be sold or closed down. GE would focus on what it was best at and cut back in the areas where it wasn't doing well instead of hanging on to them solely for their material value.

Any chess master would recognize Welch's strategy as employing the principle of improving your worst piece. He was applying Siegbert Tarrasch's dictum, 'One badly placed piece makes your whole position bad!' If you have a bad bishop you try to find a way to activate it, to make it 'good'. If it can't be rehabilitated, you try to swap it off, eliminating it. The same is true of any ineffective material. Put that bad piece, that under-performing asset, to good use or get rid of it and your overall position will improve.

Returning to our stock portfolios, we can see why the same strategies don't always apply. Any good investment counsellor will tell you to keep a balanced portfolio with a mix of risky and stable assets depending on your age, needs and income. If you constantly sell the things that aren't performing well at the moment you will inevitably be out of position at some point.

Compensation and relative value

Along with external factors we have the intrinsic quality of the forces themselves. A bishop is worth more than a pawn because it has greater mobility and control of the board. A rook is usually worth more than a knight or a bishop for the same reason. That in some positions a knight or a bishop can be more valuable than a rook is due to external factors. In a vast majority of cases a rook is stronger, so we generalize by saying it is worth more.

Soldiers with better training and better weapons have a qualitative superiority that can be worth far more in winning a battle than quantitative superiority. In the early stages of the First World War the Russian military was as poorly trained as it was poorly equipped. Russia had the largest army in the world at the time, but their quality was disastrously low. At the beginning of the war many Russian soldiers were sent into battle without rifles, hardly a morale booster. Even when they were armed things often went wrong. Sections of the army were hastily pulled back from the front lines when it was discovered the soldiers hadn't been trained to use the Japanese rifles they had been issued. Sadly, many of these qualitative mistakes were repeated in the Second World War.

Each piece and pawn, each soldier, is only a small part of the overall qualitative picture. 'Who is winning?' is a simple enough question, but the real test of evaluation is when there is no obvious advantage. First we count material. If one player has a significant advantage here we can say he is winning unless his opponent has compensation in time and/or quality. Whose forces are better developed and placed more aggressively? How quickly can one side attack and the other defend? How long will it take for reinforcements to arrive? Who commands more territory? Is someone's king in danger? These are all qualitative evaluations and they are of different degrees of significance.

By habit and survival instinct we first look at our king when considering a position. Checkmate ends the game; it is the ultimate value. No matter how many extra pieces you have, if your king can't escape, you lose. Despite its overuse as a metaphor, there is no exact equivalent of checkmate in our real world discussions. In extreme cases an army can fight on for a while without its generals; subjects can live on without a king; a corporation can file for bankruptcy protection. In real life you have time to recover from catastrophe, although without proper order there must be a restoration of some sort or eventual collapse. For the sake of argument we can refer to checkmate as 'that which must be avoided at all costs'. Any amount of material can be given up to achieve checkmate of your opponent and any amount given up to stave off your own king's demise.

Material is the next priority. All other considerations are relative to these intrinsic values, the way we say a very well-placed knight is worth a rook. After the basics of king safety and material, things become considerably more sophisticated. Evaluating the time factor requires first understanding the needs of the position. Estimating how long it takes to achieve something requires first knowing what you need to achieve. To do this, finer evaluation criteria must come into play.

Double-edged evaluation

One example of a positional qualitative element is readily comparable to a military clash: structure. A chess visual aid will help us here (you don't even need to know how to move the pieces).

Take a look at the difference between the white and black pawns in the diagram. Both sides have the full contingent of eight, so they are equal in material. The qualitative difference here is structure, the form the pawns take as a group. Whites are orderly and form a complete wall across the board. Blacks are fragmented into three 'islands'. In two cases, one black pawn stands in front of another, limiting its mobility. Thus we would say that white has a 'superior pawn structure'.

In that we would be correct, and the game would be simple if there were no pieces or kings. In a real game, the pawn structure would be just one factor in evaluating the position. It is quite possible that the holes in the black pawns could benefit black, giving him compensation for his inferior structure. A chess player who likes long-term static advantages like a solid structure would undoubtedly prefer to play the white side. But show such a position to the great David Bronstein, who challenged Mikhail Botvinnik for the world title in 1951, and he would surely prefer black! Like me, Bronstein was a dynamic player who always favoured short-term activity over long-term considerations. Here he would be content to have those structural holes because he would use them to activate his pieces.

Finer, double-edged factors like structure come into focus only when the forces are evenly matched in the essential areas. The stronger the players, the more balanced the game, the more evaluation comes down to the tiniest details. The cracks in these secondary criteria only show under great pressure and it is the mark of a great player to be able to detect and exploit them. The saying says that the 'devil is in the details', and these subtle factors are the chess player's devils.

Personal return on investment

What are the smaller issues that can have a big impact on our lives? Few of us need to worry about food and water and yet we obsess over material things as much as our ancestors. The higher concepts of utility, quality and happiness sound too vague and philosophical to think about. We think about time as something not to waste, not as something to invest.

Education is a useful refutation of that passive mode of thinking. What is going to college if not an investment of material and time for quality? We give time and money to gain skills that will raise our intrinsic value to an employer. This is an exaggeration, if an increasingly accurate one. Students often enjoy college, so it can be a matter of short-term fulfilment as well as long-term investment.

Higher education is one way we (or our parents) make material sacrifices to increase the quality of our position in the future. The more we can afford to invest the greater our return will be. If you have the money and grades to go to a top university you will be able to gain a superior education, make better contacts, and be better positioned for entering the job market.

Perhaps a more openly mercenary path, getting an MBA, is a

clearer example. An executive making £100,000 a year decides to leave a good job and spend tens or hundreds of thousands of pounds going back to college. By all accounts, going to business school isn't much fun, so short-term enjoyment isn't a motive. Considering the investment of time and material the qualitative return must be judged to be very high, since business school enrolments continue to rise.

That return in quality comes in the shape of skills and contacts, which then lead to a better job. Higher pay and more responsibility enhance the new MBA's quality of life, or at least that's the way the formula is supposed to work. There are certainly many unhappy people with business degrees out there. A new high-paying job might take up so much time that there is none left for activities that are significant components of happiness. The difficulty is in being aware of these small factors and evaluating them before we make a decision that affects them.

The questions we must ask are not only about trade-offs. Giving up material doesn't always result in a gain of time, or vice versa. At least in chess you can have it all or lose it all. The player with a winning position will usually have more pieces *and* be ahead in time *and* have superior placement and position all at the same time. Consider this the 'rich grow richer' variation.

A politician on the campaign trail is seeking happiness by way of winning the election. The candidate has a limited amount of time and a limited amount of money. His strategy is predicated on maximizing these things to have the greatest possible positive impact on the electorate, to improve his quality in their eyes. Although a huge amount of money is spent on campaigns, now more than ever, experience shows that subtle elements can still surprise. A single soundbite or gaffe can shift perception dramatically, for better or for worse. Dan Quayle's mangling of the spelling of the word 'potato' in front of a classroom full of kids while on the campaign trail mangled his political career for ever. However, such things only rarely overcome more fundamental advantages and disadvantages.

Perception of quality is quality

Stock price is a snapshot of a company's quality. Experts opine on P/E ratios, the cable news shows talk about earnings reports, and yet share prices often fly in the face of these numbers. A high share price reflects confidence in quality, the promise that a company is so well-positioned, or so well-*something*, that in the future it will be worth more in material than it is now.

Google has become such a dominant and popular brand that its stock performance has brought back memories of the dot-com heyday. As I write, the company's share price in summer 2006 is an astronomical $387 (down from over $450 at the start of the year) and its market capitalization is over 120 billion. So, according to the markets, Google is worth (or will be worth) far more than the total value of every company in Chile ($65 billion), a dubious assertion on the face of it. Chilean companies combined to create a GDP of 169 billion dollars in 2004, while in 2005 Google had earnings of a few billion dollars.

Do the people who bought Google shares at $350 and pushed its cap so high believe the company will ever earn that much money? Of course not. Stock markets aren't about the future of a company nearly as much as people would like to believe. They are about the perception of a company now. Buyers jump in to make money in the short run off a hot company's current run of success. Google is worth $380, or any number, as long as people keep buying. The number is based on the buyer's profit motive and confidence, not the actual worth of the company. The crisis, as dot-com investors learned the hard way, comes when someone points out that the emperor has no clothes, that the dot-com has no revenue. Quality as perception of quality is a fragile thing.

Computers would theoretically have an advantage in evaluation because they are immune to such games of perception. And yet programs don't in fact play the market well because it is driven by 'irrational' humans whose behaviour is unpredictable, even illogical – the same reason computers don't play poker well. In chess they do a better job, but not because they understand material, time and quality the way humans do.

The monolithic objectivity of a chess program is its greatest strength and greatest weakness. A program is told how much the pieces are worth and it plays correspondingly. If you tell it that the queen is only worth a pawn it will happily throw her away. With its value system in place, the computer does a fine job of counting material very quickly to decide the best move. It looks at all the possible moves and counts up the material at the end of each variation. Material gain is good, material loss is bad.

Next comes the king and the concept of checkmate. Computers do well with this 'ultimate value' too, although they can still be distracted by the gain of material. They can easily find and defend against checkmate by force, but the concepts of time and the initiative remain relatively fuzzy. You can mass your pieces for a huge attack against a computer's king while it is capturing pawns on the far side of the board. By the time it realizes that all the lines lead to mate or a loss of material, it's too late. A computer's sense of time cannot go deeper than it can calculate. It lacks the human ability to conceptualize what's coming in general terms.

Where computer chess programs still have trouble is with quality and the way material values change according to the position. A Grandmaster can find positions where the computer will come to an incorrect evaluation and exploit this weakness. A program might over-value rooks versus other pieces, or under-estimate weaknesses around its king. This is also true of humans, of course, but we can quickly learn from our mistakes and even use them as traps.

Nowadays the leading chess programs are 'taught' to employ fluctuating piece values instead of a hard-coded formula for the worth of each piece. It has become harder and harder to fool them, although they are still materialists at heart. Their deep calculation effectively reduces the game to its lowest common denominator, material, and they do it with a speed and proficiency that allows them to play at the level of a strong Grandmaster. On the board computers play chess well, but on the inside they are playing a very different game from a strong human player.

MTQ on the home front

Now here's a final example to set the stage for the next step, evaluating and controlling the exchanges and imbalances between all these forces in our lives. My wife Daria and I recently bought a new home, an ordeal that I would describe as involving no fewer considerations – and no less stress – than playing in a world championship match. Anyone who has bought a house or even rented an apartment knows about many of the trade-offs that frame the debate. They go well beyond the obvious one of material versus quality. Even if you believe 'you get what you pay for' and that you will get a better house for more money, there is a great deal of work to do to figure out what 'better' means, especially if you have a family, which increases the number of decisions and the number of decision-makers.

First off, it's 'location, location, location'. Just as with a knight, placement is critical. Where you live is as important as what you live in. Do you need to be near a school or near work? Is it a safe neighbourhood, and what about local shopping and entertainment? These are the obvious qualities people look for. We have equivalent maxims in chess, too. 'Develop your pieces.' 'Play in the centre.' 'Get your king to safety quickly.' These platitudes serve as useful guides for beginners. As players advance they begin to detect the occasional exceptions to the rules and this is what will, or won't, separate a great player from a good one, the ability to detect and apply the exceptions.

There is no universal formula for evaluation. We get caught up in standardized rhetoric and end up with something that doesn't fit our unique needs. For the most part we all know what we like and make decisions accordingly, but under pressure we can easily be confused and lose sight of our goals. The little things are hard to keep in mind when there are so many big things, so it's no surprise that it's the so-called 'small stuff' that causes the most problems.

Where many fail is by over-dependence on the areas they best understand. It is comforting to stick to what we know, and often we are unaware that a problem can be seen from a different perspective. If we are so focused on just one aspect of a chess position, of a business deal, of a new job or a new home, misevaluation is a near certainty.

While you can 'have it all' in chess, and perhaps even in life, that Elysian condition is not a useful one to learn from. Most of the time we will have to balance, exchange and evaluate over and over. If we do this well enough to blend material, time and quality into a multi-dimensional evaluation, we gain a clear idea of what we want and can then plan on how to achieve it. When we see all the factors we can then learn how to shift them and build them. Without expanding our powers of evaluation we risk fulfilling Oscar Wilde's famous observation: 'Nowadays people know the price of everything and the value of nothing.'

Mikhail Nekhemievich Tal (1836–1992), USSR/Latvia
Pure attacking magic

The eighth world chess champion – 1960–61. Born in Riga, USSR (Latvia). Tal defeated Mikhail Botvinnik to become the then youngest world champion ever at the age of twenty-three. He demolished the 'Patriarch' in impressive fashion, but had neither the discipline nor the good health to withstand the well-prepared Botvinnik's counter-attack in the rematch a year later. As Tal put it, 'Botvinnik understood my play better than I did!'

By the time Tal won the highest title his bold style of play had already made him a legend. A true creative genius, his name is still synonymous with beautiful, speculative attacking chess. His dynamic play served as an ideal foil for the strict science and logic of Botvinnik, and their two world championship matches are an excellent study in contrasts.

Tal remained a dangerous force for decades, despite never gaining another shot at the title. Plagued by serious kidney problems throughout his life – exacerbated by a rough lifestyle with too much smoking and drinking – he always returned to the board in excellent spirits. In 1988, well after his powers had begun to wane, the beloved 'Misha' delighted his legions of fans by taking first prize in a world blitz championship in Canada ahead of an all-star field that included Anatoly Karpov and me.

On Tal: 'If Tal would learn to programme himself properly then it would become impossible to play him.' – Mikhail Botvinnik

Tal in his own words: 'Usually, I prefer not to study chess but to play it. For me chess is more an art than a science. It's been said that Alekhine and I played similar chess, except that he studied more. Yes, perhaps, but I have to say that he played, too.'
'If you wait for luck to turn up, life becomes very boring.'

9

EXCHANGES AND IMBALANCES

Freezing the game

An imbalance is a lack of symmetry, any difference at all that can be exploited in some way. In chess this refers to the quantitative and qualitative differences between your opponent's forces and your own. Imbalances always exist when all three MTQ factors are considered because even if the pieces are completely symmetrical on the board, it is someone's turn. The player to move has an advantage in time, which breaks the balance.

Suspending the game in time is a useful way to teach students how to evaluate qualitative factors like structure and space. Showing a chess position without revealing who is to move first sounds preposterous. If the entire purpose is to decide the best move, isn't it essential to know whose move it is? The motive of this technique is precisely to remove the anxiety about choosing the next move and be able to appreciate the subtle elements in play across the board. Otherwise students immediately start making suggestions for the next move, trying one after another without thinking things through and therefore missing the big picture entirely.

My various ventures (and adventures) into the internet industry left me with some bumps and bruises, but they also exposed me to areas of expertise I would otherwise never have experienced. In 1999 we were getting ready to launch a giant internet chess portal bearing my name. As the site neared completion the designers worked with testers and focus groups to see how well the design and navigation worked in practice.

It was tragic-comic to watch the testers entirely ignore the signs and instructions carefully placed by the web designers.

Instead, following what I was told is a normal usage pattern, the web surfers would immediately click on whatever caught their eye and, if unhappy with the result, jump back and try again. Unless the menu choices were unavoidably obvious they were usually ignored. The desire to be quick and to keep moving forward overwhelms us.

Unfortunately, this mirrors how many of us go about making decisions all the time. We take our best guess and plunge forward, barely considering the options. There is a huge difference between looking at the possible moves and evaluating the situation. It is easy to get caught up in the search for options instead of doing the need-based analysis that will tell you which of the options is superior. Purely relative evaluation is better than none at all, but we can't confuse it with understanding even if the results aren't always bad.

For example, getting back to those chess students, what if one of them, through a combination of intuition and luck, hurriedly calls out the right move when presented with a position to analyse for the first time, what then? It's to his credit, but it doesn't mean he really understands the position and it may lead to the formation of bad habits. This is why it is useful to remove the time factor for a moment, to stop worrying about what to do next, what to do right now. A deliberate analysis of the situation leads us to the core necessities of the position. This in turn narrows our options and informs our decisions. That's when we start the clock up again and reintroduce the time factor.

This isolation technique is utilized in business schools to train students in various methods of evaluating a company or a case study. To start out, the class might be given only a balance sheet with no knowledge of the competition, perhaps even of the industry. Or they might be shown only the market share of the company's products relative to the competition. Introducing elements one by one attempts to eliminate gaps in education and evaluation habits. When students have the full picture they can see how all the elements combine to form a single, unique image.

Once we have frozen time we still have to know what to analyse and how to weigh that analysis. On a chessboard there are a limited number of factors to consider but an unlimited number of ways to consider them. As we discussed earlier, even very strong players will differ over the relative importance of the different elements. The simplest test is to present a position and ask someone which side he would prefer to play. White or black? Who is better and why? The position may be equal, but a human being is a creature of preference and can never be completely objective. Being aware of your own preferences and prejudices can be as critical as how well you observe the external factors.

The search for compensation

A proper evaluation is a search for advantage or compensation for disadvantage. Few advantages are unconditional, while most clouds come with silver linings. It was only a slight exaggeration when Siegbert Tarrasch wrote that 'every move creates a weakness'. Unless a move delivers checkmate, it has negatives as well as positives. The same is true of static characteristics. For example, when your pawns advance you gain space to manoeuvre your pieces, but at the expense of weakening your defences. When troops advance, lines of communication and supply can be cut or become disorganized.

Material losses, not the qualitative ones we are concerned with here, are typically the only purely negative factor, although there are extreme cases when you would rather be rid of a member of your own forces. If an army's fast-moving cavalry is hemmed in by its own foot-soldiers, a general can't just sacrifice his slower-moving troops. But in chess it's not uncommon to play a 'clearance sacrifice' by throwing a pawn into the teeth of the enemy to clear the lines for your pieces to advance.

If an asset is nearly worthless and has no prospects of improvement you might as well get what you can for it while you can. Amateurs who dabble in the stock market are famous for holding on to losing stocks all the way to the bottom, imagining that they haven't really lost anything until they've sold, a self-destructive fallacy. The cold-blooded investor knows that getting something now is better than nothing later.

At a tournament in Yugoslavia in 1983 I had the opportunity to dispose of some falling shares in the form of a bishop. In my game against the leading Hungarian player, Lajos Portisch, I was straining to find a way to exploit my slight lead in development. I wanted to use this dynamic advantage to launch an attack on his king. The problem was, all of my pieces needed to use the same central square. If I played my knight there it would block my bishop, cutting it out of the game entirely. This led to my wondering – if the bishop wasn't participating actively at this exact moment in the game, why couldn't I exchange it for something of value in the black position, such as the pawn right in front of the black king?

Giving up a bishop for a single pawn doesn't make any sense from a material perspective, but it was a time advantage I had at the moment and it was more time I needed. The bishop would be otherwise unemployed in my planned operation and this way it could be sacrificed to further increase my dynamic advantage. I gave up the bishop, and with his king exposed Portisch had to lose more time running for cover. Eventually my activity overwhelmed his material lead.

We total up all the pluses and minuses in the position and then go to work on how to improve our side of the ledger. We want to create weaknesses in our opponent's camp while strengthening our own. An essential part of this process is trying to turn our weaknesses into strengths, using them to best advantage or at least minimizing them. A theoretical weakness, a by-the-books disadvantage, that can't be exploited by your opponent is really not weak at all.

Successful exploitation of our advantages leads to greater advantages, eventually great enough to win a decisive amount of material. This is where the alchemy comes in, the transformation of one type of advantage into another. With accurate play we can turn material into time and back again, or invest both for a high return in quality.

The laws of thermodynamics, chess and quality of life

The first law of thermodynamics tells us that the total amount of energy in a system is a constant, that if we move energy into one area we lose an equal amount. That is, energy can't be spontaneously created or destroyed, only transferred from one place to another or transmuted from one form into another.

On the chessboard we are trying to break the law and to create energy, even to create material. If a pawn reaches the other side of the board it can be 'promoted' into any piece, even another queen. (Of course you can't have another king. In chess, bigamy is acceptable but monarchy is absolute.) And improving the energy of our own pieces doesn't always come at the cost of our opponent's energy level. A typical game of attack and counter-attack sees both players marshalling their forces, increasing their activity level.

If done well, each chessboard transformation increases the quality of our position. In exchange for time – say two moves – I can bring my knight over to a superior location. Or when I sacrifice a pawn my opponent has to lose a move or two to capture it, giving me time to augment my attack.

A company can view its own playing field in a similar way. An advantage in cash reserves – material – is turned into research on new products, or employee bonuses, or more advertising, or a modernized factory. Looking at the assets of our competitors helps us find imbalances we can exploit. Even if our opponent dominates in many areas we can try to develop a positive imbalance of our own. If we can detect or cultivate a weak spot in our opponent's position we can then attempt to transform our position to take advantage of that weakness.

Strategy on the browser battlefield

The expression 'browser war' was in wide use in the late 90s, when Netscape and Microsoft were battling for web market share. Netscape Navigator was first and best and Microsoft Explorer far behind in just about every respect. Its early versions were mediocre and Navigator had a large and loyal customer base.

Microsoft developed a masterful strategy of exchanges. It had negative qualitative imbalances in product quality, user base and brand recognition. But this wasn't just browser versus browser, it was company versus company, and here Microsoft had some positive imbalances against Netscape. First, it had a massive material advantage in cold, hard cash thanks to the success of its office suites and operating system software. Second, Microsoft had a placement advantage; it could bundle Explorer with its other popular software. If you bought Windows or Office the Microsoft browser was also installed on your computer.

Microsoft didn't just give the browser away with other software. Leveraging that massive amount of cash, they simply gave it away to everybody free. This was a brutally efficient exchange of material for positional quality and it worked wonderfully. To be fair, they also invested a lot of money into improving the quality of the Explorer browser itself, but that wasn't the most important factor in the race with Navigator. The much smaller Netscape saw what was going on and tried to keep up – as well as crying foul and going to the courts. But such a small company couldn't afford to give its main product away to everyone free and still maintain quality. Their attempts to bundle Navigator with other software paled in the face of the 95 per cent desktop dominance of Windows. Within two years Microsoft went from less than 10 per cent of the browser market share to over 80 per cent, continuing to gain even after that until all the competition was entirely marginalized.

Microsoft exploited its overwhelming advantage in resources, in American Civil War terms playing General Grant to the rest of the software world's General Lee. The Union's Grant wasn't the most brilliant tactician but he knew he would eventually wear down the Southern army by sheer weight of troops and supplies. A war of attrition suited Grant fine – if not his men – and he had the brutally pragmatic nature needed to fight and win such a war. With some stretching we can even make an analogy to the Cold War. By constantly increasing military spending, the USA eventually bankrupted the USSR, although in this case the Communist side also suffered from the fatal 'bug' of a bankrupt ideology.

As an epilogue, the browser war has reignited in the past year. With no competition in sight, Microsoft neglected its browser development, permitting it to be outflanked on a quality level by competitors like Firefox. Security, viruses and spyware became big consumer issues too quickly for Microsoft to react and Explorer was behind the curve in these areas. Microsoft's aggressive tactics of distributing its browser for free with other programs has also been challenged successfully in court, hobbling their distribution strategy.

Firefox – a creation of the company Mozilla, which is in part a remnant of Netscape – is a relatively small open-source project and doesn't have the commercial distribution possibilities of a Microsoft product, but here lies another important difference between 2006 and 1998: the ubiquity of the internet itself. First-time internet users are a nearly negligible market segment. Nowadays it's normal to download new software from the internet and Firefox only needs a website to reach the world. As of this writing it is approaching 200 million downloads. This model partially neutralizes Microsoft's favourable imbalance in distribution and, combined with the superior quality of the product, has led to Firefox taking a big chunk out of Explorer's market share, as high as 10 per cent in most estimates. Not coincidentally, Microsoft is making major enhancements in its next version of Explorer for the first time in years.

All change comes at a cost

This measuring of imbalances should also take into account our own operations, and not just in comparison to our rivals. In chess we talk about having harmony in our position. Our pieces work together in a complementary fashion and the development of our material is in agreement with our strategic goals. Imbalances are inevitable but we can try to get them to work together. The difficulty of achieving successful coordination increases with the sheer number of assets. The corporate mega-mergers of the past decade have illustrated this very well. Time Warner and AOL came together in a deal of record proportions in 2001 and investors are now considering separating the companies again. Bigger isn't always better, especially if it comes at the cost of coordination.

The second law of thermodynamics covers the concept of entropy, which says that since exchanges of energy are never 100 per cent efficient, some is always lost during a process unless something is fed into it from the outside. (Remarkably, this theory was in a way anticipated by a century in the preface to the 1755 edition of Dr Johnson's *Dictionary*, where Johnson quotes Richard Hooker: 'Change is not made without inconvenience, even from worse to better.') This tends to be true in chess too, and we fight to overcome this loss of energy, of quality and time. To capture a piece requires the investment of a move, so while we gain material we may lose time. We have to decide in advance whether or not that exchange represents a positive overall result for our position.

In general we are talking about roughly equal positions in which our opponent is fighting back and maintaining the balance. We must build our advantages incrementally, looking for every chance to enhance our MTQ elements. But if our opponent slips we often have the chance to dramatically increase the relative amount of energy in our position with a powerful exchange. Most mistakes underestimate dynamic factors like time and initiative, leaving the position vulnerable to an exchange of material for time gained for an attack.

Consider Napoleon's early victories, especially in his 1796 Italian campaign. His successes owed much to his opponents' outmoded understanding of dynamic factors. They held an antiquated belief in large standing armies and slow manoeuvring. They were baffled and overwhelmed by Napoleon's quicksilver attacks and innovative tactics. What he gave up in numbers he more than made up for in speed and quality.

Over-extending our reach

Getting back to physics for one last time, we finally find common ground in the principle that 'ordered systems lose less energy than chaotic systems'. If our pieces work together they can better transform one advantage into another without losing quality. A position, or a company, or a military formation, that is already unorganized can be torn apart entirely by attempting a transformation. Achieving the objective may leave us so depleted in other ways that we are quickly wiped out, a common occurrence in positions that are already tenuous.

The phrase 'hastening defeat' is a very common one in the annotation of chess games. A player in a difficult position tends to make mistakes due to the psychological pressure of knowing he's in trouble. A more concrete motive for these collapses is that an inferior position is less able to withstand the loss of energy required by an attempt at activity. If a company is in financial trouble it can gamble on a risky venture or be conservative and fail slowly. Without stability that risky venture could lead to the total collapse of the company even if the gamble succeeds in its immediate objectives.

Over-extending military resources is a readily understood concept. In the Second World War Germany tried to fight on a front that stretched from the Russian forests to the deserts of Libya. This was simply too much territory for their troops to cover and too big a picture for their generals to monitor, let alone control. Similarly, when a politician's influence is waning we say he has used up his political capital and has to pick his battles. It represents a loss of accumulated energy, in this case of favours and the ability to reciprocate with influence.

Over-extension is a concept also referred to regularly in other walks of life. The once-dominant airline Pan Am invested in new planes and new routes just as the market for air travel was about to hit a plateau, and the company was soon in serious difficulty. As usual it took a combination of negative imbalances to go from a winning position to a losing one. The global energy crisis that hit in 1973 was a critical external factor which came right on the heels of a court battle awarding important international routes to the company's competitors.

Pan Am tried to solve some of their problems with the purchase of a domestic airline, but, as so often happens, a bold move from a position of weakness was severely punished. They overpaid for National Airlines and accumulated huge debt, limiting further desperation tactics. They held on by selling assets and routes, expending their material resources and hoping for a favourable change in conditions. The company was in such a fragile state that one more negative development could knock it out. In 1988 the Lockerbie terrorist bombing of Pan Am flight 103 was the proverbial last straw. Bookings plummeted, and a further overall fall in air travel thanks to the first Gulf War led the company to declare bankruptcy in 1991.

There is no doubt that the first airline giant had more than its fair share of bad luck, but the directors of Pan Am also suffered from their own mistakes and made themselves much more vulnerable to bad luck by over-extending and by not taking care of the imbalances in their own position – no domestic routes, weak cash position, pending court cases. This analysis is not meant to serve as a recommendation to be conservative or to plan only for the worst-case scenario. Risk-taking is essential in any endeavour. It's the context of that risk that is so critical. If we are sensitive to our vulnerabilities and negative imbalances we can factor them in to our strategy. One imbalance is rarely decisive. We must be able to see when a confluence is forming and whether or not it is in our favour.

In 1993 I committed the fatal mistake of launching an attack from a position of weakness. This wasn't at the chessboard, however, but in chess politics. Ever since the international chess federation, FIDE, had interrupted my first world championship match in 1985, I had feuded with their leadership almost without pause. In the run-up to my 1993 world championship match with Nigel Short, the Englishman called me with a tempting offer, to play the match outside of FIDE and launch our own Professional Chess Association. Here at last was a chance to break away from the corrupt bureaucracy and introduce chess into the world of modern sport.

Short was the first Western challenger since Bobby Fischer in 1972. With his involvement I thought we could generate tremendous interest and rally the support of the world's Grandmasters to our cause against FIDE. Just a few years earlier the professional players' union I had created had foundered when the western GMs formed an opposition bloc. Suddenly here was Short, the last president of the Grandmaster Association, offering to join forces. Now, I thought, we could really unite the chess world. This turned out to be a terrible blunder, the worst of my career. After we made our announcement it quickly became apparent that my assumption was incorrect and that Short had no such support. We were on our own and were immediately portrayed as 'renegades' and 'hijackers of the world championship'. FIDE essentially excommunicated both of us and held an alternative world championship match in parallel to the one Short and I played in London. Thus began a schism in the chess world that has never properly healed. I was so eager to achieve my goal that I was oblivious to how unlikely the plan was to succeed.

Static factors and choosing our evils

My recent entry into the world of politics has given me new insight into the give and take of lesser evils and trade-offs. If politics is, as Bismarck said, 'the art of the possible', it is essential to first establish what can and what cannot be altered. Each situation has static, immutable factors that we must exploit or work around. There are also dynamic factors that are largely beyond our direct influence, such as our competition. It is essential to identify these factors and what they mean to our strategy. How can we transform our assets to take advantage of these external conditions? Are we streamlined to work within our environment? If the market is changing around us, we have to be prepared to adapt and invest our energy to reposition ourselves.

There may also be static factors in our own position, weaknesses that can't be remedied directly. In this case we have to seek an environment where these flaws are minimized. If I have permanent weaknesses on one side of the board, I'll consider an assault on the other side. If my structure is so bad that a long manoeuvring strategy is hopeless, I'll try to sharpen play to create a wild attacking environment where my opponent won't have time to exploit my structural weaknesses. All the textbooks tell us of the struggle for control of the Roman empire in 31 BC, in which Octavian used his nimbler navy to defeat Antony and Cleopatra's forces, which he had been unable to defeat on land after many battles. Octavian kept Antony's armies boxed in until finally he had to come out and fight at sea, where Octavian's brilliant admiral Agrippa won a decisive encounter – or so the story goes.

This struggle with imbalances and trade-offs also exists within society. Benjamin Franklin put it bluntly when he said, 'They who would give up an essential liberty for temporary security, deserve neither liberty or security.' Thanks to the threat of global terror, the American PATRIOT Act (a flashy acronym for 'Providing Appropriate Tools Required to Intercept and Obstruct Terrorism') and similar measures proposed by the European Union are the latest examples of this eternal battle between security and personal liberty. Exchanges between civil society and the state are constant, and the corporate world also participates with its many agendas.

Throughout history the state has pushed as far as possible for control, a great blunder according to Franklin. Parkinson's famous law and its axioms explain why bureaucracies expand inexorably.* When this natural tendency to inflate meets the politician's desire for power and control the citizenry had better watch out.

My decision to retire from professional chess and enter politics full-time was largely based on what I saw as the need to join the resistance to the catastrophic expansion of authoritarian state power in my home country. I spent twenty-five years representing the colours of my country and I believe I am

* In 1958, the British historian and author C. Northcote Parkinson postulated that 'work expands so as to fill the time available for its completion', along with the attendant axioms (1) 'An official wants to multiply subordinates, not rivals' and (2) 'Officials make work for each other.' Parkinson's genius was confirmed when his prediction that the Royal Navy would eventually have more admirals than ships actually came to pass.

continuing to do so. In Russia today, President Vladimir Putin is exploiting the name of security to push for the exchange of liberty for control and yet security always seems to remain beyond reach. With a lack of transparency there is little to control expenditures, and without controlling those, state expansion is endless. In Russia the citizens are now in great danger from state abuse of power because officials are beyond public reach. Any criticism of state officials can be termed 'extremism', a term separated from terrorism by only a comma in Putin's law book. Not martial law exactly, call it 'martial law lite'. The tendencies are always there, only the details change with the times.

This pattern has been well established since the rise of modern society. Mussolini employed this method to impose fascism in Italy in the 1920s. Even with such recent examples before us we allow it to happen over and over. We exchange our freedoms for promises of security and when that security fails to be delivered we are told it's because we have yet to give up enough freedom. We can see the pattern and we know the rules by which this game is played. The question is whether or not we are able to resist the temptation to make these concessions. While we cannot receive guarantees that our exchanges will work out well, we should at least keep recent history in mind.

There are imbalances in our daily lives and we constantly struggle to transform them positively. Gaining control means finding the most favourable balance and working constantly to make positive exchanges. Norman Mailer wrote that at every moment we are either 'living a little more or dying a little bit'. There is no standing still, no maintaining a perfect equilibrium. We can, however, in effect freeze time by pausing for a moment in our constant search for what to do next and instead calmly evaluate the pluses and minuses. We can flout the laws of thermodynamics to create energy and quality through positive transformations.

Tigran Vartanovich Petrosian (1929–84), USSR
Boris Vasilievich Spassky (1937–), USSR/France
Two contrasting sources of chess wisdom

Tigran Petrosian was the ninth world champion and Boris Spassky was the man who, on the second attempt, took the title from him. Together these USSR teammates acted almost like professional tutors for me when I entered the international tournament world. They were still successful players and had a wealth of experience at the top to share with an up-and-coming junior.

Their teachings came to me long before I met them by way of a book covering the second world championship match they contested in 1969. I was given the book as a gift as a child and still get pleasure from thumbing through it and from the games themselves.

Petrosian and Spassky also gave me lessons over the board. With both of them I lost my first two decisive encounters from fine positions only later to come back older and wiser to eventually even our career scores at 2–2.

Petrosian was the man who finally brought an end to the reign of Botvinnik, defeating him for the title in 1963, the year of my birth. His redoubtable defensive style was ideally suited for match play, where one win and zero losses is enough for victory. Botvinnik paid his conqueror a rare compliment, saying that Petrosian's ability to deeply evaluate a position was unsurpassed.

Spassky was a truly universal player, capable of both spectacular attacks and calm manoeuvring play. In his first world championship match he under-estimated Petrosian's ability to play in complications and paid the price. In their next match, in 1969, Spassky controlled his aggression and won. Unfortunately, he is best remembered for losing the title to the American Bobby Fischer in their famous match in Reykjavik, Iceland, in 1972.

Spassky's carefree attitude precluded his doing the immense amount of work required for a long stay at the top. A free-thinker who never accepted the Soviet mentality, Spassky married a French woman and emigrated to France in 1976. Now he proudly calls himself a Russian nationalist and monarchist.

On Petrosian: 'Petrosian has the ability to see and eliminate danger twenty moves before it arises! I was staggered by Petrosian's ability, after achieving an excellent position, all the time to find manoeuvres that strengthened it.' – Bobby Fischer

Petrosian in his own words: 'Some consider that when I play I am excessively cautious, but it seems to me that the question may be a different one. I try to avoid chance. Those who rely on chance should play cards or roulette. Chess is something quite different.'

On Spassky: 'Spassky possesses enviable health, he is a good psychologist, and he subtly evaluates the situation, his strengths, and the strengths of his opponent.' – Mikhail Botvinnik

Spassky in his own words: 'Chess, Garry, is the royal game!' – To me, regarding my attempts to democratize the sport in 1986 by creating a Grandmaster Association.

10

INNOVATION

Originality is hard work

Creativity is one of the many human qualities that is often credited with being innate and immutable, something you are either born with or can only envy in others. We often hear about someone with a 'fertile mind' that is 'brimming with ideas' and wonder how it is this person got so lucky in his genetic makeup.

Just about anyone who has come up with an idea or invention that reaches the public is endlessly asked where the idea came from. Musicians, even bad ones, are asked where they get the ideas for their songs. After a game chess players are asked how they came up with a certain idea, or how the winning move occurred to them. (Even worse, we are often asked why we played a particularly terrible blunder.)

As with untapped talent, imagination that goes unexpressed may as well not exist. Ideas can contribute merely by being launched into the atmosphere, where they mingle with others and find application. Every mind approaches every problem in a unique way because of the singular set of experiences that each person brings with them. As discussed earlier, inclination and style also have a say in the decisions we make. But this doesn't mean that solutions and innovations must come from the right person at the right time as if parcelled out from on high. Through work and a sense of purpose we can take creativity into our own hands.

En route, we will take a look at both the power and limitations of innovation. Not all novelties are of equal value and it's worth looking at a few fiascos along with the success stories. There are also different classes of innovation.

The first category is the kind that leads directly to creation and invention. It has an immediate impact, a problem solved, a product developed, a question answered. We think of Archimedes leaping from his bath and crying 'Eureka!' when struck by the idea of buoyancy and density. But this 'Eureka model' of creativity is very much misunderstood.

The second category relates to the long-term and the ideas that spark evolutionary transformations. Their effects might not be apparent for generations, which in turn means their causes can also go unnoticed. First we'll focus on the more immediate type, the discoveries and inventions that make the news instead of just the history books.

Raising our innovation index

Looking at examples of famous innovators can amount to more than a collection of entertaining stories. We can take away both inspiration and insight into what we can do to increase the 'innovation index' in our own lives. We must ask ourselves, 'Is there a different way to go about this?' Look at the goal first, then the means, and allow yourself to entertain new ideas and experiment with alternative methods. We are all familiar with the problems of our own lives, so no one is better qualified to discover innovative solutions to them. It won't happen overnight, but if we keep working on it, it will happen.

There is as little truth to the story about the apple falling on Isaac Newton's head as there is to the American tale of Washington chopping down the cherry tree. (There is of course a long history of fateful fruit in mythology.) We all like a good story, especially one that avoids mentioning all the hard work behind these so-called strokes of genius. It is only human nature to seek out the amusing and trivial aspects of greatness. If you look up Newton on the internet you would think that his inventions of the cat flap and of calculus had been of equal value to mankind.

Earlier we talked about Thomas Edison's tremendous capacity for work and his example is a typical refutation of the Eureka myth. Just about every great discovery was the product of a combination of prior knowledge, hard work and systematic thinking. The miraculous epiphany makes for a better children's story, but it's not helpful when we seek inspiration ourselves. We can strive to emulate Newton's dedication but we can't compete with a lucky apple.

Even the startling ideas that turn conventional wisdom on its head come from somewhere. A thorough knowledge of what came before is required to move forward. As we have seen, the first world chess champion, Wilhelm Steinitz, contributed a huge amount to the development of the game. His writings in the last quarter of the nineteenth century were the first to break down the component parts of a chess position and elucidate the workings of strategy. Steinitz's discoveries are well demonstrated by his own games, which changed from romantic chaos to scientific order during the course of his career as he came to understand and apply his principles.

These revolutionary concepts, however, were firmly based on his analysis of old material. Only after careful analysis and understanding of the old style could Steinitz embark in a successful new direction. He was the first to cast a critical eye on what had come before instead of accepting the status quo. He incorporated his new concepts into his own play and won the first world championship match in 1886.

The power of novelty

Innovations in specific chess games, as opposed to general theories, have a very concrete definition. They come when a move is played that has never been played before in that position, what we call a 'theoretical novelty', usually shortened to 'TN' or just 'N' in chess notation. With the depth of professional preparation and the use of computer databases, you might think it difficult to innovate these days. In some variations we may reach well past the twentieth move before diverging from known games and analysis, often over half the moves of the game.

I should point out that just because a variation has been played before doesn't mean both players are aware of that fact. A database of several million games can instantly point out where previous games diverged, but even the most well-prepared Grandmaster is occasionally surprised to later find that he spent a few hours at the board reinventing the wheel by repeating the moves of an old game.

Chess is varied and complex enough to ensure that such things are exceptions and not the rule. Many games reach original positions before move fifteen, with some breaking new ground before move ten. Like a city, chess has its main avenues and its side streets. There is still considerable room for originality on the untrodden paths, but there is also more risk. Which do we choose, the safety of Main Street or the unknown of the back alleys?

A powerful idea is like a new weapon in battle or being first on the market with a new product. The competitive advantage is maximized by the surprise factor. The English longbow was a shock-and-awe weapon in the fifteenth century, comparable to the Colt revolvers and Winchester repeating rifles of the Wild West. Not all new weapons are as fearsome as these, but the fear of the unknown is itself a powerful weapon. The V2 rockets used by the Nazis towards the end of the war, primarily against England, were less militarily effective than bombers but were terrifying due to their silence and the impossibility of defence.

The value of surprise on the chessboard is easily translatable to the battlefield. The famous military strategist of the ancient Chinese world, Sun Tzu, constantly emphasized the importance of deception and surprise in *The Art of War*. There is little room for outright deception at the chessboard, although a little tactical psychology can't be overlooked.

Let's say we've cooked up a nasty new idea in our opponent's favourite defence. Do we play quickly and confidently all the way through, gaining time but perhaps tipping him off that we have something up our sleeve? Or do we take our time so as not to attract suspicion? And when the moment comes to play the new move, do we make it with a flourish so he knows he's in our preparation trap or do we play it after some feigned thought so he can't be sure we've analysed the position at home? It's hard to disguise the truth, since there are so many signs for a professional to detect at the board. Any new, strong move is going to be suspected of being the result of preparation, especially if we've played the line before.

My opinion on all this usually coincided with that of Bobby Fischer, who said 'I don't believe in psychology. I believe in good moves.' I've never been adept at hiding my emotions at the board and if I had a powerful novelty I didn't care if my opponent knew it. As long as it was a good move that knowledge couldn't help him.

Taming a tiger

The power of a single innovation was illustrated in my 1995 world championship match against India's Viswanathan Anand. The match started out very tight with eight consecutive draws. I had been playing different openings in every game with white, probing for weaknesses and giving my team and myself material for analysis. The breakthrough came before the ninth game, when I found a spectacular sacrificial continuation against Anand's preferred Open Ruy Lopez Defence, which he had used successfully in the sixth game. It had been his main defence in qualification matches en route to our world championship battle, so we were both expecting an eventual showdown. In three of my previous efforts with white – games 2, 4, and 8 – I had avoided this stronghold. Now it was time for a frontal assault.

Of course I was very excited about this new discovery and couldn't wait to use it. The problem was that I had black in the ninth game, not white. I was so caught up with anticipation for game 10 I got wiped out in game 9, falling behind in the match. This was undoubtedly the first time a novelty had backfired on me before I had even played it! Now it was doubly important that my new idea work well in the next game.

In game 10, I played the first part of the new idea on move 14, actually following a suggestion made long ago by Mikhail Tal. Anand was clearly ready for this approach and replied after just four minutes' thought. After my next move, however, he spent a solid 45 minutes thinking, perhaps a record for the famously speedy Indian Grandmaster. The trap had been sprung and there was no way out. I was still playing all my moves almost instantaneously, happy to at last have them out of my head and on to the board.

To his credit, the 'Tiger of Madras' played like a true championship contender and survived the first wave of the attack after first falling into my snare. Only when the smoke had cleared and my advantage was evident did I slow down in order to make sure to bring home the full point. It would have been excruciating to waste such a marvellous new idea. With precise play I notched the win to level the match, which, as I have said, I eventually went on to win. The victory was worth one point, but the psychological effect was devastating. Thanks to this one novelty Anand was forced to put his primary defence on the shelf for the rest of the match. With the comfort of hindsight, some suggested that he should have avoided repeating his use of the Ruy Lopez again in game 10 despite his earlier success with it. But he had just taken the lead in the match and he wanted to emphasize his ascendancy by failing to blink in the psychological opening battle.

It took me and my analysis team days to discover this novelty and to work out all the complexities. We needed that time to absorb all the background material and the subtleties of the variation. It's not as if we sit down to work knowing exactly where the crisis lies. The key to any good solution is first correctly identifying the problem, as any scientist will tell you. As dictated by the principle of GIGO ('garbage in, garbage out') an experiment can only produce results as good as the data fed into it and as good as the questions asked of the data. Even the greatest minds can be so distracted by the search for answers that they fail to ask logical questions. It is worth keeping in mind that Isaac Newton himself devoted much of the second half of his life to the spurious pursuit of alchemy.

Our basic recipe, then, is to first steep ourselves in every aspect of the problem and then identify the questions that need to be answered. The most creative minds usually belong to those who know the most about the matter at hand.

Innovation alone doesn't equal success

Being an innovator doesn't always translate into being a great success as defined by the worlds of business or sport. That is, by the measures of making money and winning. History is so full of inventors who died penniless that the idea has become a caricature. Recognizing the significance of an innovation is critical, as is having the will and acumen to exploit it.

Chess has also had its share of original thinkers who failed to reach the top as players. It is difficult to cast them as failures when they contributed so much to the development of the game. Several such players did the next best thing to winning, they found an outlet for their creative energies by helping others win.

Anatoly Karpov and Viktor Korchnoi are names well known to every chess fan. They battled in two consecutive world championship matches, 1978 and 1981, the younger Karpov coming out on top in both. (Their matches actually go back even further, to 1974, when Karpov defeated Korchnoi for the right to face Bobby Fischer for the world championship. Their match retroactively became the de facto world championship when Fischer abdicated the title without playing.) Less familiar are the names of the coaches who assisted them in these battles, infusing their play with rich ideas in the openings.

Yacov Murey worked as one of Korchnoi's seconds and Igor Zaitsev assisted Karpov. The nature of their relationships differed in a way that often finds a parallel in the real world. Korchnoi was a very creative player himself and rarely worked with any one person for long. He needed new people around him to spark his own ideas as much as he took them from others. In contrast, Karpov harvested ideas from a stable of long-term collaborators over his long career. He had a tremendous capacity to absorb and synthesize new ideas and to maximize their effect. We can also observe contrasting approaches in business and politics. Does a new prime minister fill his cabinet with long-standing associates in order to establish a comfortable command structure, or does he surround himself with relative outsiders who will stimulate his mind, even to the point of contradicting him?

Neither Murey nor Zaitsev ever approached the world elite, but both were dedicated to finding original ways to play the opening phase. Like many great chess inventors they lent their expertise and creativity to stronger players, giving them an initial shove the way the 'pushers' on a bobsled team shove off before jumping in and keeping their heads down.

What did they have that others do not have? Why are some players, some people, more creative than others? Foremost, they shared a certain degree of impracticality. This is a problem at the board but an asset in coming up with new ideas that can be tempered by a steadier hand. They churned out ideas without worrying over whether each one was flawless. Perhaps their initial success rate wasn't high, but they produced so many ideas that, with trial and error, a higher and higher percentage proved worthwhile. They established a routine of creativity, so to speak. The constant production of new ideas feeds and hones the intuition.

Some of their inventions were so significant that they continue to bear their names. The Zaitsev variation of the Ruy Lopez was probably the last named major system introduced in the game when its eponymous inventor developed it in the mid 1970s.

Perhaps regrettably, there are no patents for chess moves, so Igor receives little benefit beyond recognition when players around the world make use of his ideas.

There are, however, many similarities between chess innovations and real world inventions. Both have been dramatically affected by the global increase in the flow of information.

The transition from imitator to innovator

When Amazon.com develops a new feature for its website, it is immediately shared with the rest of the world. Web programming isn't like the secret formula for Coca-Cola or an invention like the DVD player. Other websites, Amazon's direct competitors, can easily copy, if not the exact code, the concept and the feature itself. This has led to understandable but increasingly absurd attempts to patent every sort of idea, no matter how obvious or simple.

The concept of intellectual property rights is an important element in the attempt to ensure that inventors are rewarded for their efforts. But what about attempting to patent things like the use of smiley faces in email or the ability to buy products over the web with one mouse click? Both have been tried, by Microsoft and Amazon, respectively. Clearly this sort of thing is not what patent offices originally had in mind. But then how can we cope with the increasing commoditization of information? If everything is quickly and freely available to everyone, why innovate at all?

Of course if everyone thought like that we'd still be living in caves, but society needs its imitators too. If we can't afford an iPod we can find an alternative MP3 player in our price range. The history of technology makes it clear that we never know what's going to be a big hit. Some new ideas are flops, and we have to accept a few failures. As Thomas Watson, founder of IBM, put it, 'If you want to succeed, double your failure rate.' If you aren't failing at least occasionally you aren't taking the risks required to be an innovator.

The less visible but even more vital reason to invest in research and innovation is that you have to stay on the cutting edge if you are going to make a big impact. You can't suddenly switch from follower to leader, because only the leader can see what's coming around the bend. Even the most successful imitators eventually become innovators if they want to expand their territory and become more successful. Those who fail to make this transition are usually supplanted by other imitators. As risky as innovation can be (one of my favourite sayings is 'Pioneers get filled full of arrows'), failing to innovate is riskier still.

The transition from imitator to innovator is commonly seen at every level. Japanese goods were for many years reviled by Americans as cheap, poorly-made knock-offs of US and European products. 'Made in Japan' was almost synonymous with 'junk' in everything from radios to automobiles just three decades ago. The flood of inexpensive imports and imitations into the market rapidly created an enormous shift in the consumer electronics industry. New features and cutting-edge technology weren't as significant in the television market as lower production costs that led to lower prices for the consumer. Unable to adapt quickly enough, most American manufacturers soon abandoned the market or went out of business entirely, leaving it to Japanese companies. The Japanese were then faced with the need to produce higher-end models with the new features consumers wanted. It didn't take long for imitators to give the Japanese companies a taste of their own medicine. Korea and Taiwan were quick to move into the lower-end market as the Japanese companies spent more money on research and development. The Japanese had been forced to become innovators.

The only way to survive is to keep moving up the pyramid. You can't stay at the bottom, the competition there is too fierce. There will always be newcomers with advantages to attack at the bottom. Just like Darwinism in nature, innovation is quite literally about survival. To survive we have to keep evolving.

The innovations of evolution

It's easy enough to identify inventions like the light bulb or the television as symbols of innovative thinking. The impact of these devices on society for generations to come is not so easily measured. The most powerful innovations are relevant in the way they create a cascading effect of new ways of thinking and living. Being aware of these cascades, of how fast they are moving and where they are going, is an intrinsic part of being an innovator.

Few of us need to have the global picture of a CEO or a prime minister. Nor do we all have the vital need to be aware of the latest developments that a doctor has. That doesn't mean we won't benefit from keeping up with the many trends that impact our lives. For example, as parents we need to follow trends and new developments in education. We often try to get by with as little information as possible instead of seeking out more. How much do we know about the latest developments in the areas that affect us, our work, our family? The more information we have the better able we will be to find new and better ways to improve our quality of life.

We all have that friend who always has the latest gadgets, the newest technology in his pocket and in his kitchen, regularly replaced by the latest models. Whatever you're eating, he's just read a new study about how it's now been proven to be horrible for you – until next month when another study says the opposite. This comic character illustrates the occasionally slim difference between being an innovator and just following the latest fads. Buying the latest toys and believing the latest factoids isn't the same as thinking about what these things mean. In other words, the implications of an invention are often a truer measure of its value than its utility.

Microsoft's old slogan, 'A computer on every desk and in every home', sounds antiquated today when that is almost literally the case. It wasn't that long ago that many technology leaders were openly sceptical about the future of the PC. In 1977 Ken Olsen, President of Digital Equipment Corporation (DEC), told the audience at the World Future Society convention that 'There is no reason for any individual to have a computer in their home.' This was said in the same year that Steve Jobs and Steve Wozniak released the Apple II personal computer that began the PC revolution. Clearly DEC's president – and he wasn't alone – failed to consider the implications of the technology in which he was an expert.

Adaptation and innovation take place all around us, albeit usually on a smaller scale. For example, the ubiquitous iPod. When everyone started buying portable MP3 players, a few people wondered what it might mean when a sizeable percentage of the population was carrying the little devices around all the time. Instead of using them only to play music, a new type of information distribution was created, podcasting.

Understanding the implications of inventions

As with evolution in the natural world, this deeper effect emerges very slowly relative to the appearance of individual innovations. To stretch the analogy, long-term effects reveal the evolution of ideas while the singular shifts and inventions are analogous to mutations. If they catch on and survive in the wild, one by one they can add up to great change and subsequently lead to further changes.

The major milestones of the distribution of information are good examples of this effect. Each marked a landmark in the advance of human society. The invention of the alphabet and the written word brought man out of the stone age. Written laws, inventories and contracts revolutionized political and business life, as permanent, objective records could be created. Then the printing press democratized the spread of information, making it much harder to control. Mankind moved into the modern scientific era when information became verifiable and universal with the creation of common references.

The internet is the next step on the path of universal information access. It is well on its way to establishing boundless, instantaneous access to the sum knowledge of humankind and instant communication with anyone on earth. Its impact on our society has already been dramatic, even though it has yet to fully penetrate the underdeveloped areas of the globe where its effects will be the greatest.

We hear so much about the internet, and it has become such an intrinsic part of our daily lives, that we often fail to consider the larger impact it has on our world. Our children are not going to grow up in the same world we grew up in. Their education will be, or at least should be, entirely different. Consider the potential for early education, for unorthodox career patterns, what it means for a six-year-old to be able to find out literally anything about any subject in seconds.

Surely this is all marvellous, but what about the consequences, positive and negative? What does this mean for the development of our children's critical thinking ability? For their desire to spend time seriously studying a subject? Does the ability to get instant answers cause mental muscles to atrophy the way our quadriceps and biceps become flabby from sitting at a desk all day? Can someone in Bangladesh do your job from 10,000 miles away?

Or, more optimistically, can you stay at home and work for companies in Germany, Brazil and India?

Simply being aware of and using technology is quite different from considering its implications and incorporating such considerations into your life strategies. During my thirty-year professional chess career I always tried to ask myself how innovations might impact on my world, the chess world. Normally we might get these insights from watching the news or talking with informed friends. Sometimes they come from an entirely unexpected direction.

And a child shall lead us

In 1985 I was twenty-two years old and the recently crowned world chess champion. One of the benefits of my new stature was the ability to obtain an early personal computer, one of the few in my hometown of Baku. There wasn't a great deal one could do with it as far as I recall, but it fascinated me just the same. One day I received a package in the mail from a stranger named Frederic Friedel, a chess fan and science writer based in Hamburg, Germany. He sent me an admiring note and a floppy disk containing several computer games, including one called Hopper.

Video games weren't yet the phenomenon they had become in the United States and I enthusiastically took up this new challenge. I admit I spent much of my free time over the next few weeks practising Hopper and setting ever higher record scores.

A few months later I travelled to Hamburg for a chess event and I made sure to look up Mr Friedel at his suburban home. I met his wife and two young sons, Martin, age ten, and Tommy, age three – they made me feel quite at home and Frederic was eager to show me the latest developments on his own computer. I managed to work into the conversation that I had completely mastered one of the little games he had sent me.

'You know, I'm the best Hopper player in Baku,' I said, omitting any mention of the total lack of competition.

'What's your high score?' he asked.

'Sixteen thousand,' I replied, a little surprised when this extraordinary number failed to elicit at least a raised eyebrow.

'Very impressive,' Frederic said, 'but that's not such a big score in this house.'

'What? You can beat it?' I asked.

'No, not me.'

'Ah, OK, Martin must be the video game whiz.'

'No, not Martin.'

It was with a sinking feeling that I realized the smile on Frederic's face meant that the household Hopper champion was the three-year-old. I was incredulous. 'You can't mean Tommy!' My fears were confirmed when Frederic led his little boy over to the computer and sat him down next to us as the familiar game loaded. Since I was the guest they let me go first and I rose to the occasion with a personal best of 19,000 points.

My success was short-lived, however, as Tommy took his turn. His little fingers were a blur and it wasn't long before the score read 20,000, then 30,000. I figured I should concede defeat before we sat there watching through dinnertime. My cause was clearly hopeless.

Losing to a little kid at Hopper was easier on my ego than any loss to Anatoly Karpov, but it still gave me food for thought. How was my country going to compete with a generation of little computer geniuses being raised in the West? Here was I, one of the few people in an entire Soviet city with a computer, and I was handily out-performed by a German toddler. And what about the implications for chess? What if we could archive and study chess games the way we used our PCs to write letters and store records? This would be a powerful weapon, one that I shouldn't be the last to have.

But my first opportunity to employ what I learned from this lesson wasn't related to chess. When I signed a sponsorship deal with the computer company Atari I took as payment more than 100 of their machines to bring back to a youth club in Moscow, the first of its kind in the Soviet Union. We couldn't be left in the stone age while Tommy and his nimble-fingered compatriots took over the world.

I had also had the chance to address the other issue with Frederic: how a home computer could be turned into a chess tool. Our conversations led to the creation of the first version of ChessBase, a name now synonymous with professional chess software through the company of the same name that Frederic co-founded in Hamburg. ChessBase was the result of embracing innovation and of being alert to the trends and the possibilities. (And while Martin and Tommy have so far failed to take over the world, both are successful computer design and programming professionals.)

Computers developing a human game

While prescient about the power of a chess database tool, I failed to see the potential of another aspect of computer influence in chess. Even though, when I look back, it is hard to see how I could have foreseen the impact 'playing engines' – the term for programs – would have on the game. Chess-playing machines and programs were almost laughably weak back in the 80s. We all understood on a vague level that they would continue to get stronger, eventually besting even the human world champion, but few considered what that would mean for the sport in a broader sense.

You might forgive my under-estimation of the potential of these machines had you attended that event in Hamburg in 1985. I played against thirty-two different chess computers all at the same time, in what we call a simultaneous exhibition. I walked from one to the next, making my moves over a period of over five hours. The four leading manufacturers had sent their top models, including eight from Saitek bearing my name. It shows you the state of computer chess at the time that it didn't come as much of a surprise when I made a perfect 32–0 score, although there was one uncomfortable moment.

I realized that I was drifting into trouble in one game, and it was against a 'Kasparov' model at that. If this machine scored a win or even a draw people would be quick to say I had thrown the game to get PR for the company, so I had to redouble my efforts. Eventually I found a way to trick it with a sacrifice it should have refused. Ah, the good old days of playing computers . . .

Nowadays for fifty dollars you can buy a ChessBase PC program like Fritz or Junior that will crush most Grandmasters. In 2003 I played serious matches against new versions of these programs running on massive – but commercially available – multi-processor servers (playing just one game at a time of course) and in both cases the score ended even. That this day was inevitable was predicted by many observers and programmers decades ago. But no one understood all the ramifications of having a super-GM on your laptop, especially what this would mean for professional players.

There were many doomsday scenarios about people losing interest in chess with the rise of the machines. Others postulated that the game would be solved, i.e. a mathematically conclusive way to win from the start would be shown by the computers.

Neither of these gloomy predictions have come true, nor will they ever come to pass. But there have been many unintended consequences, both positive and negative, of the rapid proliferation of powerful chess software.

Kids love computers and take to them naturally, so it's no surprise that the same is true of the combination of chess and computers. With the introduction of super-strong software it became possible for a youngster to have a top-level opponent at home instead of needing a professional trainer from an early age. Countries with little chess tradition and few available coaches can produce prodigies, and they have.

The heavy use of computer analysis has pushed the game itself in new directions. The machine doesn't care about style or patterns or hundreds of years of established theory. It counts up the material, analyses a few billion positions, and counts it up again. It is entirely free of prejudice and doctrine and this has contributed to the development of players who are almost as free of dogma as the machines with which they train. The motto of modern play has become 'Show me.' Increasingly, a move isn't good or bad because it looks that way or because it hasn't been done that way before. It's simply good if it works and bad if it doesn't. Although we still require a strong measure of intuition and logic to play well, humans are starting to play more like computers.

Ideas reflect society

This is only the latest phase in the development of an ancient game. Chess has undergone a great deal of evolution through the centuries. The modern European version of chess – to avoid confusion with Shogi and Xiangqi, often referred to as Japanese and Chinese chess respectively – must have the oldest written record of its rules of any popular modern game. With only a little imagination we can parallel its development with that of the knowledge of humankind.

That the premier Western intellectual game has mirrored society in many ways shouldn't come as too much of a surprise. Similar parallels have been discussed in the fine arts, music and literature. The earliest leaders in the game came from the heart of the Renaissance, Italy and Spain. The author of the oldest surviving book on practical chess play, Lucena, was a student at the University of Salamanca when he produced his volume in 1497. He documented the transition from the old forms of the game to the modern rules, which have changed only slightly over the intervening 500 years.

The first great maestro, the Frenchman François André Danican Philidor, who tried to create a theory of positional play, lived in the age of the Enlightenment and the philosophy of rationalism. We could even make the case that his memorable phrase 'The pawns are the soul of the game' eerily anticipated the French Revolution.

In the first half of the nineteenth century, chess was modelled on geopolitical reality and was the arena for continual battles for supremacy between France and Britain. Midway through the century emerged the legendary attacking player Adolf Anderssen of Germany. His reckless and spectacular sacrificial style exemplified the triumph of mind over matter. As we have seen he was bested only – and briefly – by the meteoric American Paul Morphy. In just two years – 1857–8 – Morphy came out of nowhere with an energetic blend of pragmatism, aggression and accurate calculation, personifying the characteristics of his nation while becoming the first American world champion at any endeavour.

The first official world championship match was held in 1886 in the United States. This piece of trivia often comes as a surprise to Americans, who for the most part don't consider chess a serious sport. A majority of the early world championship contests were in fact held in the US, attracting considerable sponsorship and national media coverage. The stakes from the players were a fabulous 2,000 dollars each, a sum over 200 times the average weekly wage of the day. This legendary first match travelled from New York to St Louis to New Orleans, the home town of the great Morphy himself, who had recently died. The competitors were the leading exponents of the old and new schools of the game. Johann Zukertort represented the romantic age of attacking play while Wilhelm Steinitz was the first modern positional master.

Steinitz's decisive victory set a model for players to come and put a nail in the coffin of the romantic era of the game. The first world champion went on to codify his new theories of positional dogma, occasionally, it must be said, sticking to them too closely.

The next movement in chess was the hypermodern school after the First World War. Iconoclasts like Aaron Nimzowitsch and Richard Réti challenged the traditional concepts of classical play set down by their elders. The next living milestone was Mikhail Botvinnik, leader of the cold Soviet scientific approach. In 1972 Bobby Fischer was, like Morphy, a brief and powerful explosion of American individualism that shook the world and pushed chess to a new level.

The current chess era, call it modern, or dynamic, or computerized, fully represents the successful annihilation of the 'big lies' and myths of the twentieth century. The stringent ideological dogmas are behind us and so are many of the antiquated doctrines of the chessboard. Trends still come and go, but now the only real rule is the absence of rules. Look around the world today at the dynamic state of everything from information technology to transportation to warfare. Who can say that chess does not imitate life?

Fear of change is worse than changing too fast

There are few downsides to being an innovator, despite the occasional well-publicized fiasco. Being a little too far ahead of the curve, ahead of the market, will on occasion rebound on the innovator, but even these experiences tend to have wider positive effects, if not always for the person or company that made the mistake. They can spread the seeds of a new way of thinking and, like most blunders, are valuable at least in showing what doesn't work, which is often as valuable as showing what does. As my mother always put it to me, 'A negative result is also a result.' As an engineer she takes a much more sanguine and practical approach to setbacks than a sportsman.

The scientist John Carew Eccles spent much of his early career trying to prove that synaptic reactions in the brain were electrical instead of chemical, and that the mind was in some way separate from the brain. In short, he was wrong. But his arguments and experiments led to many important discoveries that derived from why he was wrong; his later work on the nervous system won him a Nobel Prize. Thomas Edison summed up such results well when he said, 'I haven't failed, I've just found ten thousand ways that didn't work.'

Of course the world of high technology is full of early implementations that fell short of the potential of the ideas behind them. After the Second World War the Northrop corporation designed a 'flying wing' aircraft for the US military that by all accounts was more efficient than its competition. But it looked too strange and had too many innovative characteristics to be trusted by the decision-makers. Some called it 'more advanced than it should have been', a strange statement in the world of technology, but accurate when we factor in realistic market considerations. After a few early setbacks the entire design concept was ignored until the 80s, when it made a successful comeback as the B-2 stealth bomber.

Things can be 'too new' for your average shopper, too. The consumer market has often failed to embrace a new product only to buy it in droves a decade later. Small changes in a product and in the culture can make the difference between a disaster and a market revolution.

Some of the computer experts I assisted in founding the Moscow computer club in 1986 were involved in developing handwriting recognition software that was eventually sold to Apple Computer, where it was used to create one of the first PDA, the MessagePad, later called the Newton. The Apple Newton would look familiar to anyone today now that we are surrounded by Palm Pilots, BlackBerries and dozens of imitators. The Newton was sold from 1993 to 1999 but was never a big hit. It was very expensive and just a little too big to fit into a pocket, a fatal flaw for a portable device.

The first Palm Pilots hit the market as the Newton was fading away. A little cheaper, a little smaller, and with better handwriting recognition, the Palm Pilot was an instant hit. (One of the creators, Jeff Hawkins, is said to have carried around a Pilot-sized block of wood in his pocket to test the practicality of its size.) So in this case the imitator was a big success and the innovator was a relative failure. But the market itself, the consumers, the technology industry, were all moved forward by Apple's 'failure'. Like Eccles, they led the way to what did work by first showing what didn't.

Evolution doesn't care about giving credit where credit is due. It doesn't care about patent infringement or the market. It cares about the survival of the best ideas in one form or another. Northrop's 'stealth' innovations were later adapted into many other designs in the way the best elements of the Newton survived in other products. Good ideas almost always survive, even if their original hosts do not.

Being too far ahead on a strategic level can bear a higher price, especially if those ideas fail to take root or provoke a backlash. Failure to innovate, to push evolutionary changes, either due to conditions or sheer cowardice, can be catastrophic.

Count Mikhail Speransky was the leading minister of Tsar Alexander I of Russia at the start of the nineteenth century. An idealist and reformer, he promoted the creation of a complex new constitutional system with regional elections and democratic representatives on a local and state level. Despite his great influence, very little came of these fantastical ideas at the time. Speransky soon ended up quite literally in Siberia, having lost his battle with the biggest interests of the day.

Russia continued to labour under feudal systems until the reforms of Tsar Alexander II in 1861, which included the freeing of the serfs, were sparked by Russia's devastating loss in the Crimean War. Lifting the lid off the pot led to greater liberties than the Tsar was willing to accept, and he quickly cracked down on the first signs of a revolutionary movement. This in turn led to assassination attempts against him. In 1881, a terrorist group succeeded in killing Alexander II on the very day he signed a document announcing his intention to implement constitutional reform, which was then not enacted. From that critical moment on, the obvious need for sweeping reforms in Russia was always overcome by the tsars' fears that they wouldn't be able to control the consequences. This instinctive distrust of change led in a more or less direct line to the takeover by the Bolshevik revolution in 1917.

The United States also suffered greatly from its inability to implement evolutionary reforms at an early stage in its history. The issue of whether or not to abolish slavery came up again and again in the earliest days of the republic and each time it was left for future generations to deal with. Thomas Jefferson, himself famously a slave-owner, often made a point of expressing his revulsion toward the institution, but came to view slavery as an intractable problem. Towards the end of his life he was sufficiently resigned to write in a 1817 letter, 'I leave it, therefore, to time.' Great thinkers though the founding fathers were, they couldn't summon the courage to risk rending the inchoate union over slavery. The slavery debate was put off until it collided explosively with the equally contentious issue of states' rights. Both issues had proved intractable for the Founding Fathers, but postponing the confrontation eventually resulted in the devastation of the Civil War.

This series of anecdotes is meant to be more than a laundry list of cautionary tales. They illustrate our ability to find useful parallels by analysing events, whether they come from the history books, the front page, or our own lives. These common threads can help us develop useful patterns for making decisions.

The courage to let go

The first step in becoming an innovator and remaining an innovator is to be aware of the changes and advances that are going on around us. Observation of the cutting edge in one area often leads to an advance in an entirely unrelated field. Trends and ideas move in packs, and this is no coincidence. A critical mass of knowledge is reached and similar ideas and innovations start to spring up around the world. We have to keep an eye on the trends if we are to benefit from them and create our own.

Releasing yourself from dogmatic thinking is much easier said than done. Originality requires a great deal of work and daring. As the German-American psychoanalyst Erich Fromm wrote, 'Creativity requires the courage to let go of certainties.' We cherish what we know, we rely on it and take pride in it. Taking our knowledge a step further into original thinking and problem-solving requires loosening our grip on that knowledge a little bit, just enough to gain a new angle, a fresh perspective. Duly inspired in our quest for creativity, we shouldn't forget the importance of properly evaluating what we have before we set off to achieve the new.

Once we have thoroughly absorbed the known we can step back from it confidently, step back far enough to see the big picture. From there we can see new paths and make new connections. New relevancies appear, old information seems fresh, and innovation becomes the norm instead of the exception.

Sir Winston Churchill (1874–1965)

The great statesman, author and wartime leader of Britain needs no introduction. I include him in order to present his particular importance to me as well as my perception of his greatness. Having heroes is not only for children.

Churchill was viewed with some suspicion in the Soviet Union. We saw him in movies about the war, but it was a skewed image of the British leader, one that included some necessary positives while criticizing him as a wild anti-Communist. The one thing every Soviet knew about Churchill was his Fulton Speech, even more than his leadership in the Second World War. In 1946, as a guest of President Truman in his home state of Missouri, Churchill warned the world about the coming 'Iron Curtain'.

Of course the story of the Second World War was very different in the USSR. According to our history books, the Allies, fighting on what we called the second front, supported us little, because they wanted the Nazis to kill more Soviets and the Soviets to kill more Nazis. Everything was presented to show that it was the USSR alone that won the war. But thanks to stories from my uncle and grandfather I learned early of the gap between the official propaganda and reality.

In the early 90s I began to read more in English and I encountered many of Churchill's powerful quotations. This led me to discover his history books and it was with these that my deep admiration for him really began.

The key for me was Churchill's ability to resist public opinion and to speak out on big ideas. Three moments in his career stand out to me in illustration of how he was right on the things that mattered most. First were his warnings of the danger of Bolshevism and his call to 'kill this baby in its cradle before it crawls out' (a line that was often cited in Soviet books as a demonstration of Churchill's prejudice against the USSR). Next was his stand against Hitler and the Nazis, in which he would even make common cause with Stalin. Then came the Fulton speech decrying the threat the USSR constituted for Europe after the Second World War: 'I have felt bound to portray the shadow which, alike in the west and in the east, falls upon the world.'

In the first case he was ignored and we are still paying the price. In the second he was heard, but not in time to save the world from the cataclysm of the Second World War. The third time he was heard, and in time to influence Truman to act more decisively in containing the Soviet threat and to save Western Europe from it, along with South Korea and Taiwan.

I encountered Churchill at an opportune moment in my life. The collapse of the USSR made the old battles obsolete and I was searching for new ideas. He inspired me to find an active role in a world in which politicians seem unable to resist the pressure of opinion polls.

11

PHASES OF THE GAME

'Before the endgame, the gods have placed the
middlegame.' – *Siegbert Tarrasch*

The first line of Abraham Lincoln's famous 'House Divided'
speech in 1858 is a fine observation on the necessity of goal-based
planning. 'If we could first know where we are going and whither
we are tending, we could better judge what to do and how to do
it.' Lincoln might have added that it's not only knowing where you
are going, but knowing where you are. Planning and innovation
both require solid grounding in the present. This is the only way to
know 'whither we are tending'. We must develop a feel for the
direction things are moving and where the trends are trending.

Over the centuries, countless theories have been developed to
simplify the game of chess for students. One of the most lasting
was the idea of breaking the game into three parts, or phases: the
opening, the middlegame and the endgame. There is no universal
way to say exactly when one ends and another begins, but there is
no question that each phase has distinctive characteristics and that
each poses problems that benefit from different modes of thinking.

Know why we make each move we make

The opening is the phase of the game where the battle lines are
drawn. The pawns establish the contours of structure, the pieces
get off the back rank and take up hostile or defensive positions.

The standard definition of the end of the opening phase is
when the king has castled out of the centre to safety and the pieces
have left their starting squares. This is a useful textbook definition,
although it has considerable shortcomings in the modern era of
chess. The opening is far more than a trivial mobilization of forces.
It establishes what sort of battle is to come and is the first and best
opportunity to move the game into channels where you are better

equipped to fight than your opponent. The opening is the most difficult, most subtle phase of the game, especially at the highest level of competition.

Here we need to distinguish between the general phase of the game we call 'the opening' and 'the openings'. We use the term 'the openings' to describe the hundreds of specific move sequences that can begin a game. These usually have names, such as the afore-mentioned Zaitsev and Dragon variations. These proper names can derive from the player who originated the variation, the city or country where the originating game was played, or a prosaic – or poetic – description of the position. (The Dragon variation is said to get its name from the way the alignment of the pawns looks like the constellation Draco.) The names of the openings make up much of a chess player's precious jargon, allowing us to discuss everything from the Sicilian Dragon to the Maroczy Bind, from the Marshall Attack to the King's Indian.

Players, even club amateurs, dedicate hours to studying and memorizing the lines of their preferred openings. The misguided idea behind this is that you don't have to think for yourself if you know what a famous Grandmaster played in this exact position back in 1962. You can just follow the games of stronger players as long as you can and if you remember more than your opponent he'll slip off the path and make a mistake.

At least that's the theory, but it rarely holds up. Long before a player becomes a master he realizes that rote memorization, however prodigious, is a far cry from understanding. He'll reach the end of his memory's rope and be on his own in a position he doesn't really understand. Without knowing WHY all the moves were made he has little idea of how to continue when play inevitably leaves his recollection behind.

In June 2005 in New York I gave a special training session to a group of the leading young players in the United States. I had asked them all to bring two of their games for us to review, one win and one loss. One talented twelve-year-old raced through the opening moves of his loss, eager to get to the point where he thought he'd gone wrong. I stopped him and asked why he had played a certain pawn push in the sharp opening variation and his answer didn't surprise me: 'That's what Vallejo played!' Of course I also knew that the Spanish Grandmaster Paco Vallejo Pons had employed this move in a recent game, but if this youngster didn't understand the motive behind the move he was already headed for trouble.

His response took me back to my own sessions with Mikhail Botvinnik thirty years earlier. On more than one occasion he chided me for committing this very same sin. The great teacher insisted that we must recognize the rationale behind every move. All of Botvinnik's students learned to become great sceptics, even of the moves of the best players. Most of the time we eventually discovered that there was a powerful idea behind each Grandmaster move, but we also found improvements.

For players who depend on memorization, the opening ends when their memory runs out of moves and they have to start thinking for themselves. This might happen on move 5 or move 30, but this method always inhibits one's development as a player. It is one thing for a world-class player to rely on memorization; he already knows all of the 'whys' behind the moves. For development it's far more important to think for yourself from the very start.

The purpose of the opening isn't just to get through it, it's to set the stage for the type of middlegame you want. This can also mean manoeuvring for the type of game your opponent doesn't want. To do this requires preparation, study and opposition research. Which openings does tomorrow's opponent play? What happened the last few times we played each other? Can I find a new idea in one of these openings that might give me an early advantage? What types of position does my opponent dislike? Which opening choice can lead us into those positions? Decisions must be made to narrow the field of view before serious study begins because we cannot prepare everything at the same time. We must prioritize.

Creativity in the opening phase is now most often manifested in the comfort of home instead of at the board. Computer databases contain almost every serious game ever played, including, thanks to the internet, what was played yesterday. You can call up your opponent's entire career in a second and look for tendencies, weaknesses and holes in his opening repertoire. Then you head to the board to face someone who has done exactly the same with you.

By the time a player becomes a Grandmaster almost all of his training time is dedicated to work on this first phase. The openings are the only phase in which there is the possibility of unique application. You can find something that no one else has found. Although the area narrows each year there remains a great deal of unexplored territory. You can set off on your own without anyone knowing what you are working on. You can look for traps and new ideas and then return from your explorations ready to spring them on your opponents. This is why, even though you aren't actually playing at the time, opening preparation demands as much creativity as dedication.

It's much like an inventor in his laboratory working on new devices and contraptions. In the nineteenth century there was a large class of amateur inventors, now a dying breed. When did you last spend a lengthy amount of time on a creative investigation of your own, work-related or not? Often you are at your most imaginative when you aren't at the office, or at the chessboard.

With so much precedent and preparation, the power of surprise is both more difficult to achieve and of greater effect. Once you have established which lines are most critical, you (and your computer!) go to work on finding new ideas with which to shock your adversaries.

Improving the product

It doesn't take much imagination to see the universal value of preparation. Only a minimal amount of investigation is required to discover precedents. It takes a great deal more effort to understand those precedents and to improve on them.

When a big company is developing a new product there is a tremendous amount of groundwork to be done. First there is the research that directs the development of the product itself. Where is there a market niche to fill? Does our competition have a hole in its product line, or do we? What do consumers want? What improvements would they like in the products already on the market? Real-world focus testing is now accepted as essential in every consumer area from food to films. If a Hollywood ending doesn't do well with test audiences it is tossed out for one that does.

Groundwork and battleground are absolutely critical in any endeavour. They are essential in order to play to our strengths and to our opponent's weaknesses. One of Napoleon's dictums was to get his enemies out of position *before* the battle began. If they were on the move ('out of their holes') they were more vulnerable to confusion.

Art is born from creative conflict

Now we come to the middlegame, where the forces are engaged. The pieces have been developed, the kings are safe (or, for more excitement, are not), and the battle lines have been drawn. It's time for the forces to meet and for blood to be spilled. It is a time for creativity, fantasy and energy. At the start of the game the pieces are inert. The opening coils the spring, putting the pieces in position to release their energies. In the middlegame come the explosions.

It is rare for one player to be exactly where he wants to be out of the opening and almost impossible for both players to be content. Your plans are always being countered and interfered with by your opponent, and vice versa. This means fresh evaluations are always required, new reports from the front always being processed. Even if you have been in this exact position in another game it is critical to evaluate it anew, especially since your opponent is also aware you've been here before and may have prepared something nasty. We survey the landscape, examine the imbalances, and formulate a strategy.

Our MTQ analysis is similar to what those in the corporate world call SWOT reports. SWOT stands for Strengths, Weaknesses, Opportunities, Threats. Both positions must be evaluated deeply before we formulate our strategy. We must also be aware of any immediate need for action. Can we create a threat that will force our opponent on the defensive and out of his game plan? Do we need to put deeper strategic concerns on hold and respond to imminent danger?

If there aren't any immediate tactical considerations we can continue the process of developing our strategy and the intermediate objectives that go into it. That process was of course started in the opening. Note that the phases of the game have no clear boundaries, only general guidelines that become less useful as we advance our overall level of play. Our cognitive gears must shift constantly depending on the situation at hand. The strategy of an ideal game forms a common thread through all the phases.

All the elements that elevate chess to an art are native to the middlegame. Poor opening research can be disguised by tactical brilliance. Deep calculations can operate in harmony with daring visions. Total disaster lurks around every corner as the dynamic force of the pieces is maximized. Battlefield commanders take over from back-seat generals. More than anything, the middlegame rewards action over reaction. It is the attacking phase and the fight for the initiative is paramount.

The middlegame requires being alert in general and being alert to patterns in particular. These are general ideas that anyone can learn with practice; the more you play, the more experience you have, the better you become at recognizing the patterns and applying the solutions. There is still great scope for creativity. This is manifested most in how we are able to relate known patterns to new positions to find the unique solution: the best move.

What little concrete study of the middlegame there is comes from its connection to the opening, one of our key transition points. The opening establishes the outlines of the middlegame and it can be very useful, even essential, to push your study of the opening phase into the 'real world' of middlegame action. This is why studying complete chess games is so important, not just looking at the opening moves. This is also why business schools have largely switched to the case study method instead of focusing on theory. All the study and preparation in the world can't show you what it's really going to be like in the wild. Observing typical plans in action, mistakes and accidents included, is superior to ivory tower planning.

With this principle in mind, it is always useful to project out beyond the initial consequences of our decisions. We should create several 'what if' scenarios that lead logically from our preparation. We will rarely if ever exactly predict the real outcome; the world is too complex for that, unlike chess. But using modelling in this way helps develop critical experience.

Make sure a good peace follows a good war

If both players survive the smoke and flame and thrust and counterthrust of the middlegame, we arrive at the endgame. Much beloved by writers as a metaphor if only for being, obviously, the final phase, the endgame is the result of piece exchanges. When the dynamic potential of the armies has diminished to a minimal level, the middlegame is over. Raw logic and calculation take over when there are only a few survivors on the battlefield.

Much of the opening phase is as yet undiscovered. The middlegame is mostly mapped out, but some areas remain relatively uncharted. The endgame is wide open and known to all, an almost mathematical exercise. Imagination takes a back seat when there are only a few pieces left on the board. Instead, cool calculation is required for this technical phase. This isn't to say that everything is predetermined. The result remains in doubt and there is always a chance to outplay your opponent. The endgame can advance towards a logical conclusion with best play from both sides, or damage can be inflicted or repaired.

The endgame represents the treaty negotiations after the fighting has ended. The masterful endgame player Talleyrand was able to save France from being dismembered at the Congress of Vienna (1814–15) after he had craftily manoeuvred to have Napoleon removed from power. After their leader's defeat France was a disgraced and occupied nation that could expect to have little influence at the Congress that shaped Europe after the Napoleonic Wars. And yet Talleyrand successfully managed to divide the conquering Allies and create new alliances that preserved most of France's territorial boundaries. (Although they were to be shifted back some after Napoleon escaped from exile and ruled for his famous 100 days before his final defeat at Waterloo.)

The opposite course is also possible. There are few things more tragic than playing a strong opening, a brilliant middlegame attack, and then having the win evaporate with one wrong move in the endgame. This happened to me on no less a stage than my world championship match against Nigel Short in London in 1993. In this case I was lucky, as the same thing happened to my opponent in the same game.

In a fierce opening duel I confronted a new opening idea Short had introduced earlier in the match. I got a significant edge out of the opening and in the middlegame successfully resisted my opponent's attempts to get things back on track. I brought a material advantage into the endgame. The game had simplified down to just one rook for my opponent and a rook and two pawns for me. (We don't count the kings, as they are always on the board.) It was a winning position and I was only waiting for Short to resign, my first mistake. We were both on autopilot for the final moves and it wasn't until after the game that it was pointed out we had both blundered horribly near the end. Even with just two pawns and two rooks on the board I had made a slip, playing a 'natural' move with my pawn that permitted a saving defensive manoeuvre by my opponent that would allow him to draw the game. But Short was also blind to the opportunity and he responded with his own 'natural' move and resigned a half-dozen moves later.

How could the world champion and his challenger both miss something so important in the endgame despite having so little material on the board to create complications? The aridity of the endgame, the lack of dynamism, is often mistaken for a lack of opportunity. The technical phase can be boring because there is little opportunity for creativity, for art. Boredom leads to complacency and mistakes.

Endgame play is binary: good or bad, with little room for style. The best endgame players find inspiration in the details, in the necessary precision. Great negotiators, even great accountants, may well be born to their tasks as much as artists and chess players.

Cautious, patient and calculating players excel in the endgame. Tigran Petrosian and Anatoly Karpov, for example, were better in this phase of the game than Boris Spassky and me. Attackers who thrive on the dynamism of the middlegame and the creativity of the opening often find a natural enemy in the sterility of the endgame, although there are always exceptions.

Eliminating phase bias

It over-simplifies to attempt to categorize the best players in history, because of course they had to excel at everything to reach the top. I freely confess that my endgame prowess fell short of my middlegame skills and my opening play. Karpov was stronger in the middle and final phases than he was in the opening, although this was compensated by his work with well-chosen coaches. (It is worth mentioning that you are allowed to receive direct assistance in the opening and not in the other phases of the game.)

Vladimir Kramnik, who took my title in 2000, can be considered as epitomizing the last of the possible combinations. His opening preparation is excellent and he shines in the endgame as well. It is in the dynamic middlegame where, again relatively speaking only, the quality of his play lacks consistency.

It can be interesting to break down our own skills and performances this way, taking some liberties with the necessary level of generalization. Where are our own strong points? Creative preparation? Fluid action? Calculating details? Do we shy away from any of these areas? Many players depend too heavily on one area or another, which limits their growth and their success. A tenable endgame is better than an inferior middlegame, but if you don't like quiet positions you may not realize this until it is too late. We must discover and work to eliminate our prejudices.

For me this has always meant controlling my desire for action and realizing when it might be counter-productive. My love of dynamic complications often led me to avoid simplification when perhaps it was the wisest choice. This tendency exceeds the boundaries of the chessboard, where my instincts were usually correct. This experience has made my transition to politics much more fluid. It has helped me recognize when it's time to stop firing the cannons and switch to diplomacy.

Don't bring a knife to a gunfight

Transition from phase to phase is often invisible. What is important is to not make assumptions about the position that depend too much on the characteristics of a single phase. What works to your benefit in the middlegame may hurt you in the endgame, a common occurrence. You also have cases of one player relaxing into a technical endgame only to find that his opponent is still playing the middlegame.

In the eleventh round of the 2002 Chess Olympiad in Slovenia I had the black pieces against the top German player, Christopher Lutz. The game slowly simplified into a position without queens and only three pieces per player. Lutz brought his knights to the far side of the board where they became tangled up in seeking relatively insignificant gains. In an endgame this temporary loss of time wouldn't be a major factor. But with his pieces on the other side of the board I saw that there was a chance to mount an attack on his king despite the limited material.

Even after it was clear what I was trying to do, Lutz under-estimated the danger. He was already in endgame mode and wasn't able to switch back into a dynamic middlegame mentality to react to the threat. My small army soon cornered his king, forcing him to resign.

Under-estimating dynamic factors is a common mistake not only on the cusp of the endgame. There are several other typical psychological problems associated with these key transitions from phase to phase. Even a well-prepared player can delay thinking critically in the early middlegame. Routine moves might pass in the opening, but they can lead to unpleasant surprises if your opponent is paying attention to more aggressive lines than you are. That is, if he is already playing the middlegame while you're still in an opening mindset.

These errors in transition find parallels across every area that involves planning and strategy, because a good planner takes all three phases into account throughout. What sort of middlegame is our opening going to lead to? Is it one we are prepared for? Is it the type of negotiation, or battle, or job, or project we have experience with?

We must also play the middlegame with an eye on the endgame. If we have sacrificed material for an attack we will almost certainly lose the endgame if the attack fails in the middlegame. Where is the point of no return? There will be a moment at which there is still a chance to bale out and be left with a reasonable position.

The Austrian Rudolf Spielmann wrote that we must 'play the opening like a book, the middlegame like a magician, and the endgame like a machine'. Our goal is to make the transitions between the phases seamless, not just to perform well in each. In the real world the phases exist only in our minds as useful study guides.

We must now take the results of all this study and evaluation and transform it into action.

Robert James Fischer (1943–), USA
A brilliant legend and a sad legacy

Ask anyone in the street to name a chess player and the odds are good you'll hear the name Bobby Fischer. In 1972, long before the internet and playing engines, back when chess was still a purely human game, Fischer became the most famous chess player the world had ever seen. His talent for chess was only matched by his talent for creating controversy, an ideal – or catastrophic – combination for the first Western chess star of the television age.

The Brooklyn-raised Fischer was a teenage prodigy of the highest order. He had an incredible will to win, a tireless work ethic and unrivalled technical accuracy. Many of his records will likely stand for all time. US champion at the age of fourteen. World championship candidate at the age of sixteen. Winner of the 1963 US championship with a perfect 11–0 score. Winner of two consecutive world championship qualifying matches with perfect 6–0 scores. World champion, besting Boris Spassky in Reykjavik, Iceland, in 1972. With little outside support, the iconoclastic Fischer rose unstoppably to wrest the crown from the Soviets for the first time since 1948.

The build-up and controversy surrounding the Reykjavik match made for perfect theatre. Fischer wasn't going to play, then he was, then he wasn't, then he was at the airport, no he wasn't . . . and on it went. Henry Kissinger even phoned to persuade Fischer to do his patriotic duty. And even after his tardy arrival in Iceland it took a great deal of diplomacy, and chivalry on the part of Spassky, to keep the event on track.

The surprises kept coming after the match began. Fischer blundered horribly and lost the first game with black. Before the second game Fischer again protested about the conditions in the playing hall, a favourite pastime. There was too much noise, he said, too many cameras. The game finally began . . . without Fischer! He refused to show up and forfeited the game. He was down 0–2 and it looked as though the match would be cancelled after all. Heroic negotiations allowed the match to continue, but game 3 took place in a back room reserved for table tennis, not on the stage. Only a closed-circuit camera allowed the spectators to see their idols. Fischer won that game, his first ever victory over Spassky, and went on to dominate the rest of the match and take the title.

The world was Fischer's oyster at that point. He was young, handsome, wealthy, and on the verge of making chess a hugely popular sport in the United States. Sponsorship offers and event invitations rolled in, but apart from a few television appearances he didn't accept most of them. And then, nothing. Fischer stopped playing chess and wouldn't push a pawn in serious play again for twenty years. He was stripped of his title in 1975 after he couldn't come to an agreement with FIDE over the rules of the next championship match. The challenger, Karpov, was installed and Fischer became a ghost.

There were always rumours of his whereabouts, stories that he was going to reappear at any moment to again dominate the chess world. But it wasn't until 1992 that Bobby Fischer, almost fifty years old, heavy and bearded, played chess again. It was an occasion both joyous and sad. He was lured back into the limelight by a multi-million dollar offer to play a rematch, in war-torn Yugoslavia, against Boris Spassky, who was semi-retired and living in France. The chess was predictably oxidized, with few flashes of the old brilliance. Worst of all, Fischer seemed irresistibly prone to making profane, anti-Semitic remarks. His fragile psyche had crumbled during his long stay away from chess, the only world he had ever understood.

After the match he again vanished, reappearing in 2004 in an even more unlikely location, a detention centre at Tokyo's Narita airport. His match in Yugoslavia had violated UN sanctions and he'd been stopped for travelling with a revoked passport. Suddenly Fischer was in the news again. After eight long months the Japanese released him to Iceland, scene of his greatest triumph and where he is still much beloved.

Despite his behaviour and the bizarre twists of Fischer's life, he deserves to be remembered most of all for his immense contribution to chess. His stay at the top was tragically brief, but he towered above his contemporaries like a modern-day Paul Morphy. Fischer's success and larger-than-life charisma brought chess to an entire generation of players, particularly in the US, where there was a huge 'Fischer boom'. I was nine years old when the Fischer–Spassky match took place and my friends and I followed the games eagerly. Although his victims were mostly Soviets, Fischer had many fans in the USSR. His chess was undeniably brilliant, but we also admired his individuality and independence.

On Fischer: 'Fischer always made a particular impression on me by the integrity of his nature. Both in chess, and in life. No compromises.' – Boris Spassky

Fischer in his own words: 'All I want to do, ever, is play chess.'

12

THE DECISION-MAKING PROCESS

'Knowing is different from doing.'
– *Carl von Clausewitz*

Everything we have considered has pointed towards the making of better decisions. For a strategy to become reality, decisions must be made. For evaluations to be turned into results, they must lead to decisions. After we have prepared, planned, analysed, calculated and evaluated, we have to choose a course of action.

Results matter, of course, and it's hard to argue that the move I make on the board is less important than the method I use to find that move. Results are the feedback we get on the quality of our decision-making. If you follow all the right steps and come out with the wrong answer, something has clearly gone wrong. Still, we can't put all our faith in a single result, good or bad. Doing things the right way matters, which is why maths teachers insist students show their working. In the basic algebra equation $5x = 20$ we can after all solve x by plugging in possible answers one after another and eventually come up with the same solution as the person who simply divides 20 by 5.

We make decisions every moment of every day and few of them require particular preparation or the development of a specific strategy. But it is still important to be aware of how these constant decisions do or do not fit in with our larger goals, with the big picture. Even trivial choices about what to eat for breakfast involve thinking about our plans for the rest of the day – and perhaps considerable agonizing if we are on a diet.

Looking closely at the means and methods we employ cannot be reserved for CEOs and politicians and others whose decisions affect multitudes. We are just as concerned, if not more so, about the quality of the decisions that affect only our own lives and the lives of our family and friends.

The development of a sceptic

When I consider my own development as a decision-maker I must go all the way back to my early childhood. I grew up in Baku, Azerbaijan, then part of the loose Soviet empire. It was a typical imperial outpost, a rich melting pot of ethnicities that was somewhat flattened by a common language and a dominant Russian/Soviet culture.

My own roots were characteristic: an Armenian mother, Klara Kasparova, and a Jewish father, Kim Weinstein – what they call an explosive combination. The atmosphere in our household was a combination of my mother's rigid pragmatism mixed with my father's contrarian creativity. The rest of the clan included my father's brother, Leonid, and their cousin Marat, a famous lawyer in Baku. Their circle largely consisted of Jewish professors and intellectuals who constantly questioned the official view, not only the blatant propaganda of the Soviet government. For them, the conventional wisdom was to be doubted out of hand – everything should be subjected to questioning.

Being a sceptic doesn't have to mean being paranoid. The essential is not to take anything for granted and to question the sources of information as well as the information itself. Whether you watch Fox News or CNN, remember that the presentation of information has an agenda. Why were certain details included and what was left out? Thinking about why a story is being told can teach us more than the story.

My mother's scepticism derived less from mistrust than from scientific rigour. She wasn't interested in telling me how to think, only that I should question everything I heard. Her upbringing and engineering background taught her always to look for the concrete facts in any given situation. Her father was a petroleum engineer and a diehard Communist but she was more interested in practical matters than ideology. We would listen to Radio Liberty and Voice of America and I remember getting into great debates with Grandpa Shagen, who did not take kindly to views critical of the state. He had spent his whole life building Communism; the food shortages of the late 1970s were to be a great source of disillusionment for him.

Between these poles I grew up reading a lot of books and asking a lot of questions. After my father died when I was seven I went to live with my mother's family. When I began to have public success in chess it seemed natural to take her family name. My teacher Mikhail

Botvinnik, himself of Jewish ancestry, added that it wouldn't hurt my chances of success in the USSR not to be named Weinstein.

My father's name did lead to an amusing misunderstanding when I first went to the Pioneer Palace to play chess. My first coach, Oleg Privorotsky, loves to tell this tale, which has grown taller over the years. When he first met me at the Pioneer chess club he misheard my name as 'Bronstein' and remarked that this was a good name for chess. After all, Soviet Grandmaster David Bronstein had been a challenger for the world championship in 1951. My uncle Leonid said that after my first session Privorotsky jumped up and cried, 'Another Bronstein indeed! We've never had such a talent here!' It must have been around this point that the mistake with my name was cleared up.

Process versus content

The processes we go through to reach a conclusion have very little to do with the content of the decisions themselves. Our morning 'Cereal or fruit?' is far removed from the world-changing decisions going on in the White House or on the world's battlefields. And yet each individual uses the same processes for every decision they have to make. If we have bad habits and negative patterns when we make decisions at work the same will be true at home. Any changes we make will impact on every aspect of our lives.

A corollary of this is that our decision-making style may be appropriate for one area of our lives but not another. My style at the chessboard was always aggressive and dynamic and this translated directly into my forays into chess politics and business, with, it must be said, considerably less success. Now that I have entered national and international politics full-time many pundits have questioned whether my take-no-prisoners approach can succeed in an environment of negotiation.

I have several reasons not to be overly concerned about this. First off, political life in Russia today is far from the democratic ideal of debate and mutual consideration. Anyone in opposition to President Putin's administration has no possibility of negotiating anything at all. Uniting people is the only effective method of dealing with impending tyranny and bringing people together requires a strong show of resolution under pressure. For this reason my combative nature is still very much required.

Second, now that I have left the competitive chess arena I have more freedom to allow my instincts to evolve toward methods more suitable for my new endeavours. It would be impossible to go back and forth from chessboard attacker to political charmer even were such a transformation beneficial. While I don't think my fundamental nature as a person and decision-maker will change dramatically, it will slowly adjust to the needs of my new activities. This happens naturally, but it helps to be aware of such needs so that we can chart and, if necessary, correct our course.

The reason I played aggressive chess and felt no need to deviate is that I was winning. My style had always worked and I only needed to make small adjustments when the situation required them. I did what I liked and what I liked worked well, so I could follow my instincts. We try to align our natural style as closely as possible with what works (and vice versa) because at the end of the day it's the objective reality, winning, succeeding, that matters most.

Now, in politics, the things I need to do don't fit my character as perfectly as chess did. This is another lesson I learned from chess: flexibility is a top priority. You have to do what it takes to win. You can't win every game with a thrilling attack. You have to be ready to play a boring endgame on occasion if that's what the position requires. My current position, in politics, requires me to work to bring others together and to see the big picture. The style of decision-making I had during my playing career has had to adapt to this new phase of my life. Flexibility in our approach is as important as the process itself.

How much information is too much?

How do we go about examining our own decision-making processes and, if necessary, adjusting them? First off is to distinguish between information and process. There can be an over-emphasis on the collection of data and its analysis. Smart people with good information can still come to incorrect conclusions thanks to poor procedures for working with that information.

More isn't always better when it comes to collecting data. Not only do you risk diluting the quality of your information by casting too wide a net, but there is also the time factor to consider. All other things being equal, few decisions don't benefit from being made sooner rather than later.

In chess, casting a wide net means considering many possible moves instead of narrowing your choice down to a few almost at the start. Looking at every single possibility is a luxury we can't afford even in the limited realm of the chessboard, where there might be five or six reasonable moves in a given position, though there are usually just two or three.

Limiting the initial breadth of our search is the first task. Our experience and preliminary calculations allow us to narrow things down almost immediately. Only if those initial options look bad after some analysis might we attempt to go back and look for new options at move one. A company choosing a new supplier starts out with a few likely candidates and follows them up. After due diligence and evaluation they can either pursue one of those options or expand their search and look for alternatives.

Starting over involves a significant loss of time and is also a psychologically difficult choice to make. We are forced to admit that our initial assumptions were perhaps flawed – and there is no guarantee the new set of options will prove to be any better than the first. This can lead to one of two opposing, but similarly destructive, decision patterns: 1) Choosing whichever path has been most deeply investigated simply because it is better known; 2) Making a panicky choice of a new, unexplored option after discovering the initial options aren't agreeable.

The first is like the old joke about the man who looks for his wallet where the light is better instead of where he lost it. There is a certain comfort in a known evil over the unknown; in some cases it is the only possible choice. If we don't have time to evaluate other options it is preferable to err on the side of the known than to step blindly into the abyss hoping we'll land on a cloud.

That describes the second trap, throwing out our analysis and going for an unexplored option at the last minute. This behaviour is common even in the disciplined world of chess masters, who so value analysis. Obviously, if the alternatives you have examined lead to catastrophe there is little to lose by trying something unexplored. But the optimist in all of us can find these leaps of faith tempting even when the analysed paths don't lead to certain doom. That same human nature leads us to forget the many times such behaviour resulted in disaster in favour of remembering the few times it led to a brilliancy.

I'm no exception to this rule. Just off the top of my head I can remember several occasions when my mental train jumped the track at the last minute. Of course the time we spend analysing other moves also contributes to our general understanding of the position, making it more likely that we might effectively stumble into something else. The problem is then having to decide whether this new inspiration is better than the lines we've been analysing.

This is why it is so critical to start out with at least two options in mind and enough time to consider them both. Diving into a deep investigation of just one alternative can leave you without enough time to consider any others, and you'll be stuck between these two negative patterns. By the time you've done that it's already too late, you're out of time.

Do you pick one way of doing something and stick with it no matter what? Do you look briefly at many different options and choose one impulsively? Do you resist the need to start from scratch even when there is time to do so? We have to find a balance somewhere between settling too early and never settling until it's too late. It's not necessary to revolutionize your thinking, even if it were possible to do so. If you are naturally conservative you will tend towards the first scenario. If you are impulsive your decision-making will lean towards the second. Our goal is to keep our own tendencies in mind so that they can be reigned in. If you are cautious, make sure you take a moment to consider a few fresh new options before taking action. If you are rash, force yourself at the very start to narrow your choices down to a select group for evaluation. Remember that in both cases this will require a little extra time, at least until you get used to it and develop a more balanced style.

Of course we can all act one way or the other at different moments; there is no universal recipe for how many options to consider or how deeply to analyse one alternative or another. The best we can do is give ourselves the time and opportunity to make the best decision possible.

Candidate moves and pruning the decision tree

One tool that can be used to discipline our thinking is the use of what chess players call candidate moves. As previously mentioned, there is a very rapid branching factor in chess; looking ahead just a few moves can lead to hundreds of thousands of possible positions, each the result of a cause and effect chain that has to be examined carefully. For each move there are several possible responses that must be calculated, and then there are the responses to those moves, and so on.

Only rarely are things made easier by the presence of what we call a forced move, when there is no alternative that doesn't lead to disaster. For example, when one player checks his opponent's king, attacking it directly, that limits the number of responses dramatically since the king cannot remain in check. Even in this case there can be several options. The attacking piece may be captured, a defending piece might interpose between the attacker and the king, or the king can flee.

With so many possibilities expanding so quickly, it is essential to limit the number of candidate moves at the start and at every step. The decision tree of 'if this then that, if that then this' has to be aggressively pruned or we will never get deep enough in our analysis to return anything useful. As always we are after balance between breadth and depth. Looking at five different options two moves deep is no better or worse than looking at only two options five moves deep, depending on the problem, the position, at hand.

A strategic situation without an immediate crisis encourages us to think more broadly, to consider a wide variety of situations. A schoolgirl contemplating which university to go to doesn't pick just one or two and perform deep research on them. It makes more sense for her to look around at a wide variety of candidates first off. Later on, having narrowed the field to just a few, a deeper comparison can be made.

But if great precision is needed and time is of the essence, selecting a narrow set of candidates and delving into them deeply is often required. We call this a sharp position, when any slip will lead to disaster. The key is to realize what sort of position we are in before we start selecting options. How much time do we have to analyse? How precarious is the situation? Is it all-or-nothing, right-or-wrong, or can we choose from a variety of alternatives based on style? True, sometimes we don't know the answer to these questions before we go a little deeper, but our intuition usually knows, if we take the time to ask it.

Flexing our intuition

Intuition and instinct form the bedrock of our decision-making, especially the rapid-fire decisions that make up our daily lives. We don't have to analyse why we turn left here and right there on the way to work, we just do it. A chess player can spot a simple checkmate in three moves without hesitation, even if he's never seen that exact position before in his life. We depend on these patterns the way we depend on our autonomic systems to keep us breathing. We are not like whales, which have to think about every breath.

We wouldn't want to consider every decision we make, and so we rely on patterns gleaned from experience. These are essential shortcuts and have no drawbacks as long as they are confined to the basic functions. The problems come when we begin to rely on patterns for more sophisticated decisions in our lives. This stifles creativity and leads to a 'one size fits all' approach to decision-making as we try to force the same patterns and solutions on to every problem we face.

If faced with a repetitive job it can be difficult to stay alert to opportunities to solve problems creatively. Your instincts slowly go numb when every analysis returns the same answers over and over. What should be a search for excellence and the best solution eventually turns into a 'good enough' mentality. We must strive to keep things fresh so we can rely on and enhance our instincts instead of falling into mental ruts. General Electric's Jack Welch once sent the senior manager of an under-performing GE sector on a month's vacation so he could come back and 'act as though you hadn't been running it for four years'. Many companies regularly rotate managers or have programmes where top executives drop in on other areas so problems can be seen through fresh eyes.

This desire to see things from the outside can sound contra-dictory, since we know how important knowledge and experience are. As usual we are looking for that elusive middle ground that is compatible with our natural instincts. We have to be prepared to recognize our own failings in our decision-making process and to shake it up when necessary. If we don't stay sharp, the edges begin to blur and subtle differences fall through the cracks, differences that can be critically important at decisive moments.

With the sheer quantity of decisions we make every day, even small improvements and adaptations in our processes make a huge cumulative difference. It's like making a tiny enhancement in an assembly line that shaves a few precious seconds off the pro-duction of each car.

Big branches in the decision tree require extra caution. These are the forks in the road that leave us with no way back. It is an old chess maxim that 'pawns can't move backwards', which is more than a simple statement of the obvious. If I put my bishop on a bad square I can later change my mind and move it back and the same goes for any other piece. But pawns can only move in one direction, forward. We often talk about 'committal moves', usually captures or other moves that change the position irrevocably. Every pawn move is of this sort and therefore must be considered more carefully.

Life's rules aren't as clear as those of chess; we can't always know when a decision will lead to irreversible consequences. As with detecting a crisis, sometimes it is obvious and at other times you have to go on instinct. It is always valuable to ask ourselves if we will be able to reverse course if it turns out our decision was a poor one. What will our alternatives be if things go wrong? Is there a satisfactory alternative course where we can keep our options open longer?

This mentality requires us to overcome the desire to release the tension. Many bad decisions come from wanting to just get the process over and escape the pressure of having to make the decision. This is the worst type of haste, an unforced error. Resist it! If there is no benefit to making the decision at the moment and no penalty in delaying it, use the time to improve your evaluation, to gather more information and examine other options. As Margaret Thatcher put it: 'I've learned one thing in politics. You don't make a decision until you have to.'

As ever, my personal preference is to err on the side of intuition and optimism. Decisions derived from positive thinking may not be any more accurate than conservative decisions, but we definitely learn more from our mistakes. Over time our decisions will become more accurate as we exercise and hone our intuition. Most of us are happier when doing, when fulfilling the human need to push boundaries. F. Scott Fitzgerald wrote, 'Vitality shows not only in the ability to persist, but in the ability to start over.' If we err and must begin again, we must. This vitality isn't only about quality of life; staying motivated and involved in the decision-making process is one key to improving it. One of the best ways to do this is to take the initiative, which puts positive pressure on you while challenging your competition. I like to say that the attacker always has the advantage.

Aaron Nimzowitsch (1886–1935), Latvia/Denmark
Savielly Grigoryevich Tartakower (1887–1956), Russia/France
Richard Réti (1889–1929), Czechoslovakia
The Hypermodernists, exploring new horizons

It is standard in discussions of chess history to speak of 'schools of chess'. Each era that has seen distinct evolution in the way the game is played is inevitably assigned a catchy title, occasionally the name of the leading player of the day. One period fully deserving such distinction is that which saw the rise of the Hypermodern School in the 1920s.

The founder of the Hypermodern movement was Aaron Nimzowitsch, whose personality and play were as difficult as his name, often shortened to 'Nimzo'. An iconoclast through and through, Nimzowitsch turned chess orthodoxy on its head with his games and his still-famous writings. He questioned the formerly fundamental principle that the centre of the board must be occupied and held by pawns, the equivalent of saying the battlefield must be occupied by infantry. Nimzowitsch demonstrated that instead of presenting these central targets, the central squares could be attacked from afar, from the flanks. This was the central tenet of Hypermodernism.

Much of Nimzo's heterodox proselytizing came as a form of resistance to the traditional teachings of one of the era's leading players, Germany's Siegbert Tarrasch. The dogmatist and the rebel, they had a running battle of ideas, words and moves that lasted decades. Tarrasch called Nimzowitsch's unusual moves 'ugly', while Nimzowitsch maintained that 'the beauty of a chess move is not in its appearance, but in the thought behind it'.

Several of Nimzowitsch's classic books remain in print today. The defensive system bearing his name has remained one of the most popular among players of every level. This 'Nimzo-Indian Defence' is only the most important of the many opening ideas he contributed.

The effectiveness and sheer boldness of these new methods quickly attracted other experimental players. One was Savielly Tartakower, an original and successful master who is best known today for his countless witticisms about the game. (His immortal 'Nobody ever won a chess game by resigning' is always brought out to encourage fighting spirit in a hopeless position.) During his curious life he travelled widely and wrote extensively. His eclectic contributions include an offbeat flank opening he dubbed 'The Orangutan' after playing it following a visit to the New York zoo. The coining of the term 'Hypermodern' in chess is also credited to Tartakower.

Of Polish descent, Tartakower led the strong Polish team at various chess Olympiads during the 1930s despite never having lived in Poland and not speaking Polish. He fought in the French resistance during the Second World War and subsequently played for his adopted homeland of France.

Tartakower's contrarian nature manifested itself at the chessboard in constant experimentation with systems that were widely thought to be inferior. This, too, was an aspect of the Hypermodern creed, to challenge conventional wisdom. Is it too much to say that it might not be a coincidence that experimental artists such as Pablo Picasso and Marcel Duchamp were coming to the forefront of the art world at the same time?

It was said of Richard Réti by Tartakower that he 'represents Vienna without being Viennese; [and] was born in old Hungary yet he does not know Hungarian'. Réti was one of many players whose origins are difficult to be precise about since they came before the map of Eastern Europe was redrawn after the First World War. He developed and incorporated Hypermodern ideas in his play and documented the development of the movement in his books.

Réti was also a fine composer of chess studies and puzzles, several of which are among the best-known in the lore of the game. As with Tartakower, his tournament results were never of world championship calibre, but he achieved a certain immortality by ending José Raúl

Capablanca's eight-year unbeaten streak in 1924. Not only that, but Réti achieved this feat with the hypermodern system of play that still bears his name.

On Nimzowitsch: 'He has a profound liking for ugly opening moves.' – Siegbert Tarrasch

On Tartakower: 'What really made him outstanding was his fascinating personality. With Tartakower among the participants, any tournament had colour and life.' – Hans Kmoch

On Réti: 'Réti is a brilliant type of artist, who battles not so much with his opponents, as with himself, with his own ideals and doubts.' – Tartakower

Nimzowitsch in his own words: 'Why must I lose to this idiot?' (attributed)

Tartakower in his own words: 'A chess game is divided into three stages: the first, when you hope you have the advantage, the second when you believe you have the advantage, and the third, when you know you're going to lose!'

Réti in his own words: 'For in the idea of chess and the development of the chess mind we have a picture of the intellectual struggle of mankind.'

13

THE ATTACKER'S ADVANTAGE

'Even a bullet fears the brave.'
– Russian saying

Equating the life of the chessboard with the real world has its risks. Even if we can agree on the language and identify useful parallels, what works in chess may not be considered appropriate elsewhere, even if it is just as effective outside the sixty-four squares. I'm very familiar with the best example of this double standard: aggression.

As I've said, my ability to move into politics was questioned because of my aggressive style of chess. If attackers are born, not made, how would I fare in an environment in which attacking wasn't effective? First off, we all have the ability to adapt to new environments. Second, is it really so wrong to be an attacker? Is it really not effective, or is it just unpopular to point out that being aggressive is just as successful in politics, business and other walks of life as it is in chess?

I became aware of this paradox of conventional wisdom as I rose through the chess ranks. Chess magazines celebrated my 'aggressive chess' and my 'violent attacks'. Such terms are provided special, almost always positive, meaning in the world of sport. We want aggressive attackers on our favourite teams even if we don't want them to move into our neighbourhood.

I received some words of wisdom on the matter in 1980, when at the age of seventeen I was awarded a place on the mighty Soviet Chess Olympiad team for the first time. We travelled to Malta for the tournament and spent two days in Rome on the way back with the gold medals we had won after a tight race with Hungarians. On average our team was over twice my age and we had very different agendas for our free days. The others took the opportunity to do some sightseeing, including a trip to the Vatican. I went to see *The Empire Strikes Back*, which I would never have been able to see in the USSR. I can't say what spiritual guidance my compatriots received at the Vatican while I watched Yoda coach

Luke Skywalker with 'Anger, fear, aggression; the dark side of the Force are they'. To be honest, at seventeen I very much sympathized with Luke's impatience at such a passive outlook. Didn't he have to go after Darth Vader and protect his friends?

The double standard breaks down occasionally. It's acceptable to refer to a CEO's management style as aggressive in a positive way. But what is permitted to Jupiter is not permitted to the ox. The average employee can't be aggressive and, depending on the field, even ambition can be viewed with suspicion. Anyone who too clearly wants to get ahead can be criticized for trying to steal attention or, worst of all, will be told he 'isn't a team player'.

At the same time a host of euphemisms are in ever-increasing circulation. Now we have 'proactive', which at least to my ear is a clinical and inferior substitute. My thesaurus also offers 'positive', 'enthusiastic', and 'forceful', as well as the unserious import 'gung ho'. (Which, ironically, means 'work together' in Mandarin.)

Stoking the competitive fires

Who runs a race wanting to come in second? Who grows up wanting to be the vice-president? Putting limits on our ambition puts limits on our achievement. Having an aggressive philosophy also applies to being aggressive with ourselves. It's not about being a nice guy or not; it's about constantly challenging ourselves, our environment, and those around us. It's the opposite of moral and physical complacency.

Sportsmen and sportswomen always talk about challenging themselves and the need to play their best game, without worrying about their opponents. There is some truth to this, although I find it a little disingenuous. While everyone has a unique way to remain motivated, we thrive on competition and that means beating someone else, not just setting a personal best. Ask the Olympic runner who breaks his personal record, or even the world record, and finishes a close second how good he feels. We don't need to wonder if he would trade a tenth of a second for a gold medal instead of silver.

We all work harder, run faster, when we know someone is right on our heels. Some of my best performances have benefited from close competition, occasionally involving an odd statistical side-effect for a few of my opponents. In several of my tournament wins other top players achieved their career-best performance and finished second or third. Just as racing dogs go much faster after a 'rabbit', we push ourselves to new heights if we have a target to focus on, a competitor to match us stride for stride to the finishing line.

From 1999 to 2001 I won the Wijk aan Zee tournament three times in a row. In each tournament, second place went to Viswanathan Anand – on two occasions tied with other players. My first win, in 1999, was one of the best performances of my career. I won eight games out of thirteen – including seven in a row near the start and lost only one. Anand charged hard near the end of the event and finished only a half-point behind, giving me the narrowest possible margin of victory.

From a statistical perspective, looking only at wins and losses instead of the podium, it was likely the best performance of Anand's career. And yet I doubt he would list this event among his finest achievements. Anand has won many important tournaments, and as a true competitor he values those victories over any second-place finish, no matter how great it may have been.

Finishing second is definitely better than finishing third and is far better than finishing last. The platitudes about winning being the 'only thing' are as banal as the ones about winning not being important at all. What concerns us is how to develop our own system of controlled aggression to make us better at what we do. Aggression in this context means dynamism, innovation, improvement, courage, risk, and a willingness to take action. We have to learn the value of unbalancing the situation and taking the initiative. You've got to bang a few rocks together to create fire.

The initiative rarely rings twice

We've touched on the concept of having the initiative before, and it is at the heart of being a successful attacker. When it's our move and we are creating the action instead of reacting, we are controlling the flow of the game. Our opponent must react, which means his moves become more limited and thus more predictable. From this lead position we can see further ahead and can continue to control the action. As long as we continue to generate threats and pressure we maintain the initiative. In chess this eventually leads to an attack that cannot be parried. In business it leads to a greater market share. In negotiations it leads to a better deal. In politics it's a rise in the polls. In all cases it creates a positive cycle of very real quality plus the perception of improved status and imminent victory, benefits both tangible and intangible. This is the attacker's advantage.

Once you have the initiative you must exploit it and feed it constantly. Wilhelm Steinitz reminded us that the player with the advantage is obliged to attack or his advantage will surely be lost. It is a dynamic factor that can disappear in an instant. A lead in initiative can be converted into material gains. Or it can be augmented into a stronger and stronger initiative until your opponent simply can't keep up and falls to your attack.

This doesn't necessarily mean massing your forces into a single overwhelming threat. That can work, but there isn't a real life (or chess) equivalent of the Death Star in *Star Wars*, a weapon capable of destroying any and all resistance. Our competitors will react and prepare defences, so we must employ the initiative creatively and maintain perspective on how we define success. An attack doesn't have to be all or nothing, or lightning quick. Sustained pressure can be very effective, and creating long-term weaknesses in our opponent's position can lead to a win in the long run. One of the qualities of a great attacker is to get the maximum out of a position without overstepping and trying to achieve more than what is possible.

Being a step ahead means we can keep our opponents off balance, shifting and moving in order to provoke weaknesses. The defender has to race around to cover the holes, but against constant pressure the job soon becomes impossible. Moving to cover one breach creates another until something cracks and the attack breaks through. In chess we have the 'principle of two weaknesses'. It's rare to be able to win a game against a strong player with only a single point of attack. Instead of becoming fixated on one spot, we must exploit our pressure to provoke more weak spots.

So a large part of using the initiative is mobility, flexibility and diversion. Building up all our armies to attack one spot can leave us as tied up as the defender. Even the Allied D-Day attack – Operation Overlord, the largest seaborne invasion in history – involved plenty of diversionary tactics to keep the Nazis guessing and unable to prepare their defences. Along with more traditional techniques the Allies went so far as to create an entirely fictional army unit with Hollywood-style sets and equipment to fool the enemy into thinking the invaders had twice their actual capabilities.

The opponent of an aggressive player is likely to be nervous and off his game. Any threat or perceived weakness will create doubts in his mind. No matter how secure his position appears to be, he will tend to focus on the possibility of losing material, on the likelihood of defeat. This inevitably leads to changes in his approach and his thinking, changes that can be exploited.

An attacker by choice

When I see my early games I look back at my development as a chess player. My friends and family look back over my life and see my development as a person, too. With so many visible parallels between players and the type of chess they play, it's not surprising to see how their lives and their chess often develop along similar paths.

Although I continued to play attacking chess by any definition throughout my career, my games became over time more concrete and less speculative. In my thirties, after a decade as world champion, I was less likely to embark on an uncertain assault and more likely to be patient. There was more at work here than the stereotypical conservatism of age; it was a reflection of the experience those years had brought me. I wasn't just playing differently, but better. I had learned that a well-timed counter-attack against an over-aggressive opponent could be more effective than always trying to meet fire with fire.

Psychologically I no longer felt I had to prove something in every game by launching a blitzkrieg. My approach had become more scientific and more professional. I was there to win, not to make a statement. Those closest to me tell me that this mirrored changes in how I dealt with the media and in my business affairs. The break with FIDE in 1993 and the collapse of the Professional Chess Association I had started took some of the wind from my sails, making me more circumspect. This break coincided with the painful dissolution of my first marriage and my separation from my wife and my daughter, Polina.

Stability on the board and in my private life returned together in the second half of the 1990s. I had a new family, with an infant son, Vadim. Owen Williams joined me as my full-time business agent. In different ways both additions to my 'family' made me more aware of the broader and long-term repercussions of my actions. In 1999 I launched an internet company bearing my name, turning it quite literally into a global brand. I could no longer pretend I was the rebel fighting the establishment when in many ways I had become the establishment. When this happens it can be difficult to keep the combative edge necessary to stay on top. It becomes necessary to remind ourselves how we achieved our successes and to remain true to those fundamentals.

Despite these transformations, my best results on and off the board were still the products of an attacker's mindset. The difference was that what came naturally to me at twenty-two often required conscious decision at thirty-five. Greater knowledge brings the burden of more things to consider, giving doubts a chance to creep in. Over-thinking can numb our instincts and turn what should be a quick decision into a mental committee meeting. The last thing I could afford was to be sitting at the chessboard, or in a business meeting, wondering, 'What would the young Garry Kasparov do?'

I used to attack because it was the only thing I knew. Now I attack because I know it works best. My new experiences in politics haven't altered this evaluation. The knowledge that there is a time and a place for diplomacy hasn't changed my belief in negotiating from a position of strength whenever possible.

The threat is stronger than the execution

A concept related to the initiative was elucidated elegantly by Aarton Nimzowitsch, who wrote that 'the threat is stronger than the execution'. An attack doesn't have to come to fruition to have a devastating effect on the enemy's position. If our opponent has to lose time rushing to defend one area it may lead to an opportunity to win elsewhere. Prior to D-Day, Allied double-agents led the Nazis to believe the main attack was coming at the Pas de Calais, causing Hitler to send Rommel and his elite forces well away from the actual invasion site.

Nimzowitsch's famous phrase is also about perception, something akin to the old Wall Street line 'Buy the rumor, sell the news.' Anticipation of something happening can be more powerful than the event itself, or, put another way, is inseparable from the event itself. Impact is impact. Shouting 'Fire!' in a crowded theatre causes, at least in the short term, the same reaction whether or not there really is a fire.

Even on the chessboard the initiative isn't a completely zero-sum concept. While we typically say either one side has it or it is balanced, it is also possible to divide the initiative across the board. White having more active pieces on the kingside while black is crashing through on the opposite wing is one common example. In these situations defence is barely relevant; only the attack matters. Both sides do everything they can to exploit their advantage as quickly as possible.

Divided advantages don't necessarily mean geographic divides. In the retail business, for example, it can stand for market segments and product categories. If we can dominate in one area, no matter how small, we can thrive and, perhaps, use even a single square as a launching pad for expansion.

A word for the defence

The aggressive mentality for successful attacking requires a readiness to upset the status quo, even a passion for it. Taking the lead means pushing into the unknown instead of being able to wait, see and respond. There is a level of uncertainty here that many find uncomfortable. This leads to a wait-and-see approach that can seriously limit our potential.

To be fair, defence is more rational than attack in many ways. An old military maxim says that a successful attack requires three times the resources of the defender. (In chess we will usually settle for a simple majority.) Defending involves conservation of resources and minimum exposure, both natural human tendencies. The defender also has fewer angles to cover, needing only to make sure his own weaknesses are protected. A rare genius like Tigran Petrosian could succeed with an almost entirely reactive style. But that was in a game in which each player gets a turn no matter what. In real time, initiative is compounded. As the pace of the world accelerates, the advantage is moving steadily towards the attacking side.

The art of military defence is nearly obsolete today, nearing its end after a rapid decline brought on by advances in technology. The First World War was the last stagnant war of attrition due to the advent of heavy mobile armour. At the start of the Second World War German tanks blitzkrieged across Europe, often taking more territory in a single day than the German army had taken in months twenty-five years earlier. Fast-forward to today and we have laser-guided bombs that can destroy a cement bunker 100 metres underground. Static defence is dead. Today's warfare is about hitting first and hitting hard.

This trend is mirrored across the rest of society. With things moving so quickly, passivity in investing and corporate strategy is as obsolete as siege fortresses and trench warfare. If we don't stay aggressively in front we are quickly left behind. It's not necessary to go back very far to find examples. Does the name AltaVista ring a bell? It was one of the many search engines pushed to the margins first by Yahoo! and then by the Google juggernaut. Yahoo! was ahead of the curve enough to diversify its business. When Google came along and made other search engines almost irrelevant, Yahoo! had already moved into content and services. AltaVista and others like Lycos and HotBot were absorbed by larger concerns and now exist mainly as nostalgic brand names.

Risking success

With defence on the run, the other side of the coin is that attacking has become more rewarding. It used to be that being first was great, but being second wasn't so bad. Nowadays being second could mean irrelevance. Attack is still risky, but the rewards are greater in an accelerated, high-tech world and the punishment for not attacking is more severe. Getting back to our MTQ terminology, time is more important than ever and attack is all about time.

Witness the latest Apple iPod, the 'Nano'. Apple replaced one of the most popular electronics products in history, the 'Mini', while it was still the best-selling item they had. They didn't wait for other companies to bite into their margins or for sales to slow. They stepped right over their own product to release a better one, no small risk. In contrast, as we have seen, Microsoft waited two years to begin work on a new Explorer browser, only making the effort when their market share had already started to fall significantly.

Unlike Microsoft, most of us cannot afford such mistakes.

They have the resources to absorb a 10 per cent drop in market share and fight back with new product development. An equivalent slip would get most employees fired. Taking chances in a superior position isn't really a risk when sitting still guarantees failure. It is better to risk success than to risk someone else succeeding at your expense.

Only with regular practice do we become used to accepting greater degrees of risk. The tougher the competition, the higher the stakes, the more risk is likely to be required to succeed. Some chess players, even a few quite successful ones, adopt a safety-first approach, waiting for their opponents to slip up. Mikhail Tal, whom we have seen as one of the greatest attackers in the history of the game, had this to say about a young player who had quickly risen into the elite in the 1980s: 'He's like a football forward who waits by the opposing team's goal to kick the ball in.' The creative aggression of Tal had no patience for an opportunistic mentality.

A small edge, a tiny lead, is a big leap away from a win. It is very common to achieve a great many of our strategic goals only to find that we have what we call a 'small plus', written in chess notation as +/=, just a little bit better than equal. Naturally this is better than being in an equal or inferior position, but it can be psychologically difficult to convert +/= into a decisive advantage. This is partly due to a tendency we call 'falling in love with your position'. We are so pleased with our advantage that we don't want to risk losing it. We manoeuvre around, trying to maintain the pluses in our position without doing anything significant. Against strong opposition this is likely to lead to the dissipation of our initiative. Without genuine risk it is almost impossible to make progress.

We often refer to chess positions by their risk factor by saying, for example, 'Now white is playing for three results,' meaning as a result of the player's risky plan it is now possible to win, lose or draw. When a player makes a move that heads into unknown territory he is taking away the safety net. Playing for two results means trying to play with little or no risk, only to win or, at worst, draw. This means maintaining a safety net, a way to bail out if things don't go as planned. Since it is almost impossible to win at the top level without significant risk, playing for two results is often just playing for one: sterile equality and a draw.

Such over-cautious behaviour is another form of complacency, a common side-effect of modest success. When we're in serious trouble we know instinctively that we'll need to take risks to survive. But when we are doing well we become hesitant to give anything up and, as we have seen, transformations are usually required to augment an advantage. Cash must be invested, soldiers sent to the front, and small advantages risked in order to gain large ones. Risking to win also means risking to lose, so courage is the most critical ingredient.

Boldness has magic

'What you can do or think you can do, begin it. For
boldness has magic, power, and genius in it.'
— *Goethe*

Attacking requires perfect timing as well as nerve. Knowing the right time to attack is as much an art as a science, and even for the best it's often guesswork. The window of opportunity is usually very small, as with most dynamic factors. No neon sign appears to say that there is a big opportunity right around the corner.

A common way for chess players to improve their basic attacking and tactical skills is by solving puzzles. These can be taken from real games or specially composed problems, akin to business school case studies. The solver is usually instructed to find the winning move in the given position. This makes for fun and useful practice in learning a wide variety of tactical patterns quickly, but it isn't very realistic. During a real game there is nothing to tell you there is a winning blow available. Vigilance is the next essential instrument in the attacker's toolbox.

Detecting opportunities requires letting go of assumptions of all kinds. The patterns and automatic assumptions we rely on to save time can also prevent us from identifying the best opportunities. This is especially true in quiet positions, those periods of stability that seem unlikely to produce attacking chances. We must also avoid making too many assumptions about our competition. We are often reminded never to under-estimate our opponents, but over-estimating them also leads to missed opportunities.

The 1953 world championship qualifying tournament in Zurich saw one of the most remarkable double blunders in the history of top-level chess. America's Sammy Reshevsky, famous for his early years as a child prodigy and now a contender for the championship title, was defending against Hungary's top player, Lázló Szabó. Szabó attacked Reshevsky's king with his knight, putting him in check and leaving him with only two possible moves. He could either capture the knight or move his king away. Even with so few options, Reshevsky made the wrong choice. (To be fair, Reshevsky was famously always in time trouble.) He quickly captured the knight, allowing himself to be checkmated by force in only two moves, something any casual player could spot in a moment.

Stunningly, Szabó missed it too! Instead of checkmating his opponent he recaptured the piece. The game dwindled to a draw a few moves later and the astonishing double blunder was revealed. Afterwards the befuddled Szabó could only blame his opponent, saying he could never have expected the great Reshevsky to blunder so horribly.

Remaining alert for attacking chances requires the evaluation of any and every change in your position, in the environment, in the competition. A small change that doesn't seem relevant at first can combine with a later transformation to create a weakness and an opportunity.

Even in a balanced position, an opponent on the defensive is more likely to make a mistake. Pushing the action gives us more options and a greater ability to control our fate, which creates positive energy and confidence. This energy we create, our mental adrenaline, is no small thing. Mikhail Tal once said that perhaps the worst move of his life was one he didn't make, a speculative sacrifice he pondered for forty minutes before uncharacteristically declining. Attackers may sometimes regret bad moves but it is much worse to forever regret an opportunity you let pass by.

Savielly Tartakower contributed as many aphorisms and colourful stories to the chess world as he did victories, which is to say hundreds. One of my favourite 'Tartakowerisms' is 'The first essential for an attack is the will to attack.' All our planning and evaluation skills are academic if they aren't combined with the nerve to employ them and to strike when the opportunity arises. There are concrete practical benefits to having an aggressive approach. If you're already in a fight you want the first blow to be the last, and you had better be the one to throw it.

PART III

14
QUESTION SUCCESS

Success is the enemy of future success

We know that complacency is a dangerous enemy. Satisfaction can lead to a lack of vigilance, to mistakes and missed opportunities. Generally we are interested in curing the disease, not just treating the symptoms, but in this case we run into something of a paradox. Success and satisfaction are our goals, but they can also lead to negative patterns of behaviour that impede greater success and satisfaction, or even to catastrophic failure at a key moment.

On 9 November 1985 I achieved my lifelong goal of becoming world champion (if it is proper to discuss lifelong goals when they are attained at the age of twenty-two). During the celebrations I was taken aback by the words of Rona Petrosian, the wife of the former world champion. 'I feel sorry for you,' she said. 'The greatest day of your life is over.' What a thing to say at a victory party! But I often heard those words in my head in the years that followed.

The gravity of past success

The next fifteen years were a constant battle to augment my strengths and eliminate my weaknesses. I was always convinced that if I worked as hard as I could and played to the best of my ability no one could defeat me, and I felt that way until the day I retired in February 2005. So how then to explain my loss to my countryman Vladimir Kramnik in our 2000 world championship match? We have already looked at his success purely at the chess level, at how he managed to select the battlefield for our contest. This strategic failure on my part had deeper origins, however.

I had always known that psychology played a role in chess,

but it took the loss of my title to show me just how big a role. One of the strongest points of my game had always been the ability to adapt to meet new challenges, and Kramnik's strategy used that against me. Despite feeling uncomfortable in the positions he led me into, I insisted that I would be able to adjust during the match in time to recover and win. Realistically there wasn't enough time for this in a match of only sixteen games. In my first world championship match, against Anatoly Karpov in 1984–5, there had been no limit to the number of games. I had had time to adapt and recover. I wouldn't have that chance in London.

It was difficult for me to realize this because of where I was in my career at the time. In the two years prior to the October 2000 match I had been playing some of the best chess of my life, refuting the critics who had predicted the end of my reign at the top of the rating list. They pointed to my advanced age – at thirty-five I was already a decade older than most of my opponents. In 1999 I pushed my record rating to new heights and was in the middle of a 'Grand Slam' tournament winning streak when I started preparations for my world championship match. I felt as though I could move mountains at the chessboard; how could this infuriating Berlin Defence of Kramnik's slow me down?

My years of success had made me vulnerable to such a trap. When faced with a new threat I assumed my old methods would get me through. I was incapable of acknowledging that I was in serious trouble, that I had been out-prepared by my young opponent. When the realization finally hit me it was already late in the short match and I went from feeling sure I would recover to believing it was impossible. I managed to put up a little fight towards the end but it wasn't enough. I lost the match without winning a single one of the fifteen games while losing two.

My loss stemmed from over-confidence and complacency. Even while it was happening it was difficult for me to credit my one-time student with the ability to outfox me in preparation for the match. Perhaps I paid too little attention to the fact that he had been one of my own assistants in my 1995 world championship match against Viswanathan Anand. I had been playing so well and winning so many events coming into the 2000 match that I couldn't conceive of any serious weaknesses in my game.

This is what I call the gravity of past success. Winning creates the illusion that everything is fine. There is a very strong tempta-tion to think only of the positive result without considering all the things that went wrong – or that could have gone wrong – on the way. After a victory we want to celebrate it, not analyse it. We replay the triumphant moment in our mind until it looks as though it were completely inevitable all along.

Similar sins accumulate in our daily tasks. The old saying 'If it ain't broke, don't fix it' should be left for plumbing and kept well away from how we lead our lives at home and at work. We must question the status quo at all times, *especially* when things are going well. When something goes wrong we naturally want to do it better next time, but we must train ourselves to want to do it better even when things go right. Failing to do this leads to stagnation and eventual breakdown.

Competition and anti-complacency tactics

Failure due to complacency comes in many forms. In competitive environments such as the military and the corporate world it almost always springs from doing 'business as usual' while our competition is catching up and passing us by. The consequences of resting on reputation and outdated experience can be tragic.

In 1941, in the first months of the German invasion, the Soviet troops were led by Red Army civil war veterans who still believed that horses were paramount. Marshal Kliment Voroshilov – a favourite of Stalin – employed the same tactics with massed cavalry units that had been so effective in 1919 against the White Guard. Unsurprisingly, they were completely ineffectual in preventing the Nazi armoured divisions from encircling Leningrad. Even worse, this duplicated the blunder made by Russian commanders early in the First World War, when an observing newsman wrote, 'Today I watched a wave of Russian flesh and blood dash against a wall of German steel.'

Horses were no match for tanks and artillery. American car companies in the 70s were no match for new Japanese manufacturing and management techniques. Constant reinvention is a necessity in fast-moving areas like technology. Ignoring what the competition is up to can leave us looking like George III, whose diary for 4 July 1776 read, ironically, 'Nothing of importance happened today.'

Competition should be the foremost way we keep ourselves motivated. It would have been impossible for me to reach my potential without a nemesis like Karpov to push me every step of the way. When a new generation of chess players emerged in the nineties and Karpov ceased to be the main threat to my dominant position, I had to refocus and find new sources of inspiration. My new theme was to fight back the new wave of talented young stars, something few world champions had managed to do for long.

Other players have their own methods. The amazing Viktor Korchnoi is still playing high-level chess well into his seventies and he has kept his competitive fires burning. 'Viktor the Terrible' has led a difficult and colourful life both on and off the board, defecting from the USSR in 1976 after years of battles with the Soviet authorities. He became even more of a thorn in their side after he fled to the West, first to the Netherlands and then in his current home, Switzerland. It became very difficult for the Soviet censors to keep the defector's name out of the news when he was winning so many tournaments and defeating the top Soviet players. Three times he faced the much younger Karpov in world championship contests, failing each time but assuring himself of the bittersweet title of 'the strongest player never to become world champion'. Korchnoi has had a revenge of sorts by continuing to play competitive chess while Karpov – twenty years younger – has largely retired from the rigours of tournament play. When he was the age at which I retired, Korchnoi was not yet at his peak!

Despite his impressive career, Korchnoi has always been able to play as if he has something more to prove. Defying age is not nearly enough for him; he is not content just to turn up and move the pieces around. Korchnoi enjoys showing players a half-century his junior that they still have something to learn from him. At one tournament in 2004, Korchnoi defeated the Norwegian prodigy Grandmaster Magnus Carlsen, a triumph of a seventy-three-year-old over a fourteen-year-old.

Korchnoi has maintained his drive by refusing to look back at what would be glory days for just about anyone. He is still driven by the game of chess and by an earnest desire to beat his opponent, not merely to do his best. It is essential to have these benchmarks in our lives to keep us alert. In chess and other sports we have ratings, opponents and tournaments, so things seem clear, but more is required.

We have to push ourselves, create our own criteria and raise them all the time. It can be a bit of a paradox to have the confidence that we are the best and still compete as if we were outsiders, underdogs. It is just as hard to change a working formula, but anyone who wants to excel over a long career will find it necessary to do both things. Despite winning eight gold medals over three Olympics, Carl Lewis still wanted more at the age of thirty-five. In order to qualify for the 1996 Olympic Games in Atlanta he embarked on an entirely new training programme, leaving behind everything that had worked for him up to that point. He knew that his age and injuries created new challenges. He went on to win another gold and a silver in Atlanta and he did it by not being afraid to change what worked.

Finding ways to maintain our concentration and motivation is the key to fighting complacency. Maybe we don't have a rating system at work or at home, but that doesn't mean we can't develop one. What metrics can we contrive to measure our performance? Certainly money is one, if a bit cynical. Perhaps a 'happiness index' or a comprehensive and realistic list of goals similar to those so many of us invariably produce each New Year can help. I doubt becoming a compulsive list-maker has ever led anyone to fame and fortune, but a few lists, be they mental or on paper, about what motivates us and what we really value can certainly help.

Before we can fight we have to know what we are fighting for. Everyone says they want to spend more time with their kids, but how many people know, down to the hour, how much time they actually spend with them each week, each month? How many hours at work are wasted playing solitaire or surfing the web? What if we knew? Then we would have a target to pursue, a helpful technique for that vast majority of us who don't find 'Just Do It' sufficient. Anticipating Nike's ad agency by two centuries, Goethe wrote, 'Knowing is not enough; we must apply. Willing is not enough; we must do.'

Finding and fixing the flaws

Together with motivation comes the search for weaknesses in our own camp, examining the way we go about our business, our day-to-day lives. If we are aware of the negatives, the worst-case scenarios, the potential crises, we can work to eliminate those weaknesses now and by so doing improve the quality of our performance overall. We cannot wait for disaster to strike before making changes. 'Find and fix' has to be our mantra.

In recent years self-scrutiny has become the norm in politics. The Clinton campaign team hired investigators to dig up dirt on their own candidate so that they could pre-emptively disarm the news and prepare defences against the allegations to come. If they couldn't avoid the scandal at least they could anticipate it and have their campaign 'war room' ready to respond immediately.

Naturally it is difficult to focus on our own flaws, just as it is painful to examine our defeats and blunders. No one likes to relive difficult setbacks, but at least we understand that analysing them is essential. It is even harder to look for mistakes in our successes. Our egos want to believe that we won brilliantly against tough opposition, not that we were lucky, that our opponent missed several chances, and that things could have been very different.

We've already looked at examples of bad strategy winning with good tactics and vice versa. Knowing why we win is as essential as knowing why we lose; not doing so throws away valuable study material. Questioning success again means asking what should be our favourite question: 'Why?' We must be brutally objective with our successes or we will surely slip into stagnation.

We often refer to the mistake of 'analysing to the result'. This means assuming that since white won, he played better and scored a deserved victory. Of course black's plan was mistaken; after all, he lost. It is terribly difficult to avoid doing this, since we already know the outcome of the game when we sit down to analyse it. Each move by the winner looks a little bit better because we know it all worked out in the end. Even great chess writers like Aaron Nimzowitsch and Siegbert Tarrasch fell into this trap. They wanted the games to prove their theories and to provide a tidy narrative to illustrate the conclusions they already held.

Fifty years before the brutal objectivity of computer analysis helped my generation with this problem, my mentor Mikhail Botvinnik established a system for avoiding this trap. He deeply analysed all his games and published all his analysis so that it could be checked and criticized by the public. The threat of an embarrassing public correction was stronger than his desire to appear infallible, so he developed a strong sense of detachment in his game annotations.

I confess I could have done a better job of remembering this particular Botvinnik lesson when I began work on my series of chess books in the late 1990s. A combination of editorial haste and our confidence that our analysis was better than any that had come before led to our publishing the first volume of *My Great Predecessors* without enough regard for the attention the book would receive in the chess community, and what that attention signified.

The first volume appeared in the summer of 2003. My in-depth look at the first four world champions and their closest rivals quickly got its own in-depth examination from tens of thousands of chess players around the globe. Nowadays this also means tens of thousands of powerful chess computers going deeply into every move, every line of my analysis. The internet allowed this distributed network of analysts and ad hoc book critics to collect and present a remarkable, and humbling, number of corrections.

I've done my best to deal with this turn of events in a way that would make Botvinnik proud of his former star pupil. At my insistence we began to collect and do our own analysis of the corrections so that they could be incorporated into later editions of the book. In fact, many changes were ready in time for translations of the book into other languages, so, for example, the Portuguese version, which came out a year later, is far more accurate than the first Russian edition. At the same time we made our analysis and fact-checking processes much more rigorous for the subsequent volumes and each one has been better than the last in this regard. Part V, on Karpov and Korchnoi, was published in early 2006 and I'm proud to say that the vast audience of eager would-be critics has been gratifyingly quiet!

This improvement in quality would never have happened without a willingness to accept criticism and the will to do something about it. I took it as a challenge, not as an insult. Nobody enjoys disapproval, of course. During my twenty years at the top of the chess world I endured a constant barrage of both condemnation and praise, and the temptation is always to ignore the former and embrace the latter. We must fight our own egos and defensive instincts to appreciate that some criticism is deserved and constructive and that we can use it as a tool. We can't always win that fight, but it is vital to realize that there is a battle going on.

There is a great danger in trying to avoid criticism and to shield ourselves from its impact. This is a challenge not only for individuals, but also for businesses and governments. A company that can't respond to the demands of its customers is certain to fail.

A key test of the validity of a government is its ability to receive and respond to critics and to improve its systems and reactions.

Inner strength is required to question success, to face failure, and to accept that changes are needed. Further strength is necessary to enact those changes. Churchill said 'Success is not final, failure is not fatal: it is the courage to continue that counts.' This courage can be inspired by competition or any number of external factors, but in the end it has to come from within.

Vladimir Kramnik (1975–), USSR/Russia
My nemesis

Perhaps it is better left to the next generation to write about the man who took the world championship from me. The strong emotions that swirled around our 2000 title match in London, and my subsequent attempts to gain a rematch with my former protégé, make objectivity difficult. Regardless, he was an important figure in my personal development as a chess player and a decision-maker and thus cannot be disregarded.

I was one of the first to recognize the towering teenager's remarkable talent, back when he was a student at the Botvinnik–Kasparov school. He came from the small Black Sea town of Tuapse but there was nothing small about him or his chess. I championed his participation in the prestigious Russian Chess Olympiad team in 1992, overriding the objections of the press and some of our teammates who said Kramnik was too young and inexperienced for such an important event. He surpassed even my high expectations by scoring eight wins and one draw and a new star was born.

His rise was steady and he soon became one of the top three players in the world, a leader of the new generation that supplanted my old foe Anatoly Karpov. In 1995 I selected him to be on my team of analysts when I beat Viswanathan Anand in our New York world championship match. While helping with my preparation and analysis, Kramnik was also learning my habits and methods, knowledge he would use to great effect five years later.

By October 2000 Kramnik had gone from being my second to being my opponent for the title. We met in London in a match scheduled for sixteen games. He had done his homework very well and immediately took the initiative. He demolished my main defence with the black pieces as early as game two. For his own games with black Kramnik had devised a brilliant concept, using an old and relatively unpopular defence that he knew played to my weaknesses. He had mastered the intricacies of the Berlin Defence and I had no time to do so. He defeated me two wins to none, with the other thirteen games drawn.

Kramnik had defeated me for the champion's title and his next quest was to surpass me on the international rating list. But it turned out that the conservative style of play he had perfected in order to beat me was less effective in the tournament world and his results were rarely up to his old standards. He had trouble staying motivated after reaching the peak so early in his career. Kramnik remained, and remains, an elite competitor, but he has been outshone by younger players and others of his own generation even while he defended his increasingly devalued title by drawing a championship match in 2004. Only time will tell if his physical and psychological health will recover enough to bring him back to the top.

On Kramnik: '[In London] Kramnik used a very good strategy and managed to carry it off. He's not the first with the idea of trying to contain Kasparov as he did, but it's another thing to be able to do it as well.' – Viswanathan Anand

In his own words: 'You must have good health, a strong nervous system, and you must hate losing a game. Only then you may have a chance to become world champion.'

15

THE INNER GAME

The game can be won before you get to the board

South American liberator Simón Bolívar said that 'only an inexperienced soldier believes that all is lost after being defeated for the first time'. In the weeks and months after my defeat in London I had time to absorb what Vladimir Kramnik had achieved and how he had done it. I worked to cover the weaknesses he had exploited and to turn the flaw-finding tables. We played over a dozen games after that match, all of them draws but one. The lone victory was mine.

With no small irony, that victory came in the final round of a supertournament in a game I had to win to overtake Kramnik for first place, and the opening was the very same Berlin Defence that had so frustrated me in our London match. Combined with my maintaining a substantial lead on the rating list, this added up to a small consolation for the bitter defeat in London.

Finding the holes in my game was only one element in recovering from the loss of my world championship title. At the same time there was a period of psychological recuperation. Getting back into the ring after a bruising loss is never easy, especially when we know our opponents are emboldened by a perceived weakness.

There are few things as psychologically brutal as serious chess. It involves spending five or six hours in total concentration in direct competition with another mind, with a ticking clock and nowhere to hide. There are no teammates to share the load, no referees to blame, no unlucky dice or cards to turn over. Chess is what is referred to as a 100 per cent information game: both players know everything that is going on all the time. When you lose it's because the other player beat you, plain and simple. In this, chess has much more in common with boxing than with other pastimes, and it can take even longer to recover from a loss. As my 1993 world championship challenger Nigel Short once said in an interview, 'Chess is ruthless: you've got to be prepared to kill people.'

As much as some players try to downplay it, the importance of psychology cannot be over-estimated in chess or in any endeavour. Every skill and talent we have requires the fortitude to develop it and the courage to employ it. Even a game like chess, which has the appearance of a mathematical puzzle, benefits greatly from the proper mindset at every step, not just at the board.

The storm before the calm

Preparation requires the ability to self-motivate and to work long, lonely hours. Constant study can feel like a Sisyphean task when you know that perhaps only 10 per cent of your analysis will ever see the light of day. We know that all our work pays dividends indirectly, but that's easy to tell ourselves and yet difficult to use as motivation, the way we couldn't see much possible use for algebra in school.

Next we have the run-up to the game and the battle to control our nerves, fears and adrenaline. Some players lose sleep or appetite, some do last-minute preparation and focus on the game, while others watch a movie or take a walk to clear their heads. I always knew something was wrong if I wasn't on edge before a game. Nervous energy is the ammunition we take into any mental battle. If we don't have enough of it our concentration will fade. If we have a surplus the results can be explosive, either for us or our opponent.

Several times in my career I had an extraordinary feeling before a game, that no matter who my opponent was or what he did I was going to tear him limb from limb. I had one such experience in 1993 before my game with Anatoly Karpov in the Linares supertournament in Spain (a rough equivalent of 'Grand Slam' in tennis or 'Major' in golf). Although I played with the black pieces in the game, I was bouncing off the walls in anticipation; I had a strange feeling that something phenomenal was going to happen.

My established rivalry with Karpov was accentuated in this case by our being tied for first place with only four rounds to play.

My then trainer Sergey Makarichev could confirm that I was extremely optimistic before the game, boasting that I was going to wipe Karpov out this time. Indeed that was what happened, although there was a comedic twist at the conclusion that no one could have predicted.

After sacrificing a pawn and seizing the initiative I reached a dominating position. Karpov's pieces were quickly pushed back against the first rank, a highly unusual situation. On move 24 I promoted a pawn, saying 'queen' and looking over to the referee to deliver me a second queen, which should have been on the table already. But before I received a response Karpov played his move, an illegal one! He claimed that since I hadn't actually placed a new queen on the board yet, he could choose which piece it was, and that it was a bishop, a piece much weaker than a queen. The little farce was quickly resolved. I got my new queen and Karpov resigned three moves later, although he demanded and received a few extra minutes on his clock in compensation for the supposed confusion. That win was part of a five-game stretch I consider one of the best series of tournament rounds of my life, four wins and a draw against the world's top players to clinch the tournament victory.

There is more to such premonitions and results than the power of positive thinking. Creative and competitive energy is a tangible thing, and if we can feel it, so can our opponents. Our confidence level is reflected in how we move and talk, not just by what we say, but how we say it.

If you want to be taken seriously, take yourself seriously

I was always credited with – or accused of – a terrible level of intimidation at the board. Bobby Fischer was similarly attributed with causing 'Fischer Fear' in his opponents, while during his best years Mikhail Tal allegedly hypnotized other players with his magnetic glare, which often wandered up from the board to his opponent's eyes. One of Tal's opponents, the Hungarian-American Pal Benko, once went so far as to wear eye shades at the board to protect himself from the Latvian's gaze. In response, Tal, always with a quick wit, borrowed a huge pair of sunglasses from Tigran Petrosian and put them on, much to the amusement of the spectators and other players. Even Benko had to laugh a little, at least until he resigned the game.

Less successful players are never accused of intimidation or hypnotism, so I took it as a compliment. If other players felt great pressure sitting across from me it was because they knew my games and reputation, something that became more of a factor as the players I competed against became younger and younger. Before I retired I had the dubious pleasure of facing several opponents who hadn't yet been born when I won the world championship. To them I was almost a piece of living history, although this didn't stop one of them, Teimour Radjabov, a teenage prodigy from my own home town of Baku, from beating me in 2003 in Linares. While some critics suggested that my opponents played poorly against me because of my reputation, I'm certain that at least an equal number were instead motivated to play at their very best.

If I had a threatening demeanour at the board, it came from my belief that chess was serious business and that it was my responsibility to show my opponent I was going to do everything I could to beat him. This was equally true in elite tournaments and at exhibitions against amateurs, where I was often encouraged by spectators to smile for the cameras while I was playing. I did try on occasion, making a few courtesy draws with high-ranking politicians or celebrities, but in general I felt I would be cheating my opponents by not playing my best and making it clear that I took the games seriously.

When I played, say, twenty-five games at the same time in a simultaneous exhibition (known in the chess world as a 'simuls'), I took it as my duty to try to make a clean score, or a 'dry score' as we say in Russian: 25–0. Wearing my 'game face' whenever I was in front of a chessboard was an important part of my psychological preparation. I did not want to get out of the habit of being completely focused at the board.

My hard-nosed attitude in these exhibitions has other origins as well. Against strong competition, playing many opponents at the same time is an opportunity to indulge creatively, free from the constraints of one-on-one play. Some masters view these exhibitions solely as entertainment, but I never wanted to miss an opportunity to learn something, to gain a new perspective. Simuls also require complex decision-making, as you have to consider your overall score and how each game might affect the others.

In May 1995, I gave a simul at the legendary Central Chess

Club in Moscow. It was the fiftieth anniversary of VE Day and I played against thirty Soviet Second World War veterans. I believe my youngest opponent was seventy-three! But it wasn't a walk in the park. Many were quite reasonable players, and some had played in chess clubs in the 30s and 40s. It was quite an impressive array, with some of the veterans wearing their medals. There was even a general present in full uniform.

My game with the general didn't go well for me and it was beginning to distract me from the other games. I could have kept playing, but the position was complicated, and so when I saw a chance to force a draw I made a practical decision to do it so that I could concentrate on the other twenty-nine games. It was the first game to finish and I immediately sensed anger from other players. They thought I gifted the general a draw because of his rank, which was not the case at all.

Instead of having the weight of that one thorny game on me throughout the event, I found a way to relieve the pressure early at a small cost. It was a purely pragmatic decision. If I had continued that game I might eventually have won, but it would have distracted me from all the other games. This sort of situation is one we often face, when one tricky problem, be it personal or professional, begins to dominate our thoughts, making it impossible to focus on other things. If it's possible to do so we should resolve it quickly, even if the resolution isn't entirely in our favour. Consider it as comparable to selling a losing stock before it drops even further.

There was an amusing conclusion to that simul with the veterans. I made a few more draws after a big fight, playing nearly five hours. In the very last game we had reached an endgame where I had an extra pawn and good winning chances, but with a long way still to go. My opponent was quite exhausted as well, and I thought I had pushed hard enough and offered a draw, which he accepted. He got quite excited as I signed his scoresheet and he said he would remember this draw for the rest of his life, as well as he remembered his simul draw against Lasker in 1937!

The ultra-competitive Viktor Korchnoi takes his exhibitions even more seriously, at least judging by this story from his collection of games. In 1963 he was in Cuba with a squad of other Soviet GMs for a tournament and a few of them gave well-attended simuls. Korchnoi's opponents included none other than Che Guevara, and before the game an official suggested to Viktor that it would be a good idea to give Guevara a draw. Back at the hotel, Mikhail Tal asked him how his simul had gone and he must have been a little surprised to hear Korchnoi say that he had won all his games. 'Against Che Guevara too?' Tal asked. 'Yes,' Korchnoi replied. 'He doesn't have the faintest idea what to do against the Catalan Opening!'

Maintaining a suitable attitude, inward and outward, makes a great deal of difference to our success. It's not as simplistic as convincing ourselves we are geniuses, or that we are invincible. We must aim to give our best effort at all times and acknowledge that doing less is the real failure. Platitudes and office posters about 'giving 110 per cent' can't inspire us if we cannot first inspire ourselves to give 100 per cent. That proverbial extra 10 per cent comes from the knowledge that we are ready and able to do everything we can. When that happens we are often surprised to find that we are capable of more than we thought.

How we perceive ourselves is also a critical element in how we are perceived by others. A nice suit and a firm handshake must be backed up by the look in our eye and the timbre of our voice. Sociologists have claimed that women may unconsciously find married men more attractive because they exude a certain type of security and confidence that many single men lack (so pretending to be married doesn't work). People who interview others for jobs and university admissions remember the way the candidates acted far better than they recall what they had to say.

How do people remember you? Everyone is self-conscious to a certain degree. As Mark Twain wrote, 'There are no grades of vanity, there are only grades of ability in concealing it.' The sad result is that the more we worry about how others think of us, the worse our presentation becomes. To take Twain at face value, we 'conceal it' best by staying focused on our quality, our preparedness, our achievements. It is a healthy sort of pride that stems from hard-earned success and the sincere belief that more success is to come.

Don't get distracted while trying to distract

As with just about everyone on earth, real chess players fall between the literary caricatures of the ultra-rational Bond villain Kronsteen and Vladimir Nabokov's psychotic Luzhin. My impression is that they are bunched towards the rational end of the bell curve, but there are notable exceptions. The incredible stories around Viktor Korchnoi's 1978 world championship match against Anatoly Karpov in the Philippines are enough to make anyone wonder if chess players might indeed be crazy.

Tensions between the sides at the match were already at peak level. The 'hated defector' Korchnoi was challenging the full might of the Soviet machine and its champion Karpov. Countless petty protests were filed by both sides before the match had even started. They argued about the flags on the table, the height and style of the chairs, and the colour of the yogurt Karpov was brought during the games. None of these were as bizarre as the story of Dr Vladimir Zukhar, a psychology professor who came to Baguio City as part of Karpov's entourage.

Zukhar sat in the audience and stared directly at Korchnoi during the games of the world championship. His association with Karpov and his apparently disconcerting mien led the superstitious Korchnoi and his over-protective team to suspect foul play of a supernatural kind. Zukhar was accused of being a para-psychologist who was attempting to disrupt Korchnoi's thinking. Korchnoi's team asked that Zukhar not be allowed to sit too close to the stage, while the Soviets fought every request and responded with their own demands. Thus began a bizarre epic that saw Zukhar changing seats daily, often flanked by members of Korchnoi's delegation. Prior to game 17 of the match, Korchnoi even refused to play unless Zukhar moved further back, a protest that cost the challenger eleven minutes on his clock, time he could have used when he blundered to lose the game after missing several winning continuations while in severe time trouble. Later, Korchnoi brought in his own 'parapsychologist, neurologist, and hypnotist' to combat Zukhar's powers.

The saga continued in similar fashion throughout the match. Was it all posturing or is it really possible that the two greatest chess players on the planet, and/or their closest associates, were distracted by such sideshows during the most important match of their careers? Karpov won the thirty-two-game match by a single point, winning the final game (with Zukhar returning to again sit up front, for the record). It's worth wondering how much better Korchnoi would have done had he not invested so much energy in responding to Karpov's provocations and wondering whether or not Karpov was receiving secret messages in his yogurt.

Incidentally, Karpov's first victory came in game 8, which was when he startled his opponent and the fans by refusing to shake Korchnoi's hand before the game.

The importance of taking control

The loss of mental energy is reflected in the physical as much as the reverse. Depression and lack of focus cause enervation as real as running a mile. 'Empowerment' may be an overused word these days, but it is a crucial concept in our personal and professional lives. When we feel in control we are literally stronger. A macabre example comes from an experiment I read about that used two mice in adjoining cages. At random intervals an electric shock was sent through the floor of the cage, affecting both mice. In one of the cages there was a lever that, when depressed, stopped the current. Both mice received the same shock, but the mice in the cage with the lever far outlived the mice in the cages without a lever. When faced with random and uncontrollable events even mice lose their will to live and without that the body doesn't last long.

These days we read about 'stress chemicals' and other things that show what we have always suspected, that mind really does control matter. Feeling in control of our fate at the chessboard, at home, in school, at work, has rewards in mental and physical well-being. This means better performance on a wide scale. The management revolution that started in the 1970s stripped away layers of management and decentralized the corporate decision-making process. Small units closer to the sources of information could make better decisions faster and also had much higher morale.

We often hear laments about having too much responsibility, but the alternative is far worse. The brief sense of relief at having decisions made for us doesn't last very long, especially if they are about things that directly impact on our quality of life – if not necessarily electrical shocks. Too often our instinct is to let things happen around us instead of taking the reins. This is taking the default path, asking, at most, 'What happens if I don't do anything?' instead of getting involved. Avoiding responsibility in this way starts out as a labour-saving device but inevitably leaves us far from our goals.

Breaking the spell of pressure

Years of competition got me used to the tension that came with each game and each event. It wasn't so easy for me at the start of my career, however. In January 1978, at the age of fourteen – an ageing prodigy – I participated in the Sokolsky Memorial tournament in Minsk with the hope of making a score good enough to qualify for my master title. I also needed to follow up my junior successes. After clinching two consecutive national junior titles I had failed to win the world under-sixteen championship in 1976 and 1977. Meanwhile, my closest junior rival, Artur Jussupow, had just won the world under-twenty title. It was highly unusual for a junior to be invited to play in a strong event in another Soviet republic – from Azerbaijan to Belarus in this case. I was allowed to play only at the insistence of my mentor, Mikhail Botvinnik, so success was critical for both our reputations. Therefore I had many reasons to be nervous about the possibility of failing in the event; I was also a bit scared of some of my experienced opponents.

My mother came up with an idea. 'Garik,' she told me the day before the first round, 'you can do well here, but before each game I want you to memorize some lines from Pushkin's poem *Eugene Onegin*. It will sharpen your senses.' I followed her instructions, and with my anxiety distracted by this 'magic feather' I won my first games and my confidence returned. I ended up not only scoring enough points to qualify for my master title but I also won the tournament – with a little help from our national poet.

Feeling a little uneasy when under pressure is completely natural; it's when we begin to feel nonchalant about new challenges that it may be time to worry. If everything seems easy, we aren't pushing ourselves hard enough or being challenged enough. If we don't keep up our psychological strength we won't be able to respond well when faced with setbacks. Psychological muscles atrophy from disuse just like physical and mental ones. If it has been a while since you experienced the nervous thrill of trying something new and unknown, perhaps you've been avoiding it all along. We need a regular diet of change and healthy nervous energy to maintain our defences.

We must have those defences in good working order when failure strikes. It is very difficult to learn from a tough loss and still come out the next day believing we are the best. It takes a strong mind to balance these somewhat contradictory storylines, especially after a particularly crushing defeat. Our theory of mind over matter can also work against us if we are convinced things are hopeless. One defeat quickly leads to another, and then another. This can happen over a single tournament or even a career, resulting in us falling into a rut of failure.

Staying objective when the chips are down

In my 1986 championship match with Karpov in Leningrad I was well in the lead when I suddenly crashed to three losses in a row, leaving the match tied with five games remaining. After the third loss, in game 19, I had an emergency session with my coaches about what to do with white in game 20. Should I force a quick draw to stabilize myself and recover or fight as usual? 'Why not fight,' I said. 'I've just lost three, how could I possibly lose four in a row?' Grandmaster Mikhail Gurevich, who has plenty of experience of both chess and casinos, replied, 'Playing the odds doesn't work like that. When you play roulette you can lose many times in a row by betting on black every time.' It's sad but true; it makes no sense to believe that faring poorly now means you'll do better later. There are no cosmic scales that will eventually balance out on their own. I took his advice and made a short draw in game 20, drew game 21, and then, fully recovered, scored a crushing victory in game 22 to retake the lead and hold on to my title.

Casinos often put up digital signs next to roulette wheels showing the last dozen winning numbers, encouraging people to believe that they can gain an advantage with this information when in reality it is literally worthless. The wheel doesn't know how the last spin came out. It is very dangerous to fool ourselves into believing that something is due to happen when there is no relation between past and present. If we fail to shake off these false trails we are doing little more than following superstition.

The concept of an individual's nemesis is much discussed in the chess world, where the transitive principle rarely holds true. Player A can beat Player B, who beats Player C, who beats Player A. Some players are what we call 'good customers'; we beat them seemingly no matter what they do. I maintained very good scores against many of my leading competitors, but Alexei Shirov was without a doubt my best customer. Over twelve years of encounters encompassing nearly thirty games he suffered fifteen straight losses – not counting draws – without ever winning a game against me. (Meanwhile, Shirov has a good score against my nemesis, Kramnik.)

Such a degree of dominance over one of the most talented players among the elite must find its explanation somewhere beyond the chessboard. After so many losses we begin to doubt if it is even possible to dream of a win, and thereby we seal our fate to lose yet again. After his thirteenth loss Shirov bravely joked that since thirteen was my lucky number it was clearly time for the streak to end. This psychological gambit wasn't a bad idea, but alas for him it didn't turn out that way.

When our best isn't good enough

A defeat can be doubly damaging when we feel we've done our best and still failed. This is contrary to every parent's words of consolation to a child whose football team has lost: 'You did your best.' We are supposed to feel better, knowing that even if the outcome wasn't positive, we couldn't have done any more. And yet, someone with aspirations to be the champion of the world does not want to hear that he did his best and was still beaten convincingly. Indeed, could there be anything worse?

The Soviet Andrei Sokolov and America's Russian-born Gata Kamsky were both made to face this ugly reality in matches against Karpov and in both cases the effect was devastating. The twenty-three-year-old Sokolov was playing the best chess of his life in 1985–6 and made an impressive run at the world title. After two qualifying match victories he faced Karpov in the candidates' final match in 1987; the winner would go on to face me in the world championship. But Sokolov more than met his match; he was unable to win a single game, while Karpov scored four wins. After that debacle Sokolov was an entirely different player. The sun had melted his wings and he fell to earth. His results were barely mediocre for several years afterwards. He never again approached the world title or made strong scores in elite events. On a happier note, Sokolov is still playing good chess these days, now from the pleasant surroundings of a life in the French provinces.

The story of the last American player to reach world championship level is both more and less tragic. Gata Kamsky achieved far more, but his potential and record of success made his eventual fall all the more painful. He was brought to the United States by his father in 1989 and as a teenager enjoyed a meteoric rise in the chess ranks. In 1996 he reached the final of the FIDE world championship, where he faced Karpov. (As mentioned earlier, in 1993 my challenger Nigel Short and I broke away from the international chess federation, leading to the existence of two world championship titles: the 'classical' title I held and the 'official title' endorsed by the federation, which was held briefly by Karpov.)

We will never know what Kamsky, then only twenty-two, might have achieved had he stayed with chess after the crushing loss Karpov dealt him in their match. But he, or perhaps his notoriously irascible father, decided that if he wasn't going to be number one at chess he should try something else. He promptly retired from the game, eventually taking up the law as his predecessor Paul Morphy had done.

Meanwhile, Karpov at his peak was a perfect example of someone who could be totally objective both during and between games. His cool pragmatism allowed him to play each move as if looking at the board for the first time. He never allowed himself to be distracted by a bad move, a lost game or a poor result. Tomorrow was always another day for Karpov.

My much more emotional style never allowed for such logical expediency. I tore into every game and paid a heavy psychological price for a loss. I relied on a tremendous store of energy to get me back on track for the next game, expelling all my anger and regret in a burst before recharging again. We all have to find the best way to deal with failure, to learn from it and to come back fighting twice as hard. Trying to put a setback entirely out of our minds is only a recipe for repeating the mistakes we are refusing to learn from.

Pretenders to the crown and fatal flaws

Along with the eternal 'who was the greatest ever' debate, one of the most popular discussions at any chess club – or these days internet message boards – is who deserves the dubious title of 'greatest player never to be world champion'. Throughout chess history we come upon great players who came very close, but who never conquered the chess Olympus. These legends were not lacking in chess skills, and indeed they created many of the game's enduring masterpieces.

When we ask why these great players never quite made it to the top we have to go beyond shrugging our shoulders and blaming it on fate. Each case is different, and while we can never say exactly where to place the blame, each case offers insight into the psychology of failure.

Supporters of the dynamic Russian player Mikhail Chigorin cannot say he did not have his chances. Twice he jousted for the world championship against Wilhelm Steinitz towards the end of the nineteenth century, losing both times. Throughout his career Chigorin fought against the conventional wisdom, sometimes to a fault. He was never able to harness his wild creativity in a practical direction. Proving his point was more important to him than winning, and this lack of competitive pragmatism prevented him from making it to the top.

Chigorin teaches us that we cannot sacrifice results to a blind belief in our methods, no matter how innovative they may be. There is a strong, and not necessarily unhealthy, tendency to respond to a setback by telling ourselves that we didn't follow through enough, that if only we had gone even further in the same direction things would have turned out better. We must rely on our inner observer to look at the results dispassionately, to push ego aside long enough to question our approach. Had Chigorin been able to rein in his fantasy on just a few occasions the world might have had its first Russian champion decades before Alexander Alekhine.

If any chess player can be forgiven for cursing the Fates it would be Akiba Rubinstein. Now, nearly a century after he joined the elite, the quality of his chess is still above reproach. A certain sporting impracticality cost him dearly on more than one occasion. Rubinstein was unwilling or unable to consider the tournament situation as well as the game at hand, losing sight of the big picture and taking unnecessary risks. But his more consequential failings were away from the board, where a championship contender in the early twentieth century needed charisma and a knack for cultivating sponsorship as well as chess skills.

Despite his many tournament successes Rubinstein never succeeded in putting together the money needed to challenge Emanuel Lasker. The posturing and heated public exchanges typical of such negotiations were simply not in the timid Pole's repertoire. José

Raúl Capablanca soon surpassed him as the number one contender, something the bold Cuban was quick to proclaim.

It's facile to say that in a perfect world only chess skills would matter, not fundraising and politicking. The best-qualified candidates would always win the elections and the most elegant software would outsell the rest. This dream world of presumed objectivity ignores the complexity of any competitive environment. The moment we believe we should be entitled to something is exactly when we are ripe to lose it to someone else who is fighting harder for it.

Rubinstein wasn't the only leading player never to even get a shot at the world champion. Paul Keres spent decades as a leading player before and after the Second World War. The Estonian-born Soviet was hindered by political and historical factors both broad and narrow. His best chance to challenge for the title was interrupted by the outbreak of war. Later, the 'good Russian' Mikhail Botvinnik was preferred by the Soviet authorities.

Fate aside, however, Keres had multiple chances to qualify for the world championship and he always came up just short. I hesitate to assign any particular failing to his chess, but I am very sceptical that he would have been a match for Botvinnik under the bright lights of the world championship stage.

David Bronstein did earn a shot at Botvinnik. Their 1951 match ended in a draw, meaning that Botvinnik retained his title as defending champion. (Traditionally the incumbent had 'draw odds', meaning the challenger had to clearly defeat the champion to take the title.) Bronstein liked to tell students that if he hadn't lost the penultimate game of that match they would listen to him with much more respect, 'as if to the Oracle of Delphi!'

The young Bronstein arrived at his match against the living legend Botvinnik already having achieved, for him, a great victory. Having set his sights on reaching the match, he found it impossible to raise them to winning the match itself. Taking pride in our achievements mustn't distract us from our ultimate goals. A marathoner who makes good time over twenty-six miles isn't going to get credit unless he finishes the last 385 yards.

Thomas Szasz, the so-called 'anti-psychiatrist', wrote that 'there is no psychology; there is only biography and autobiography'. We don't live our lives with motivational tricks and ploys; we cannot fool ourselves for long. We must not be relegated to a supporting role in our own lives by refusing to seek out new challenges and by avoiding responsibility. The inner game IS the game. It's not psychology. It is life as it should be lived, an autobiography in progress.

The pretenders to the throne
Mikhail Chigorin, Russia (1850–1908). The father of Russian chess, Chigorin was one of the world's top players until the turn of the century. He twice attempted to take the crown from Wilhelm Steinitz, in matches in 1889 and 1892, but was both times defeated. His play was energetic and creative, but his chess was too inconsistent and his character too undisciplined for the rigours of match play. Chigorin also clashed with Steinitz's dogmatic theories and insisted that chess was too rich to be summed up by concise rules.

Apart from his national and international tournament successes, Chigorin did a great deal to popularize chess in Russia. He founded a club in his native St Petersburg and travelled and wrote extensively in his native land.

Akiba Rubinstein, Poland (1882–1961). Born the youngest of twelve children in a small Polish town that was then part of Russia, Rubinstein was one of the top players in the world for fifteen years. His play seemingly lacked nothing; many of this games stand out today as works of the highest chess art.

Until the international chess federation took control in 1948, matches for the world championship were organized between the champion and the challenger, who inevitably had to come up with considerable funding. Rubinstein was never able to get the backing for a match with Emanuel Lasker despite many years of excellent results. His peak years were interrupted by the First World War. By the time he restarted his career, Rubinstein had several other contenders to deal with, including the great José Raúl Capablanca.

Rubinstein was a fragile and emotional figure, tendencies that developed into serious handicaps later in life. At one stage he would make a move and then stand off in a corner of the room awaiting his opponent's reply.

Paul Keres, USSR (1916–75). 'Paul the Second' was the tragic title acquired by perhaps the greatest name and world figure ever produced by the Baltic state of Estonia. Certainly Keres is the only chess player to adorn his nation's currency – the five krooni note bears his likeness. Another whose peak years were interrupted by a world war, Keres still came very close to qualifying for a title match multiple times, four times in a row finishing second in candidates' events. The one time he did take first place, in the legendary 1938 AVRO tournament in the Netherlands, negotiations for him to face Alexander Alekhine were disrupted by the outbreak of hostilities across Europe.

Estonia has shared the fate of other Baltic nations, to be traded between great powers. Estonia was occupied by the Soviets, then fell to the Nazis. When Estonia returned after the final Soviet takeover in 1944, Keres was disciplined by the Soviet authorities for what they deemed his collusion during the war by playing in German events. He was told not to disrupt Mikhail Botvinnik's attempts to arrange a title match with Alekhine. When the 1948 world championship tournament was arranged after Alekhine died holding the title, Keres was one of the five participants. His terrible results against Botvinnik in the event have led some to believe that he was officially pressured to help make sure Botvinnik won the title.

David Bronstein, USSR (1924–). While Rubinstein and Keres never got a chance to play for the championship, Bronstein came as close to becoming champion as possible. He not only reached a match with Botvinnik in 1951, but played the 'Patriarch' to a draw, five wins each with fourteen draws. A single win from the title, and we might say a single move from it as he lost a critical game late in the match with a careless manoeuvre. Bronstein never again made it to a world championship match.

Bronstein was always a tremendously creative player and he often reached superior positions against Botvinnik in their match. It was his lack of technique that cost him dearly against Botvinnik, although it is possible that psychological factors were just as significant. He later wrote that just reaching a match against the 'god' Botvinnik was such a huge triumph that it was difficult to sustain his drive. When Botvinnik first won the Soviet national championship Bronstein was a boy of seven, and from 1931 to 1951 Botvinnik ruled like a king. It takes rare resolve to face one's childhood hero in a direct confrontation.

Viktor Korchnoi, USSR/Switzerland (1931–). How could a player remain among the elite for thirty years and never become world champion? 'Viktor the Terrible' has led a defiant life. He survived the siege of Leningrad, battled with Soviet authorities until defecting in 1976, and continues to defy age by playing strong professional chess at the age of seventy-five.

Unlike some of the others on this list, Korchnoi had his opportunities. He faced Anatoly Karpov in three consecutive world championship matches, in 1974, 1978, and 1981. (The first became a de facto world championship match retroactively when Bobby Fischer declined to defend his title against Karpov.) He lost the 1978 match by a single game. This match was marked by great tension and many distractions away from the board. The Soviets would do anything to ensure the 'hated defector' did not take the title, and Korchnoi was not one to avoid provocation.

His decades of excellence earn Korchnoi the title of the greatest player never to hold the title of world champion. He was unfortunate, if that is the correct word, to have peaked exactly as the new star Anatoly Karpov took centre stage.

On Chigorin: 'A genius of practical play, he considers it his privilege at every convenient opportunity to challenge the principles of contemporary chess theory.' – Wilhelm Steinitz

Rubinstein in his own words: 'Sixty days a year I play in tournaments, five days I rest, and 300 days I work on my game.'

Bronstein in his own words: 'It is my style to take my opponent and myself on to unknown grounds. A game of chess is not an examination of knowledge; it is a battle of nerves.'

Korchnoi in his own words: 'I don't study; I create.'

16

MAN, WOMAN, MACHINE

'The well-bred contradict other people. The wise
contradict themselves.' – *Oscar Wilde*

Contradicting ourselves

As with most platitudes, 'opposites attract' is dragged out for the
few cases where it seems to be true and left on the shelf the rest of
the time. Attraction usually comes from likes and affinities. Apart
from the diehard depressives among us, we have to like ourselves
to survive, and when we like ourselves we tend to like our
characteristics in others as well. A shy man could surely benefit
from dating an outgoing woman, but we tend to end up with
partners with whom we have much in common. Maybe it's just
that the phrase 'likes attract' sounds redundant.

This isn't only in romantic life. Friends and associates will
seek out people with similar outlooks, and it's the rare boss who
doesn't surround himself with people who think the way he does.
It's that rare leader, however, the boss who instead brings in
people who think differently and who will challenge him, who has
the potential for greater success.

Such people are exceptional because no one enjoys being
contradicted or corrected. It takes great willpower and self-
confidence to willingly surround ourselves with people we know
will confront us. If not handled correctly it can lead to loss of
authority, or to an anarchy of mixed messages. We must trust our
ability to use the opposition to make ourselves stronger and our
information more complete. The dread of being challenged is
closely related to the childish fear of simply being wrong. Both
fears can be crippling to our development and success.

Ralph Waldo Emerson wrote, 'Let me never fall into the
vulgar mistake of dreaming that I am persecuted whenever I am
contradicted.' Like a monopolistic corporation grown inefficient
and sluggish after years of an absence of competition, we become

over-confident and oblivious if we aren't fed a steady diet of new challenges, contrarian attitudes and information.

When someone agrees with us and supports our point of view it feeds our confidence, not a bad thing. No one could survive being battered every day, definitely not just for the sake of building character. This is yet another of the balances, the blends, the syntheses that are so critical for achieving at our highest level. That we learn more from our defeats than from our victories doesn't mean we would be well served by losing all the time.

Feudal and caste systems might be dying out in most places but they are alive and well in the chess world. National and international federations have classes and categories based on rating that allow players to compete for prizes against opponents of a similar level. First category players aren't allowed to participate in the second category competition, any more than a twenty-year-old could play in the under-twelve championship. Of course there are no restrictions in the opposite direction. An ambitious novice is free to get killed in the 'open' section where the highest-rated players are. No one could complain that it was unfair when I won the Soviet national under-eighteen tournament at the age of twelve.

If it is challenges that help us improve, why then – apart from prize money –shouldn't everyone want to play in the open section of the tournament? Would we not learn more from nine losses to very strong opponents than from six wins and three losses against players roughly our own level? This question has become relevant even with players who never attend tournaments, thanks to chess software. A PC program at its maximum strength will wipe out any casual player without mercy. Ironically, the main task of chess software companies today is to find ways to make the program weaker, not stronger. The user can pick from different levels and the machine will try to make enough mistakes to give you a chance. So how much of a chance should be asked for?

Finding the correct balance between confidence and correction is up to each person. 'Lose as often as you can take it' is a good rule of thumb. Playing in the open section and scoring 0/9 every time is going to crush our spirit long before we get good enough to make a decent score. Unless we have a superhuman level of ego, or a total lack of one, a constant stream of negativity will leave us too depressed and antagonized to be able to make the necessary changes.

As much as we enjoy winning, and winning every time out would obviously be ideal, it is important to realize that setbacks are both inevitable and required if we are to make progress. The art is in avoiding catastrophic losses in the key battles. This awareness is even more important in the real world because, if well insulated by our supporters, we can be right virtually all the time. It's not only dictators and pharaohs who are always right. Politicians and CEOs naturally tend to both attract and acquire the like-minded. They gain energy by talking with their avid supporters, while critics are accused of not being supportive. When things go wrong the blame can simply be assigned to others. It is dangerously easy to go from succeeding because we are often correct to being told we are correct because of who we are.

The difference between better and different

If we can learn to accept criticism and acknowledge contrary information we can also learn to incorporate new methods. Much of our discussion has focused on how we all have unique ways of solving problems. Our method is a product of our experience and is enhanced by consciously taking note of what works and what does not. We can hold ourselves back if we adhere too strongly to our own methods at the expense of different, yet equally valid, ways of doing things. If we learn to see the value in other methods we can take what we need from them to improve – not replace – our own.

In May 2005 I was in Bogotá, Colombia, to give a speech at a conference on business strategy. Renowned business consultant and writer Tom Peters, a popular guest at such events, spoke the day before I did. Backed by several PowerPoint diagrams, Peters told a humorous anecdote about the difference between men and women when they go shopping for trousers. The first illustration was the layout of a shop with the route a man would take. A few lines showed the man entering, going to where the trousers were located, going to the cash register, then leaving.

The next slide showed the 'woman's route' in the same shop. It depicted a spider web of lines, showing the woman going to every part of the store and eventually buying a dozen different items. I won't address the correctness – political or otherwise – of the gender stereotype on display; what interested me was how one method, the man's, was presented as clearly superior.

To stretch Peters's anecdote well beyond its intended point, I wondered what happened after the shoppers had left the store. When I spoke to the same audience the next day, I joked that perhaps the man had left the shop, gone directly to the local pub with friends and gambled the rest of his money on the day's football games, while at least the woman had spent the money on useful things. Humour aside, there are also genuine questions to be asked here. Is the 'man's method' as described actually superior? Perhaps the woman saved time buying all those other things on one trip instead of single-mindedly buying one item and having to return later. Or, instead of trying to get the task over with as quickly as possible, maybe she shopped around to get the trousers at a better price.

Pandering only a little to the many businesswomen in attendance, I asked the Bogotá audience whether Peters's story might be an illustration of the woman seeing the bigger picture. Instead of being narrowly focused on one thing, buying trousers, she treated the task as only one part of her day. In the twentieth century, four nations selected female leaders at moments of crisis and transition: Margaret Thatcher in the UK, Golda Meir in Israel, Indira Gandhi in India, and Corazon Aquino in the Philippines. All led their countries through times of turbulence and reform, times when creativity and adaptability were essential. The 'male' system of stringent and linear thinking described by Mr Peters is not always best, any more than any one particular method of behaviour can always be the best.

In the twenty-first century, talking about a female style is rapidly becoming as obsolete as the novelty of female leaders. There are no hard and fast rules about styles of problem-solving, any more than there are rules about gender. Germany, in urgent need of reform, just elected its first female chancellor, Angela Merkel, who is best known for her straightforwardness and pragmatism. And let us not forget that it was once said about Margaret Thatcher that she was 'the only real man in the cabinet'!

Creating a universal style

In chess we often talk about being a complete player, or having a universal style. This doesn't mean being perfectly balanced, equally competent at every aspect of the game. As we have seen, every player has strengths and weaknesses, relatively speaking. Instead it refers to the ability to detect and apply the method appropriate to the position, to know when it is right to attack and when it is necessary to defend.

Having a universal style makes it very hard for our opponents to employ any psychological tricks against us based on our preferences. If a player has a reputation as an attacker he may avoid an objectively superior continuation to get the sort of position in which he is more comfortable, a tendency that can be exploited. A player who is comfortable in any chess terrain is able to be more objective and is therefore less predictable.

I of course always enjoyed wild, complex positions and my long-time coach Alexander Nikitin fought to keep me from trying to complicate games at every opportunity. During my early teens he would tell me, 'Garry, you have to learn how to excel in the simple positions. If you play them confidently your opponents will try to complicate things and they will fall right into your favourite territory.' By not forcing play into my preferred positions I set a trap for my opponents and at the same time strengthened the weaker areas of my game.

The list of chess players who reached the elite with play spanning just one or two dimensions is surprisingly long and includes many of the most entertaining players in the game's history. Mastery of one or two phases of the game can be enough to excel, although it is rarely sufficient to reach the very top. Austria's Rudolf Spielmann was a throwback to the romantic age of chess. He was called 'the last knight of the King's Gambit' for his devotion to that most romantic opening of a bygone era of wild sacrifices. Spielmann was a tremendous attacker whose greatest successes came between the world wars and on his best day could beat anyone in the world – but only on his best day. In an insightful observation he once lamented that he could play attacking combinations as well as the then world champion Alexander Alekhine, but he couldn't reach the same positions Alekhine did in order to play them. That's the catch. Being great at applying the finishing touches isn't good enough if we have nothing to finish.

Even in the modern game, where balance and flexibility are paramount, there is ample room for style. Players like Alexei Shirov and Judit Polgár made it into the top ten primarily by virtue of their excellence in conducting direct attacks. No one rises so high without being strong in every phase of the game, but their preferences at the board are always readily apparent.

Polgár in particular has gained fame for her sparkling attacking chess. If, based on Polgár's games, to 'play like a girl' meant anything in chess – a sport with very few women among its practitioners – it would mean relentless aggression. (Polgár is the only woman among the top 300 players on the rating list, largely reflecting the tiny, if growing, fraction of women in competitive chess.) Such skill at handling the initiative can come at a cost if it is gained at the expense of not being comfortable playing without the initiative. Polgár rarely errs in attack, but her losses show that she will go to great lengths, including making poor choices, to avoid going on the defensive. When preference overrides objectivity to too great a degree, our growth is inhibited.

Of course Polgár's games and style receive even more attention because she is the only woman among the elite, the only woman ever to reach the top ten. If you think this is noteworthy now, imagine how it was when she first came on the international scene at the age of ten. At twelve she was winning open international tournaments and in 1991 she broke Bobby Fischer's thirty-year-old record to become the youngest Grandmaster ever at the age of fifteen.

(That record has since become a popular target and, thanks to the proliferation of the once-rare GM title, has been broken many times. It is now held by Ukraine's Sergey Karjakin, who in 2002 became a GM at twelve years, seven months. Veteran GM Walter Browne, six-time US champion, likes to joke that when he was awarded his Grandmaster title by the annual FIDE Congress in 1970 in accordance with regulations, 'only two of us got the title that time, and they weren't too sure about the other guy. The other guy was Karpov!' Nowadays dozens of players receive the title each year, though few ever reach the top 100.)

Is greatness born or bred?

Judit Polgár's rise to the world elite is only one part of a remarkable story. She also has two chess-playing older sisters, Susan and Sofia. Susan, the eldest, was the first woman to participate regularly in strong 'men's' tournaments, and was one of the first women to receive the 'men's' Grandmaster title. After her youngest sister she is currently the second highest-rated woman in the world. Middle sister Sofia was also a strong international player for many years. At the age of fourteen in Rome she scored one of the most astonishing tournament results on record, battering a field of Grandmasters. Their father László gave his three daughters an experimental home education to prove his theory that 'geniuses can be created'. It focused on chess, and it's hard to argue with the results.

The issue of nature versus nurture has always been a hot topic in chess. I suppose that since the three Polgár sisters share many of the same genes they don't resolve the debate either way, but their upbringing and development certainly make a good case for 'nurture'. For most of the game's history the few women who played chess competently were regarded as curiosities. Enclaves like the former Soviet republic of Georgia, where women's chess was a tradition, produced some very strong players. Two of the first women to make inroads into the international chess world in the 60s and 70s were both Georgian: Nona Gaprindashvili and Maya Chiburdanidze. But they mostly concentrated their efforts on women-only events, especially in the critical early years of their development, which sheltered them and limited their growth.

The Polgárs changed all that. Susan was pushed out into the rough-and-tumble world of international tournament chess as a teenager. With a few exceptions for official events like the women's Chess Olympiad – where the sisters twice composed the first three boards of the winning Hungarian team – they shunned women-only events and sought out the toughest competition. Susan, who now lives in New York, came equal second in the 1986 'men's' Hungarian championship, an event later won outright by Judit. After winning the national championship in 1991 at the age of fifteen, Judit said she would only consider playing on the 'men's' Chess Olympiad team. What could the Hungarian federation say? Thanks to the Polgárs the adjective 'men's' before events and the 'affirmative action' women's titles such as 'Woman Grandmaster' have become anachronisms, though they are still in use. Judit once remarked that another change she and her sisters inspired is that now men can no longer make use of the women's bathroom at tournaments.

The rapid rise of the Polgárs dispelled most of the remaining myths about women chess players. Whether by temperament or upbringing, few women are attracted to serious chess at any level, but the Polgárs showed that there was no built-in limitation to their aptitude – an idea that many enjoyed postulating right up to the point at which they had to fear being crushed by a twelve-year-old with a ponytail. Perhaps the last myth was laid to rest only in 2005, when Judit returned to chess after taking a year off to have a child. Her first tournament after her return was a tough one, the Corus supertournament in the Netherlands, and she finished with a positive score and gained rating points. On the October 2005 rating list Judit Polgár, at twenty-nine, was ranked number eight in the world, just four points behind Vladimir Kramnik. However, due largely to her lack of universality of style, it is highly unlikely that Polgár has in her another surge that could take her to the world championship title.

It would be hasty to say that the success of any one individual, no matter how impressive, has entirely dispelled the many interesting questions about gender and chess success. Men and women go about solving problems in very different ways from an amazingly early age. With so many obvious biological differences between the sexes it is impossible to say confidently that the disparity in various endeavours, chess included, is due only to upbringing and tradition.

I admit I haven't always handled the issue sensitively on the many occasions when I've been asked by journalists why there are so few strong female chess players. But while I wish I had sometimes phrased things more delicately, my opinions on the matter haven't changed. Be it due to physiology, psychology, or education, the plain truth is that very few women seem to possess the single-minded fighting impulses that are required to become a top chess player. Indeed, these urges are required in order to be seriously attracted to the sport in the first place. That said, I concede that it may well be argued that they have found more practical uses for their energies!

Enter the machines

Of all the opposites that do attract, few have received as much attention as the 'man versus machine' debate. My six-game matches against the IBM supercomputer Deep Blue in 1996 and 1997 received unprecedented attention around the world. The official website of the 1997 rematch received traffic that was similar in scale to that of the website of the Atlanta Olympic Games, an event that lasted three times longer. *Time* and *Newsweek* ran cover stories and a thousand subplots were developed. Was Deep Blue really artificial intelligence? Was I the defender of humanity? What were the implications of my win in 1996 in Philadelphia, of my loss in 1997 in New York, and of IBM's refusal to play a third, deciding match?

Being human, I was unable to ignore all of these distractions, something my silicon opponent did not have to worry about. Worse than the loss of the final decisive game in 1997 was IBM's blow to the scientific and chess communities by deciding to immediately shut down the Deep Blue project. For half a century chess had been considered a unique field for the comparison of the human and machine minds, of intuition versus calculation. To this day the six games I played with the multi-million-dollar machine are the only ones ever made public. It was as if they had gone to the moon and not taken pictures.

The tragedy of IBM's hurried dismantling of Deep Blue overshadowed disappointingly questionable behaviour on their part during the match. IBM was not only my opponent at the board in the 1997 rematch, but also the organizer of the event. There was so much antagonism, and so many unanswered questions about what was going on behind the scenes, that it was easy to wonder just how far they would go to win.

Before I am accused of being a sore loser I will plead guilty to the charge. I hate losing, especially when I don't understand the reason for the loss. When we analyse those six games today we find that for the most part Deep Blue was not superior to today's programs. Only in a few key moments did the IBM computer play uncharacteristically subtle moves, moves that even today make one question how they emerged from the same machine that lost game 1.

The closed nature of the contest created the potential for human interference, although in the pre-Enron era it sounded like paranoid folly to suggest that a corporate giant might resort to subterfuge to gain billions in free publicity and a huge surge in its stock price. Despite these remaining sour feelings, I was amazed at the enormous appeal the match clearly had for the general public. I knew I wanted to continue the adventure, although in the future the environment would need to be much more open and scientific.

If you can't beat 'em, join 'em

My enthusiasm for finding new ways to use computer technology to promote the game of chess did not disappear when IBM betrayed the great experiment and pulled the plug on Deep Blue. As mentioned above, in 1998 I turned to a new experiment, humans fighting together with machines instead of against them.

Grandmasters play chess by combining experience with intuition backed up with calculation and study. Computers play chess by brute calculation with study simulated by access to a gigantic database of opening moves. At present there is a rough equilibrium between these methods; the best computers play at around the same strength as the best humans. As microprocessors have got faster, so humans have learned new tricks to expose the weaknesses of computer play. Inevitably the machines must win, but there is still a long way to go before a human on his (or her) best day is unable to defeat the best computer.

The concept of Advanced Chess, which I briefly mentioned in Chapter 5, is an effective illustration of the costs and benefits of human + computer collaboration. What would a combination of human intuition and computer calculation produce on the chessboard? Would they combine into an invincible centaur or an uncoordinated Frankenstein's monster? In Advanced Chess, two Grandmasters with powerful computers at their sides faced off across the board. In June 1998 the first such match was played when I took on Veselin Topalov in Spain.

Although I had done some preparation for the format, our six-game match was full of strange sensations. We all use computer programs in our analysis and training, so we know what they are capable of and what weaknesses they have. But having one available during play was both exciting and disturbing. First off, being able to access a database of a few million games meant not having to strain our memories nearly as much in the opening. But since we both had equal access to the same database, the advantage still came down to creating a new move at some point, and making sure it was better than what had been played before.

In the middlegame, having a computer engine running meant never having to worry about making a tactical blunder. With that taken care of, we could concentrate more on deep planning instead of on the precise calculations that take up so much of our time in regular games. Again, since we were both using computer engines it was a matter of how well we used them to check our plans and whose plan was more effective. As when I played against Deep Blue, there would be no way back if I made an error. The machine would not forgive any mistakes by making one of its own in return.

It was difficult to find the best way to utilize the machine's abilities. For me it was a race to check the validity of the computer's evaluation. It gives its opinion instantly, but its recommendation changes as its analysis goes deeper and deeper. Like a Formula 1 driver knowing his own car, you have to learn the way the program works. There is a strong impulse to follow the machine's evaluation automatically if it looks like something the computer would usually play well, a dangerous habit. If it goes against conventional wisdom I would find myself more ready to contradict it.

This metaphor extends into everything we do, now that almost all our daily activities require the use of increasingly sophisticated tools. Most of us learn just enough about the devices we use to get by, only reading an instruction manual or asking a question when we encounter difficulties. Typically this makes us very inefficient. How often do we say, 'There's probably a better way to do this,' and continue to do it the old way?

Despite the human + machine formula, my games with Topalov were far from perfect, mostly due to the rapid time control that towards the end left us with no time on our clocks to consult the machines for more than a few seconds. Putting that flaw aside, the games were very interesting and the experiment continued in León in later years with other players. The result was also notable. Just a month earlier I had defeated the Bulgarian 4–0 in a match of regular rapid chess. Our Advanced Chess match finished in a 3–3 draw.

An added benefit of the format is that the computer created a log of every variation the players examined during play. This left a diary of the players' thoughts during the game, quite fascinating for spectators and valuable as a training tool. Normally it is forbidden to take any notes during a game, but in Advanced Chess there was a complete map of the path the game took through the players' minds.

In 2005 the ethos of Advanced Chess found its true home on the internet. The online play site Playchess.com hosted what it called a 'freestyle' chess tournament. Players could compete in teams with other players, computers, anything they liked. Lured by the substantial prize money, groups of strong Grandmasters working with several computers at the same time entered the competition.

At first, the results seemed predictable. Human plus machine was totally dominant against even the strongest computers. The mighty chess machine Hydra, hardware-based like Deep Blue, was no match for a strong human using a relatively weak laptop. Human strategic guidance combined with the tactical acuity of a computer was invincible.

The surprise came at the conclusion of the event, when the winner was revealed to be a pair of amateur American chess players using three computers at the same time. Their skill at manipulating and 'coaching' their computers to look very deeply into positions effectively counteracted the superior understanding of their Grandmaster opponents. Weak human + machine + superior process was greater than a strong computer and, remarkably, greater than a strong human + machine with an inferior process.

The 'freestyle' winners took advantage of superior co-ordination of contrasting methods. They understood their tools and how to best get the most from them. A manager might say they built an effective team from a group of individuals with disparate skill sets. An army commander would recognize that a well-coordinated force will triumph over a numerically superior enemy lacking organization.

Staying out of the comfort zone

Opposite pairs working in harmony have often come up in our quest to perfect our decision-making process. Calculation and evaluation. Patience and opportunism, intuition and analysis, style and objectivity. At the next level we find management and vision, strategy and tactics, planning and reaction. Instead of one versus the other we must balance them to pull in harness together.

The only consistent method for achieving such a balance is to constantly seek to avoid our comfort zone. Negative imbalances and bad habits develop when we become over-reliant on one area, usually because it has worked well. We stick with what we know best instead of looking for better ways. The one way to be sure we are learning something is when we are nervously attempting something new, even if it is solving a routine problem in a new way. If you want an illustration of how deeply we are set in our routines, try brushing your teeth left-handed, or putting on your trousers left leg first. Our mental routines are no less ingrained and have more profound consequences.

Engaging the weakest points in our game is also the best and fastest way to improve. Working to become a universal player doesn't always have an obvious immediate benefit, especially if we are in a very specialized field. But in my experience it is very much an 'all boats rise' situation. Gaining experience in one area improves our overall abilities in unexpected, often inexplicable ways.

I was lucky in that I was virtually forced by Anatoly Karpov to become a more positional, strategic player. It was sink or swim for me: either I broadened my style and my understanding or I wouldn't be able to beat him. The situation is not so clear for most people. We can go through our day-to-day lives without changing our habits and nothing terrible will happen to us. The problem is that it is also very unlikely anything at all will happen to us. Successfully avoiding challenges is not an accomplishment to be proud of.

When I was in the fifth grade the greatest mystery that school held for me was drawing. To me it seemed like an occult science; I just couldn't draw and still cannot today. Instead of working at it as I did my other subjects I – cleverly I thought – convinced my mother to do my drawing homework. She was quite good at it in fact, good enough to catch the attention of my teacher with a fine picture of a bird in a tree that I could no sooner have drawn myself than I could have painted the *Mona Lisa*. My teacher asked me if I would be interested in entering a drawing competition, a competition at which I would have to perform in front of judges, not at home. If you think this is the end of the story you haven't realized how proud and competitive I was even then.

Instead of confessing, I spent the next few weeks at home training myself to draw the picture of the bird exactly as my mother had. I spent hours on it, reproducing it line by line as if memorizing a chemical formula. This was no substitute for being able to draw, but eventually I could manage a quite reasonable facsimile. Sweating nervously, at the competition I produced a bird almost identical to my mother's original. I don't doubt that that bird was the only thing I could draw in the world.

Of course now I wish I had done my drawing homework myself and actually learned to appreciate the skills it requires. It has long been fashionable to talk about left-brain and right-brain activities, even left-brain and right-brain people. It doesn't require a discussion of biology to see that indulging our creative side and letting our minds wander in artistic pursuits can be very helpful in breaking us out of our problem-solving routines.

The great physicist Richard Feynman is a perfect example of a brilliant man who refused to be boxed in by his own achievements. When Robert Oppenheimer was in charge of the Manhattan Project, which produced the atomic bomb, he described Feynman as 'the most brilliant young physicist here'. He was also the greatest troublemaker. He saw everything as a challenge, as a puzzle to be solved. Feynman enjoyed picking the locks in the top-secret offices of Los Alamos just to see if he could. He became a serious amateur painter and musician and loved to perform as a drummer at Brazilian carnival celebrations.

There can be no doubt that Feynman's free spirit and playful mind were assets to his scientific work, not detriments. In his popular books he insisted that science was a living subject, not just a cold set of formulae. He excelled in combining techniques and transforming a difficult problem into a comparable one that was easier to solve. This skill was directly related to how he stayed open to new ideas in every aspect of his life.

Today great emphasis is placed on specialization and focus. Students used to go off to university with the idea of broadening themselves; now it has become a mostly vocational experience. We place so much stress on being good at what we do that we fail to realize that getting better at what we do might be best achieved by getting better at other things.

It sounds strange to say that being a better artist might make me a stronger chess player or that listening to classical music can make you a more effective manager. And yet this is exactly the sort of thing that Feynman had in mind when he said that being a drummer made him a better physicist. When we regularly challenge ourselves with something new we build cognitive and emotional 'muscles' that make us more effective in every way. If we can overcome our fear of speaking in public, or of submitting a poem to a magazine, or of learning a new language, that confidence will flow into every area of our lives. We can't become so caught up in 'what we do' that we stop being curious human beings. Our greatest strength is the ability to absorb and synthesize patterns, methods and information. Intentionally inhibiting that ability by focusing too narrowly is not only a crime, but one with few rewards.

Computer chess

As soon as man invents a machine it seems the next step is to turn his creation into a chess player. Throughout the history of mechanical and digital computing, chess has been near the forefront. That so many legendary minds were also chess players – if not always good ones – is without question one reason for this. Another is that chess has always maintained a position as, in Goethe's words, 'a touchstone of the intellect'. Just about everyone who created a 'thinking machine' was quick to put it to the test of mastering the world's most respected game.

This impression of chess as the height of human intellect hasn't been limited to technologists. It has also been widely held as such by the general public, which led to the fame of the first chess-playing automaton, 'The Turk'. In 1769 the Hungarian engineer Baron Wolfgang von Kempelen built a chess-playing machine for the amusement of the Habsburg Empress Maria Theresa. It was a purely mechanical device beneath a majestic mannequin dressed as a Turk. Naturally its outstanding playing strength was in fact supplied by a chess master cleverly secreted inside the device. The machine was a fake.

The main problem of chess programming is the very large number of continuations involved. In an average position there are about forty legal moves. So if you consider every reply to each move you have 1,600 positions. This is after two ply (half-moves, one white and one black), one move in chess. After two moves there are 2.5 million positions, after three moves 4.1 billion. The average game lasts forty moves, leading to numbers that are beyond astronomical.

Remarkably, the first computer program was written before computers to run it existed. Its creator was the British mathematician Alan Turing, widely considered the father of modern computer science and the man who led the group that broke the German 'Enigma' code during the Second World War. He developed a series of instructions for automated chess play, but since there was as yet no machine to execute this first-ever chess code, he did it himself, on paper. Around this time, in the US, another great mathematical mind, Claude Shannon, outlined several strategies computers could use to play chess.

In 1950 the nuclear laboratory of Los Alamos was the unlikely site of the next advance in chess computing. When the gigantic machine 'MANIAC 1' was delivered, the scientists tested it out by writing a chess program. After playing against itself and then losing to a strong player (despite being given an extra queen), the machine beat a young woman who had just learned the game. It was the first time a human had lost to a computer in a game of intellectual skill.

The next advances came in smarter programming, teaching the computer how to avoid wasting time looking at inferior move options. The mathematical 'alpha-beta' chess algorithm was developed, allowing the program to rapidly prune out weak moves and so see further ahead. This is a brute force method in which the program stops focusing on any move that returns a lower score than the currently selected move. All programs are based on this search method, around which programmers build the chess evaluation function. The first programs using this method, running on some of the fastest computers of the day, reached a respectable playing strength. By the 1970s, early personal computers could defeat most amateurs.

The next leap came from out of the famous Bell Laboratories. Ken Thompson, creator of the Unix operating system, built a special purpose chess machine with hundreds of chips. His machine 'Belle' was able to search about 180,000 positions per second while super-computers could only manage 5,000. Seeing up to nine moves ahead during a game, Belle could play at the level of a human master and far better than any other chess machine. It won just about every computer chess event from 1980–83, before it was finally surpassed by giant Cray supercomputers.

Consumer chess programs with names like Sargon, ChessMaster and Fritz continued to improve while benefiting from the rapid increase in processor speeds provided by Intel. Dedicated machines made a comeback thanks to a generation of chess machines designed at Carnegie-Mellon University. Professor Hans Berliner was a computer scientist as well as a world champion at correspondence chess (played by mail). His machine HiTech was later surpassed by the creations of his graduate students Murray Campbell and Feng-Hsuing Hsu. They took their computer champion 'Deep Thought' and joined IBM, where their project was re-christened 'Deep Blue'.

The Deep Blue machine I faced in matches in 1996 and 1997 consisted of an IBM SP/2 server equipped with a large number of special chess chips. This combination was capable of searching 200 million positions per second. As with all modern chess machines, Deep Blue also had access to a vast database of preprogrammed opening positions culled from human Grandmaster play. Containing millions of positions, these opening databases imitate and of course surpass human knowledge and memory of the openings. Often a program will play well over a dozen moves before it begins to compute for the first time. Without the benefit of this human knowledge in the openings the programs would be considerably weaker.

There are also databases that operate only at the end of the game. These 'endgame tablebases', another creation of Ken Thompson, record every possible position with six or fewer pieces. (Some sets with seven now exist.) With many hundreds of gigabytes of storage, they allow machines to play these positions flawlessly. With the aid of these oracles we have discovered positions that require over 200 accurate moves to force a win, a level of complexity previously undreamt of – and still impossible for any human to master.

Fortunately, the two ends – opening research and endgame databases – will not meet. It is highly unlikely that anyone will ever see a computer play its first move 1.e4 and announce checkmate in 33,520 moves.

'Chess is thirty to forty percent psychology. You don't have this when you play a computer. I can't confuse it.' – Judit Polgár

'When the two opinions collide over the board, the ingenuity of one supremely talented individual will be pitted against the work of generations of mathematicians, computer scientists and engineers. We believe the result will not reveal whether machines can think but rather whether collective human effort can outshine the best achievements of the ablest human beings.' – From a statement by Feng-Hsiung Hsu and the other members of the Deep Thought/Deep Blue team

'The Brain's Last Stand' – Title of Newsweek cover article on the 1997 Kasparov–Deep Blue match.

17

THE BIG PICTURE

We have to see the whole board

There are contrary schools of opinion as to whether it is God or the Devil we find in the proverbial details. The young Albert Einstein indicated his great ambition when he said he wanted to skip mere details and know 'God's thoughts'. The broader our knowledge, the broader the potential scope of our understanding. We begin to see connections that weren't previously visible and everything else comes into sharper focus. Pushing these boundaries is more than a self-improvement exercise. Imagine looking at only a four-square corner of the sixty-four-square chessboard and trying to understand what is happening in the game. To succeed, to even know how to define success, we have to look at the whole board.

Just about everyone has made use of a 'to-do' list at least once. Many people use them constantly and might find it hard to imagine functioning without them. These are typically short lists of basic tasks or reminders for things that might otherwise be forgotten. A new one can be produced every day, with satisfying lines drawn through each item as it is completed, like a shopping list taken to a supermarket. At work they are for clean-cut chores and tasks. A manager's list might include phone calls to make and papers to sign. A higher-level executive might have a list of decisions that need to be made within a specific time frame.

Big things rarely get put on lists. Nobody writes 'evaluate our strategy' on a to-do list. Far-reaching decisions or things that will take an indefinite amount of time are not put on to-do lists. We won't see a reminder to consider the long term implications of our decisions or a Post-it note that says 'examine broader repercussions' attached to a project proposal.

The usual tendency is to plan for a while and then move on

to the implementation phase as if they were entirely disconnected. Even assuming that there is a good level of strategic planning and long-term assessment, this is often switched off as soon as the first steps are taken. This makes it very easy to slide off course. All the care that went into the construction of the *Titanic* didn't help when she was out at sea.

Making the connections

Seeing the big picture means much more than simply acquiring more information. We must see how the information is connected as well as how our own actions are connected. Today it is more important than ever to improve the efficiency of our decision-making. We are inundated with more and more information, the supply of which has increased faster than our ability to absorb it. Teenagers intuitively click through thousands of pages and channels faster than the eye can follow. Selective data surfing is their native tongue and it is quickly becoming the essential lingua franca. The rest of us have to learn it like any new language and this requires dedication.

To drive on a motorway it is enough to be a good driver, but when you come to a crossroads you need directions – and direction. It's fine to be a detail-oriented manager most of the time, but at some point during the day we need to step back from the details and the day-to-day and look both wider and deeper. This is necessary to keep our strategy on course and to notice the icebergs in our path before it's too late. We can't be so intent on developing a laser-like focus that we don't know whether or not we are focusing on the right things. The little things can be going right while at the same time the big things are going wrong.

Having too narrow a view also makes it difficult to diagnose problems correctly even if we discern that something is wrong. There are so many interconnections in almost everything we do that it requires both a wide view and sharp vision to be a successful problem solver. Too often when something goes wrong we rush in to fix that one thing without considering whether or not it is just a small part of a larger problem.

Consider it like a zoom lens on a camera. We need to combine wide-angle with a macro focus and use them both, in and out. There is no one perfect distance or one ideal perspective; we have to stay on the move. Seeing the big picture isn't sitting at a desk far behind the front lines looking at a map. We have to be at the front lines and looking at satellite imagery at the same time. Just as our evaluations must encompass material, time and quality, our range of views has to be able to answer everything from the 'What?' to the 'Why?' all the way down to the 'How?'

It is now routine to talk about the increasing level of inter-connectedness and globalization today, particularly in economics and business. Our computers contain parts made in a dozen countries, and a crop blight in Florida affects citrus prices far from where Florida oranges are sold. The Ford Motor Company recently had to delay the US launch of a major new car line because of trouble at a factory in Mexico.

The pros and cons of specialization

With the increasing role of technology in every endeavour from medicine to banking and investing, there is more and more dependence on tight focus and detail. The guiding theory of this method is that one key detail, one tiny piece of information, can inform and guide us regarding larger issues.

One of the oldest and most clichéd business metaphors is taken from the old fable about the six blind men all touching different parts of an elephant. One touches the tusk and says the elephant is like a spear, the man touching the trunk says it's like a snake, et cetera. This is trotted out to show how we must have a view of the big picture to really understand anything. But this ancient fable is obsolete. After all, nowadays we can perform a DNA test and know the animal is an elephant from just a few cells.

With so much data there is a trend to attribute a great deal of meaning to information simply because it exists. Micro-analysis can undoubtedly produce positive results, although they tend to be only incremental. One problem is that this trend is increasingly making its way into boardrooms and CEOs' offices. The increasing use of tight focus can lead to the loss of visionaries, of true leaders. The mathematician-philosopher Alfred North Whitehead, a collaborator of Bertrand Russell, warned about the danger of increasing attention to detail at the cost of losing coordination between specialties. In a series of lectures at Harvard in 1925, Whitehead spoke about the risk of the new educational professionalism. Let me quote his far-seeing prediction: 'The dangers arising from this aspect of professionalism are great, particularly in our democratic societies. The directive force of reason is weakened. The leading intellects lack balance. They see this set of circumstances, or that set; but not both sets together. The task of coordination is left to those who lack either the force or the character to succeed in some definite career.'

Whitehead's words could be considered a direct verdict on the worst of today's politicians and CEOs, saying that when our best minds become specialists, the job of coordination will be left to weaker people. And yet in the eighty years since this warning this is what we have seen happen. Where are the great minds who become our great leaders? Leadership is not a specialty, it is synthesis and coordination. But today we depend on a hundred different specialists creating and absorbing a huge flow of data.

An over-reliance on data quantity also makes us vulnerable to the prejudices that come with every fact. We must be as aware of the sources of all this information as well as the potential outcomes. The same event reported by Fox News is likely to sound quite different when reported by CNN. But because we know so much data is available we want to wait and collect more, attempting to attain a perfection, and an objectivity, that is unreachable. We have all these wonderful new tools to collect and analyse information but these tools cannot make decisions for us. The means are not the solution, and in fact they can be a distraction that interferes with our ability to see the broader patterns and to develop our intuition.

Global thinking and global war

Current events provide us with useful case studies for big picture thinking. If the web of the global economy is taken as a given, one might think the global impact of political decisions would be blatantly obvious. When the United States invaded Iraq in 2003 the consequences were soon felt around the globe, apparently surprising many politicians. Had the US moved to pre-emptively warn and work with the local governments of countries with substantial Muslim populations? Only well into the Iraq campaign did the US attempt to evade this iceberg of international outrage.

Any shift in the status quo causes ripples, and the bigger the rock thrown into the pond, the bigger those ripples will be. With instant television and internet access the pond is now the size of the planet and the Iraq invasion was a massive rock. Some consideration had been given to angry responses in the immediate region, but what about Indonesia, the largest Muslim nation in the world? Its geographical distance from the Persian Gulf did nothing to prevent huge protests and outbreaks of violence and terror.

Attempts to address one part of a problem without treating it holistically can actually make things worse. A key strand in the war on terror web is the fact that the Islamic terrorists are largely funded by oil money. We could make a strong case that while not all oil money goes to terror, almost all terror money comes from oil. Around the globe, authoritarian governments are propped up by income that is derived from the world's dependence on oil. Calls for energy independence rarely illustrate this connection; it would offend too many important friends in energy companies and in oil-producing nations. The world can't stop using oil overnight, but there are tragic levels of hypocrisy and futility in attempting to bring democracy to places where Western consumers are themselves funding the anti-democratic forces.

Once we accept this, cutting our dependence on oil becomes crucial not only for financial and environmental security, but for physical security. Lenin and Trotsky launched the Comintern, the Communist International, in 1919. Today we see an 'Oilintern' and 'Gasintern' that are proving to be just as menacing. Iran, Saudi Arabia, Sudan, Venezuela, Algeria . . . and, sadly for me, Russia.

It is said of guerrilla war that if you aren't winning, you are losing. There is no happy status quo. This war against terrorists has become one of attrition, and our enemies now possess almost unlimited resources. Deprived of oil-based revenue, the terrorist networks would be starved. Tiny, remote Iceland is not exactly on the front line of the so-called 'war on terror', but it may provide one of the best examples of how to fight the long-term strategic war. Iceland recently announced that the entire country will be oil-free by 2050. Sweden followed with a similar announcement this year, planning to almost completely eliminate oil usage by 2020. Now imagine the United States Congress approving a request from the President to make such a programme a national priority for the US. Such announcements, backed by political will and financial commitment, would create more concern among the terrorists and their backers than all the American troops in the world.

Even in best-case scenarios, where oil money doesn't go directly to fund terror and instability, it can retard innovation. There is little incentive to focus on education and technology when your needs are met by natural resources such as oil and gas. Oil-rich Norway is obviously a best-case scenario and certainly isn't suffering from any lack of democracy. Norway has the third-highest GDP per capita in the world, thanks to the company Statoil, and yet it doesn't have a Nokia or Ericsson like its oil-less Scandinavian neighbours.

We can leave more obscure 'butterfly effect' discussions to university economics professors. There are more than enough concrete examples of global cause and effect to illustrate the importance of keeping an eye on the big picture. We must look forward, outward, and, to see how well we've been performing so far, we must also take the occasional look back. How well have our recent decisions turned out? How accurate were our evaluations? Hindsight has to be useful for more than regret.

Playing the whole board

For nearly three decades, for me showing up to work meant showing up at the chessboard. Tournaments, matches, preparation . . . it was all about the next event, the next opponent, the next move. There are sixty-four squares on a chessboard. It forms a simple plane, a two-dimensional battlefield for the sixteen pieces and sixteen pawns. There is no air power to add a third physical dimension, though it is appropriate to add the element of time as another critical factor that must be considered.

But chess has its own version of seeing the big picture; we call it seeing the whole board. Earlier we talked about how a move in one section of the board could have an impact on the opposite side, but our discussion focused on the concrete aspects of creating weaknesses and rapidly moving from one side to the other. This is definitely one part of seeing the whole board, and all the great players mastered it. In fact, I would consider it one of the hallmarks of the world champions.

Alexander Alekhine was my earliest chess idol. His game collection was a constant companion, and I dreamt of imitating his fantastic combinations and devastating attacks. He left a legacy of original concepts and powerful play that was considered superhuman by his peers. One of them, the Estonian-born Soviet Grandmaster Paul Keres, later said, 'It was impossible to win against Capablanca; against Alekhine it was impossible to play.'

Alekhine's play is often called original and surprising, words that are not used lightly in our traditional game. Originality is typically contrived by deep preparation, and how can we expect to surprise a world-class player? Alekhine managed this by never losing sight of any corner of the board. You might think it's impossible to launch an ambush on a chessboard, but Alekhine did it all the time. He had the ability to take in every piece on the board as a whole and to discover potential where no one else could see it.

Two of his games stand out for me in this regard. One was against the unheralded Hungarian player Karoly Sterk in Budapest in 1921. The other came in 1922 against a German player who would later mount two unsuccessful challenges for Alekhine's title in 1929 and 1934, Efim Bogoljubow. Both games show Alekhine at his full-board best, pressing on one wing only to suddenly shift to the other side with devastating effect. Poor Sterk found himself with all his pieces bunched up on one side of the board, only to see Alekhine launch a lightning attack on the other flank. Alekhine's pieces materialized as if by magic right in front of the black king and the game was decided in an instant.

If the Hungarian was outclassed, it took one of the most brilliant games of Alekhine's career to finish off Bogoljubow at the classic Hastings tournament in 1922. Alekhine beat the Russian-born German 'Bogo' twice at the seaside resort tournament, and his win with the black pieces has become a jewel of chess literature. The crowning combination is so legendary that it is often overlooked how Alekhine outplayed his opponent on just about every square of the board before administering the masterstroke. His kingside initiative was stymied, but with a rapid redeployment he broke through on the queenside while most of Bogoljubow's pieces were still around his king, far from the new front. They arrived only in time to take part in one of the truly immortal finishes of chess history.

Near the end of the game none of white's pieces could move without causing his position to collapse, a curious condition known as 'zugzwang', a chess term of German origin that can be vaguely translated as 'the unfavourable obligation to move' ('movicide' was a clever attempt to coin an English equivalent but it never caught on). As a rule time is an advantage, but in a few very specific situations it can actually be worse to have the move.

Most players find it very difficult to give up a slight advantage in one area of the board, especially if they are on the attack. Alekhine had the ability to transfer the energy of his pieces with remarkable fluidity, never becoming fixated on one action or area. Even his greatest rivals could not resist Alekhine's unique gift for dynamic full-board play. While all the greats could play on the whole board, there is a lineage of players who infused this ability with more dynamism, a line in which I include my own style of play. (That old book of Alekhine's games served me well.) Positional masters like Tigran Petrosian and Anatoly Karpov looked at the whole board, detecting weaknesses and the potential to exploit them in the long term. Players like Alekhine, Mikhail Tal and myself were more interested in the immediate prospects.

Developing this vision requires practice and a degree of detachment. One of the first things to go when we become too obsessed with a problem is the ability to see it in context. We shouldn't become absorbed in the details to the point where we are unable to change perspective as required. We aren't going to be able to see the wood for the trees if we are continually worried about one of the trees falling on our head.

Whole board thinking in the real world involves seeing the elements, how they are connected, and how those connections might change over time. Being able to accept a short-term loss in exchange for a long-term gain is one of the signs of mastery. Today's political environment has forgotten this almost entirely. Ten-second soundbites and overnight poll numbers are considered more important than achieving serious goals that might take time, even sacrifice, to achieve.

One of the canniest of politicians ever, Benjamin Disraeli, understood the difference between winning to lose and losing to win. His manoeuvres to promote both the welfare of the country and his own Conservative party often resulted in far-sighted successes, despite coming at the cost of a short-term defeat. We might also admit that he had an unhealthy obsession with frustrating his nemesis, William Gladstone, but Disraeli usually managed to successfully combine these goals. For years the two heavyweights fed on each other's energy in the first great duel of modern politics.

In 1866 the Conservative party took power when the Whig government resigned after failing to pass a second Reform Act, scuttled largely thanks to Disraeli's machinations. Once in control

Disraeli promptly introduced his own Reform Act, even more radical than the one just defeated. It extended the franchise to a million and a half new voters, nearly doubling the electorate. This move horrified the Tory base and the Conservatives were thrown out in a landslide in the 1868 elections, bringing Gladstone and his party to power.

But Disraeli had seen further. He realized that without an infusion of new voters the Conservatives would remain forever a minority party of lords and the upper classes. Although the 1867 Reform Act cost the Tories one election, it made them a viable party in the long run. The 1874 election was the first in which the newly enfranchised working class would be allowed to vote, and Disraeli had calculated that they would vote Conservative out of gratitude. This gratitude would persist, building a bridge between the upper-class traditional Tories and the working class and trade unions. He was proved to have calculated correctly when in 1874 he was returned to power with a full mandate thanks to the newly expanded rolls. Disraeli's government rapidly passed a broad set of labour and health reform bills that transformed the nation. He proved somewhat less adept at managing the Empire abroad – or at least at managing the perception of it at home – and setbacks in Afghanistan and South Africa were largely responsible for the defeat of the Conservatives in 1880.

The Disraelis are now extinct on the political scene. Today's political minds are dominated by short-term goals and interests. Budgets are filled with projects to make a few backers happy in the present at the cost of bankrupting the economy in the future. This is also often the case with companies worried more about today's stock price than about tomorrow's revenues. Unquestionably, this has permeated to the individual level as well, which is what most concerns us because it is where we can make a difference.

Focusing exclusively on short-term satisfaction and on the symptoms of our problems keeps us on a path of constant struggle and leads to very little actual enjoyment. We must take a conscious decision to stop, to step back and extend our senses. Instead of worrying so much about what is right in front of us, we need to look around the borders. Only if we occasionally force ourselves away from acquiring more information, away from calculation and analysis, will we be able to uncover the causes and connections and develop our intuition.

The big picture cannot be understood by sheer analysis, no

matter how deep. Only our experience and instincts can combine all the objective factors into context, a complete view not only of how things work, but of why they work that way. Intuition means understanding, not just knowing. All our memories, talents and skills come together to produce what a dictionary defines as 'knowing without the use of rational processes'. Agatha Christie said of intuition that 'you can't ignore it and you can't explain it'. But it is more than enough to recognize how important it is and to investigate how we can develop ours to its maximum potential.

The fight in Russia today

On 10 March 2005 I played my last professional game of chess. Thirty years after I had played my first major event at national level, nearly twenty years after I became world champion, I retired at the age of forty-one. I left after winning my final tournament in my beloved Linares and still as the top-ranked player in the game, inevitably leading to numerous 'Why?' inquiries from all quarters.

Faithful to my own preaching I had looked deeply at this critical move. The most important part of the answer is that this was not a spontaneous move but to me a logical step. My shift to becoming a full-time member of the Russian political opposition movement reflected both the needs of my country and my desire to make a difference in the world around me. I was fortunate enough to have attained most of the ambitious goals I had set for myself in the chess world. New challenges and new ways to make an impact were waiting for me in politics and, I hope, in writing.

One of the constant themes of this book has been how essential it is to continually challenge ourselves. The only way to develop is to venture into the unknown, to take risks and to learn new things. We must force ourselves out of our comfort zone and trust our ability to adapt and thrive. Everything that I have written here led me to retire from the chess world. I craved new challenges and I wanted to be where I felt I was wanted and needed. In fighting for the survival of Russia's fragile democracy I found a precious cause, a worthy challenge, and a new way to channel my energy.

This decision was not about running for higher office, nor was it a personal vendetta against Vladimir Putin or anyone else. Mine is a mission of positive change. Putin is only the current symbol of what we are fighting against. I don't want my nine-year-old son to worry about Russian military service in an illegal war such as Chechnya or to fear the repression of a dictatorship. I want to have a chance to offer my vision, strategic thought and fighting spirit to prevent those things from happening.

Many ask about the dangers involved in opposing this Kremlin regime and whether this is a foolhardy move on my part. After all, having his father attacked or jailed won't be of much benefit to my son. To this I can only say that there are some things that simply must be done. Succeed or fail, this is a fight that must be fought. As the Soviet dissidents famously put it: 'Do what you must and so be it.' There are millions like me in Russia who want a free press, the rule of law, social justice and free and fair elections. My new job is to fight for those people and to fight for those fundamental rights.

To achieve these ends my colleagues and I have formed a broad non-ideological coalition of true opposition groups and activists. I am working inside Russia and abroad to bring attention to the decimation of Russia's democratic institutions. My chess fame and the skills I developed in the chess world have proven equally vital to this task.

'Not Free' – Status accorded Russia in the Freedom House report 'Freedom in the World, 2005'

'Here I stand. I can do no other. God help me. Amen' – Martin Luther before Emperor Charles V at the Diet of Worms, 1519

What follows is a lesser-known passage from Churchill's great Fulton, Missouri speech of 5 March 1946. While the Iron Curtain he famously spoke of no longer exists, the mission he describes here is still paramount. 'When American military men approach some serious situation they are wont to write at the head of their directive the words "over-all strategic concept". There is wisdom in this, as it leads to clarity of thought. What then is the over-all strategic concept which we should inscribe today? It is nothing less than the safety and welfare, the freedom and progress, of all the homes and families of all the men and women in all the lands.'

18

INTUITION

We know more than we understand

Despite the best efforts of psychologists and neurologists, human thought is still best described by metaphor, poetry and the other devices we use to express what we do not fully understand. Not being a poet, I will aim to concern myself with the more practical mission of what we might call executive brain management.

Aldous Huxley, ignoring Freud and writing long before the invention of brain scans, endorsed this approach and defined experience as 'a matter of sensibility and intuition, of seeing and hearing the significant things, of paying attention at the right moments, of understanding and coordinating. Experience is not what happens to a man; it is what a man does with what happens to him.'

We definitely have an active role to play. We can't sit around and expect wisdom to accumulate along with grey hair. Learning from our mistakes is the least of what we should ask from our experience. To get more we must demand it, cultivate it, and go looking for it.

Intuition is where it all comes together – our experience, knowledge and will. Contrary to popular belief, we cannot truly be said to have intuition in a field we have little practical knowledge of. Even the vaguest hunches are based on something tangible. A positive impression of a new co-worker can stem from a deeply embedded recollection of another's voice, face or name. That we cannot explain it or understand it does not mean this powerful force does not exist.

Discussing human intuition risks running into the dilemma summed up by the one-time head of the Spanish royal household, Sabino Fernández Campo, who said, 'What I can tell you is not interesting and what is interesting I cannot tell you.' Instead of theory I had best to stick with examples that might convince you to have more faith in your own instincts. This is the essential element that cannot be measured by any analysis or device.

Intuition versus analysis

During my work on *My Great Predecessors* I have gained not just deeper respect for the achievements of the world champions but a greater admiration for chess players in general and for the way the game of chess can bring out the best in the human mind. Few activities are as taxing to our faculties as a professional chess tournament. Memory is in overdrive, rapid calculation is essential, the outcome hangs on every move, and this goes on for hour after hour, day after day, all with the world watching. It is the ideal scenario for mental and physical meltdown.

When I began to analyse the games of my world champion forebears I was, therefore, prepared to be a little forgiving. Not in my analysis, but in my attitude towards their mistakes. Here I was in the twenty-first century, standing on the shoulders of giants with gigahertz of chess processing power at my fingertips. With these advantages and the objectivity of hindsight I shouldn't judge my predecessors too harshly, I told myself, even as I would hope to receive some forgiveness for the mistakes I made in the heat of competition.

An important part of the project was to collect all the relevant analysis that had been done on these games before, especially the published analyses of the players themselves and their contemporaries. The principal theme of the series is to illustrate the evolution of the game, so the commentary of the time is in many ways as valuable as the games themselves in revealing the mentality of the players of the era.

One would assume that the analyst, working in the calm of his study and with unlimited time to move the pieces, would have a much easier job than the players themselves. Hindsight is 20/20, after all. One of my first discoveries was that when it comes to chess analysis in the pre-computer age (before 1995, roughly), hindsight was badly in need of bifocals.

Paradoxically, when other top players wrote about games in magazines and newspaper columns they often made more mistakes in their annotations than the players had made at the board. Even when the players published their analysis of their own games they were often less convincing than when they were actually playing.

Game 7 was the decisive encounter of the 1894 world championship match between fifty-seven-year-old champion Wilhelm Steinitz and his German challenger, the twenty-five-year-old Emanuel Lasker. The first phase of the match was held in New York before moving on to Philadelphia and then Montreal. They had split the first four games two wins apiece, followed by two draws. Then came lucky number 7, at least that is the way it was described by commentators at the time. But how much was chance really involved in this critical contest?

Lasker misplayed early on with the white pieces and Steinitz exploited his chances effectively to have a clean pair of extra pawns when the smoke cleared at move 20. If a Grandmaster today resigned in such a position it wouldn't much surprise the viewing public. Play was much less scientific a century ago, and of course Lasker had nothing to lose by playing on, if only to tire out his older opponent for the next encounter. Already a shrewd psychologist of the chessboard, it is also likely that Lasker wondered if his sheer bravado might disturb the dogmatic veteran.

The standard story of the game as reported at the time goes roughly as follows: Steinitz, as black, had a clearly winning position. Lasker launched a desperate attack against black's king, sacrificing a piece. Under some pressure but still winning, Steinitz committed a suicidal mistake that cost him the game. The shock of blundering so badly affected Steinitz so much that he went on to lose the next four games in a row and the world title.

So goes the narrative according to most nineteenth-century analysis, which has largely been echoed ever since. The revised story would go something like this. Steinitz had an objectively winning position but he made a few errors that allowed Lasker to launch a dangerous attack and the position became quite complicated. The challenger's subsequent play and piece sacrifice set black many practical problems. Steinitz failed to defend accurately under constant pressure and lost. Steinitz's final mistake came in a position where he was already losing. The psychological blow of being outplayed from a superficially simple and winning position stunned Steinitz and he was unable to recover in the match. More than his self-confidence had been shaken by the loss. The principles of sound and logical chess that Steinitz held so dear had seemingly betrayed him. He was sure he had been winning and he had played according to his philosophy, and yet he had lost.

How could so many strong players miss in analysis what Lasker sensed during the game? Even Lasker himself never challenged the official story in his later observations, but his intuition had led him correctly during the game! It turns out that this is not at all unusual, even a century later and including my own games and my own analysis. It is impossible to replicate the level of concentration reached during a game, for one. Moving the pieces around can be a crutch that leads us to use our eyes instead of our minds. When seated at the board we have no choice.

Over and over again these legendary figures, at the most crucial moments of their careers, intuitively found the best moves. Competitive pressure made them push deeper; when we aren't under that pressure some of our senses are turned off. Analysis is akin to a sighted person trying to learn Braille. The things we think of as advantages – time, information – can short-circuit what matters even more: our intuition.

How long is long enough?

This example is not intended to encourage a simple gut instinct mindset but to illustrate the power of concentration and instinct. The biggest problem we encounter is in not trusting these instincts enough. Too often we rely on having all the information and then doing exactly what the information tells us to do. This effectively reduces us to the role of a microprocessor and guarantees that our intuition will remain stunted.

Everything comes at a cost. Challenging ourselves in new ways inevitably leads to a few failures. More than once our instincts will all point in one direction and that direction will turn out to be a dead end. So we err, we learn, we make fewer mistakes, we gain more confidence, we trust our instincts more readily and we continue the cycle. The consequences of trying anything are failure and success; they are inseparable. If we wish to succeed we must brave the risk of failure.

When the dot-com stock market bubble began to balloon in the 1990s it set off the alarm bells of just about every 'old economy' analyst. Surely this couldn't be real; companies without revenue simply were not worth billions of dollars of market capital. Five years later, after the markets had plummeted and thousands of companies went bankrupt, it was easy to say that those sober analysts had been correct all along. They trusted their intuition and stayed well away from the wild side of the tech market. Others, though aware that the dot-com stock trend went against just about everything they had ever experienced, jumped all the way in anyway and got badly burned.

But were the conservative doomsayers really right? It can be difficult to resist jumping into the pool when all the other kids are doing it, but after a while it can become a habit and you never jump in at all. More credit should be given to the few who played it well, whose intuitions told them to go in and just how long to stay in. For all the famous disaster stories – and my own dot-com venture is somewhere on that list – there were investors who ran into the burning building, filled their pockets with internet gold, and got out before it collapsed.

There is a strong intuitive element in any discipline in which data is limited and the time element is a major factor. Stock analysts search for visual patterns in stock charts, shapes like 'teacups' and 'rising wedges', the way chess players look for checkmating patterns. Intuition doesn't just tell us the what and the how, but also the when. As they develop, our instincts become a labour-saving and time-saving device, cutting down the time we need to make a proper evaluation and shortening the time we need to take action. We can collect and analyse new information forever without making a decision. Something has to tell us when the law of diminishing returns is kicking in, so we pull the trigger.

I can ponder my move for ten seconds, ten minutes or one hour – which do I choose? A well-developed intuition keeps us on a pragmatic course while letting us know when we have reached a critical juncture that requires more time and special attention. The pattern recognition function that chess players rely on is essential in every walk of life. In every situation we have to wonder whether or not what we are dealing with is a trend or something unique. Detecting trends, preferably before anyone else, is often based on intuition and intangible elements. Has it happened before? Will it develop the same way this time?

The perils of ignoring a trend

Figuring out whether an event is a one-off, a new trend, or a new look on an old trend is essential in the political world. According to the media and the campaigns, every election season brings a half-dozen 'new paradigms', although very few turn out to be both new and relevant. In the US presidential election in 2004 the Democrats looked back at Al Gore's defeat in 2000 and guessed wrong when it came time for the critical selection of John Kerry's running mate.

The choice of John Edwards might have made sense in the Kerry campaign headquarters, but it turned out to make no sense at all on the electoral map. Bush had dominated the South in the 2000 election and there was no reason to believe that Edwards could carry even a single southern state for the Democrats. On Election Day 2004 the Democratic 'blues' again lost the entire South, even dropping Edwards's home state of North Carolina by the same thirteen points Gore lost it by in 2000. To add further insult to injury, the Democrats had spent heavily in North Carolina in order to make it a respectable loss and save face for Edwards.

The Democrats had hoped that Gore's loss in the South had been an aberration. This led them to follow a disastrous path in the eyes of a 'material, time, quality' analysis. They were punished for their poor choice of battlefield, their mismanagement of resources, and their failure to recognize a trend. If they had seen the 2000 loss of the entire South as the trend it turned out to be they might have selected Dick Gephardt instead of Edwards. The addition of the Midwestern stalwart would have created a good chance of flipping Iowa and Missouri and their eighteen electoral votes from red to blue, providing Kerry with a 269–268 victory over Bush despite the loss of Ohio.

Distinguishing between an anomaly and a movement can't be done with polls and data alone. We have to focus our attention on any new event and extend all our senses. What exactly makes it new? In what ways is it like something we have seen before? How has the environment changed? If we can answer these questions we will have an excellent chance of knowing whether or not a single snowflake is about to become a blizzard.

19

CRISIS POINT

'Everything is condensed into one single moment. It
decides our life.' – *Franz Kafka*

What would intimidate you more, being told, 'Solve this problem,'
or being told, 'Find out if there's a problem'? Solving problems
could almost be described as easy compared to figuring out
whether we have a problem in the first place. It's hard to say we're
lucky when we face a crisis, but knowing that action is called for
is reassuring. The truest tests of skill and intuition come when
everything looks quiet and we aren't sure what to do, or if we
should do anything at all.

Anyone who has sat for a multiple-choice exam knows the
most feared option is 'none of the above'. Suddenly it's open-
ended. Maybe there is no solution at all, who knows? Try this
short mathematics test, which won't require a calculator.

$$13 \times 63 = ?$$
a) 109
b) 819
c) 8,109

No trouble at all, of course. The answer is found by a simple
process of elimination. Our intuition tells us instantly that we
don't have to calculate anything. But if we add 'd) none of the
above', we have to do the work and solve the equation no matter
how obviously wrong answers a) and c) are.

Earlier we touched on this with regard to composed chess
puzzles. You are presented with a position and stipulations. 'White
to checkmate in three moves' is very strict. 'White to play and win'
is more open-ended, but in both cases we know before we start
that there is something to be found. We turn the matter over to the
problem-solving section of our brain and can safely turn off the
higher evaluation and vigilance functions.

In such cases, no longer slowed by doubt, we can perform these tasks with remarkable efficiency. In 1987 I was invited to a special reception in Frankfurt held by Atari. All of their managers were there and the master of ceremonies was the head of their German division, Alwin Stumpf. It was an informal and entertaining evening where we discussed politics as well as chess and computers. In fact, I've since been reminded many times that during the evening I acquired the friendly condescension of almost everyone with my prediction that as a consequence of the changes in the USSR, the Berlin Wall would soon fall, perhaps in as little as five years. 'A fine chess player, but he doesn't know anything about politics!' was probably the consensus. It turns out that my forecast was two years too late.

After the banquet was finished Herr Stumpf took the microphone and grandly pronounced that we were about to see something extraordinary. I had no idea what he was talking about when he went on to say that he had seen me perform this amazing feat on television and now I was going to do it in person. He pointed to a long table on the other side of the room that we had passed on the way in. Stumpf explained each board was set up in a position from a historic game of chess, each selected from 150 years of games by a local chess player and journalist. In front of each board there was a face-down card with the date, place and names of the players. I was to be tested by seeing if I could identify each game by looking at the position on the board. Stumpf walked over to the boards and invited me to join him in order to begin the challenge.

He was disconcerted when I remained in my seat. He hadn't told me about this exercise in advance and he feared that I had been annoyed by his little surprise. I said, 'I'm honoured you are interested in understanding the human mind, but I hope you will forgive me if I stay seated.' Stumpf's face fell. I was going to ruin his big moment! I continued by saying that I hadn't been able to help glancing at the boards when we walked into the hall and that I would like to try to name all the positions from my chair across the room. One by one I named the players, tournament, and even the next move of each game represented on the ten boards.

The effect was satisfactorily jaw-dropping for the guests, and looking back I try to forgive myself this youthful display of the dramatic. What I did not explain, and likely did not pay attention to at the time myself, was how they had made it easy for me. Not with the game selection, as not all of the positions were taken from world-famous encounters. But of course each selected position was from the critical moment of each game. After all, without such moments games do not become well-known in the first place. No self-respecting chess fan would select a nondescript position from a deservedly forgotten game when there are so many fascinating and famous positions to choose from.

It was enough to know that since the first position was the key moment of a known game from history the others were likely similar. Had the positions appeared uninteresting or trivial perhaps I would have assumed the participants had been playing some casual games before I had arrived. When I glanced at the boards I quickly recognized that I didn't have to evaluate the positions, only look them up in my memory.

Knowing there is a solution to find is a huge advantage; it's like not having a 'none of the above' option. Anyone with reasonable competence and adequate resources can solve a puzzle when it is presented in such a way. We can skip the subtle evaluations and move directly to plugging in possible solutions until we hit upon a promising one. Uncertainty is far more challenging.

Crisis in Seville, a case study

After winning the world championship in 1985 I had very little time to savour the taste of victory. The traditional cycle called for a title defence every three years. During that time the challenger would be produced by a rigorous qualification process of regional tournaments, giant 'interzonal' tournaments and finally a series of candidates' matches. This process was so gruelling that by the time the challenger arrived at the final there could be no doubt he was a worthy contender. In fact, since 1950 when the qualification system began – then just a single tournament – only two players to have reached a world championship match failed to become champion.

This process was interrupted in my case, however, thanks to an old rule that FIDE reintroduced to the books in the 70s under Soviet pressure to favour Karpov: the rematch clause. If he lost, the champion had the right to an automatic rematch a year later with no qualification process. This rule had been abolished after Mikhail Botvinnik made good use of it to beat Vassily Smyslov in

1958 and then Mikhail Tal in 1961. Botvinnik had poor scores in world championship matches but was devastating in the rematches, a skill that twice enabled him to come back and limit his vanquisher's reign to one year.

To avoid the same fate I would have to beat Anatoly Karpov again in 1986. Bear in mind that we had already played the longest championship match in history in 84–5 before I took the title in our second match in 1985. I narrowly won the rematch in 1986, but the ordeal was still not over. The qualification cycle had started on schedule in 1985 despite our cancelled marathon match, the rescheduled match and the rematch. This meant that I was due to face the scheduled challenger in 1987, exactly a year after beating Karpov. And who would my opponent be this time? Karpov.

Evading the main qualification process, my nemesis had been dropped into a 'superfinal' and had duly demolished the leading contender, Andrei Sokolov. In October 1987 we sat down in Seville, in Spain, to begin our fourth world championship match in three years. If I thought I was tired of looking at Karpov back in 1984, I was really sick of him by now. At least this time there were no more tricks. If I won this match I wouldn't have to see him or any other title challenger for another three years.

Detecting a crisis before it's a crisis

Detecting a crisis is a separate skill. Here I don't refer to crisis as catastrophe. It doesn't take skill or intuition to realize when things have gone horribly wrong. In a 1959 speech in Indianapolis, John F. Kennedy famously observed that the Chinese word for 'crisis' is composed of two characters, one meaning danger and the other meaning opportunity. It turns out that this is not literally true, although it is a poetic and memorable way to illustrate a very useful concept.

The English definition of the word is good enough on its own, I was somewhat surprised to discover. From its common usage we might assume it means something like 'disaster', which needs no further synonyms. 'Crisis' really means a turning-point, a critical moment when the stakes are high and the outcome uncertain. It also implies a point of no return. This signifies both danger and opportunity, so the Kennedy speech was accurate where it mattered.

The greater danger is often in trying to avoid crises entirely, which often only means postponing them. It would be pleasant, if boring, to forever take our boat down calm and straight streams, never encountering rapids or bends in the course. Great success with minimal risk of failure is a goal held by many, especially in the modern political and commercial environment. It may even be doable if we have many advantages to start with, the way an heir to a fortune goes into business. But for the vast majority of us success depends on detecting, evaluating and controlling risk. Of these three things, detection is often the most important and always the most difficult. Important because without it, instead of controlling risk we end up fighting to survive when the crisis hits. Difficult because it requires an alertness to the most subtle changes.

World champion Boris Spassky once observed that 'the best indicator of a chess player's form is his ability to sense the climax of the game'. It is virtually impossible to always play the best moves because accuracy comes at the expense of time and vice versa. But if we can detect the key moments we can make our best decisions when they matter most. The moves we make on the chessboard have far from equal importance and we must rely on intuition to tell us that here, at this precise moment, we need to spend some extra time because the game may hinge on this one decision.

Apart from an indicator of good or poor form, the ability to detect these crisis points is a gauge of overall strength in a chess player – and in a decision-maker. The greatest players are distinguished by their ability to recognize both specific and general crucial factors. Analysis of past games illustrates this well, despite the aforementioned difficulties of comprehending today what was going through the mind of someone 100 years ago. One of the beauties of chess as a cognitive laboratory is that we can do this. We can't be positive that Emanuel Lasker knew a certain move was the climax, but we can tell from analysing his play when he found the best moves and when he didn't. Usually we also know how much time the players invested in each move.

Must-win strategy

Perhaps my eagerness not to have to play another match with Karpov for three years is what led to such a turbulent start to our match in Seville. Four of the first eight games were decisive, two wins each, and there were four draws. I was disappointed with my uneven play and my inability to put any distance between us. After a terrible Karpov blunder I won the eleventh game from a very dubious position to take the lead for the first time in the match, scheduled for twenty-four games. After four draws Karpov won the sixteenth game to draw level. At this point I began to think only of my title and the 12–12 score I needed to retain it. I went into defensive mode and stopped pressing him. After all, a drawn match would give me three years of peace. A stretch of six quite uneventful draws followed, setting up a showdown in the final two games.

If the match ended this way, all even, I would retain the title. Hardly the convincing victory I had hoped for to end our marathon, but beggars cannot be choosers. I didn't want to push and Karpov didn't have the energy to do so. Two more draws seemed the most logical result. It turned out that members of my analysis team thought so too. They didn't tell me about their side wagers until after the match had ended, but GM Zurab Azmaiparashvili made a bet against GM Josef Dorfman regarding the conclusion of the match. Dorfman got phenomenal odds for taking any outcome other than two more draws to finish the match.

It would have done my heart a great deal of good had Dorfman lost his bet, but unfortunately the string of draws would end at six. After a tough, prolonged defence I suffered one of the worst hallucinations of my career and blundered to a loss in game 23. Suddenly Karpov was up by a point and was only a draw away from taking back the crown he had lost to me two years earlier. The very next day after this catastrophe I had to take the white pieces into a must-win game 24. Caissa, the goddess of chess, had punished me for my conservative play, for betraying my nature. I would not be allowed to hold on to my title without winning a game in the second half of the match.

Only once before in chess history had the champion won a final game to retain his title. Emanuel Lasker beat Carl Schlechter with his back against the wall in the last game of their match in 1910. The win allowed Lasker to draw the match and keep possession of his title for a further eleven years. The Austrian Schlechter had, like Karpov, a reputation as a defensive wizard. In fact, his uncharacteristically aggressive play in the final game against Lasker has led some historians to believe that the rules of the match required him to win by two points.

In 1985 the situation had been reversed. I had gone into the final game leading by a point and Karpov needed to win to tie the match and save the title he had held since 1975. As discussed in Chapter 3, in that decisive game Karpov started out with an all-or-nothing strategy of attack. At the critical moment he was betrayed by his own instincts and failed to find the best moves. He had started out the game playing in my direct style only to slow down to his own more cautious approach in midstream, with predictably poor results.

When preparing for my turn on the other side of this situation, I recalled that critical encounter. What strategy should I employ with the white pieces in this must-win final game? There was more to think about than game 23 and game 24, of course. These were also games 119 and 120 between us, an extraordinary number of top-level encounters between the same two players, all played in a span of thirty-nine months. It felt like one long match, with this final game in December 1987 the climax of what we had started in September 1984. My plan for the final game had to consider not only my own preferences but what would prove most difficult for my opponent. And what could be more annoying for Karpov than my turning the tables and playing like Karpov?

Complexity, forks, blurriness and stakes

In just about any other endeavour, historical insight becomes a matter of opinion. Recent history is spun and debated by partisans, and ancient history is a web of myths with only sporadic basis in demonstrable fact. These legends are passed on from textbook to textbook until we all assume they are true. An even more harmful myth is that there is a single, objective answer to big, complicated questions. For example, in conventional wisdom the First World War is often blamed on the assassination of a single archduke, as if history and life itself could be broken down into a multiple choice test.

Alfred de Vigny wrote that history is a novel written by the people, and how can we imagine a novel without crisis and conflict? History is the story of crisis points, one after another. My favourite succinct definition of crisis is 'a moment at which questions cannot be answered'. Crises are periods of uncertainty and inevitable sacrifice. Over time our instincts will interpret our experience to better detect these moments as they approach. We can also postulate analytical guidelines that are as applicable to a business deal or a treaty negotiation as they are to a chess position.

As with many of the themes discussed throughout this book, the onset of a crisis is a sensation we feel instinctively but usually fail to anticipate and deal with rationally. If we are alert we can recognize the warning signs and take measures to minimize the damage and maximize the opportunities that can arise out of crisis.

Complexity can be measured by the number of elements of a situation and, more crucially, the number of possible interactions between them. At the start of a chess game there are thirty-two pieces on the board but no one would call the initial array complex. The pieces are separate and without any interaction. When elements combine like an unpredictable chemical reaction, we have complexity. When the density of complications and connections peaks we are at a point of crisis. We must also remain aware of our decision-making load level and the relative difficulty of those decisions. Another sign to watch for is when paths begin to diverge increasingly. Everyone likes to keep their options open for as long as possible and this natural tendency is not a wholly unhealthy one. The difficulty comes when keeping our options open becomes a matter of postponing an inevitable decision. We have to recognize the point at which there is nothing further to be gained by postponing a choice.

It's rare to come around a blind corner into a wide fork in the road; stark choices usually approach with time enough to anticipate them. If we give in to the temptation to put off such committal decisions for as long as possible we squander the advantage of seeing them coming. We must take advantage of time to prepare. If we can see a crisis forming well in advance we can place our forces correctly.

Every crisis has a time factor, by definition. Even global warming, an issue that is literally glacially slow, presents humanity with a series of deadlines. The reverse is not necessarily true, however. It's possible to be in a time crunch without being in a crisis. If little is at stake or if no negative result is possible, this is simply a question of anxiety.

A chess player down to his last seconds is moving pieces and banging the clock as fast as his hands can move. At this point chess looks more like Nintendo. It is critical not to let time become such an overwhelming factor that all other factors are tossed aside.

A racing driver's car goes in circuits that don't require much in the way of anticipation, though of course the other cars do. In real life we are racing down a highway with countless off-ramps, one every second. Every off-ramp is a decision and few of them have clear signs above them. When the signs start to blur or disappear altogether, that's another crisis indicator.

In other words, the more difficult it is to tell the qualitative difference between options the more likely it is that the situation is getting out of control. We can distinguish such a situation from complexity because it can happen even if there are only two paths from which to choose. Franklin Roosevelt observed that the most difficult decision he made during the Second World War was selecting who would lead the D-Day invasion of Europe. To many the position should have gone to George Marshall, FDR's most trusted commander. Instead it went to Dwight Eisenhower, for the touching reason that Roosevelt couldn't bear to let his closest aide (and most effective planner) leave his side during the critical moment of the war.

Along with its complexity and point of no return nature, the Normandy landings were also a crisis point for the most obvious of reasons, the investment of resources. If the stakes are high and the consequences of failure severe, the situation is a critical juncture no matter how high the chances of success.

Ethicists, psychologists and logicians enjoy composing puzzles that force us to balance crisis factors. Imagine you are the leader of a group of 1,000 soldiers caught in a snowstorm. There are two routes out, a long trek through a snow-filled valley or a short but unstable ledge around a mountain. If you go through the valley you will lose 40 per cent of your men. If you try the mountain pass there's a 50 per cent chance of saving them all and a 50 per cent chance almost everyone will be killed. Which do you choose? How would the percentages have to differ for you to change your selection?

A CEO must decide whether to downsize 40 per cent of the workforce or avoid layoffs and risk his company collapsing entirely. In everything from investing our savings to planning a holiday we must decide when to gamble and when to play it safe. Our decisions will in the end depend on our character and how comfortable we can be with a given level of risk. Calculation should always be a factor because some paths are genuinely superior. Following your gut reaction immediately instead of doing the necessary analysis crosses the line from intuitive thinking to mental laziness.

A staple scene in Russian fairy tales involves the hero coming across a magic stone bearing inscriptions. It presents him with three options, each of which offers serious drawbacks. Danger is imminent, and the question is only which risk to take. In life our choices are rarely so clear-cut. Our decisions are always a balance of opportunity and sacrifice. We must not be so blinded by what we might gain that we ignore what we will lose.

What should our reaction be in such situations? A common tendency is to attempt to cut through the knot instead of untying it. According to legend this method worked well for Alexander at Gordium, but we can't take a sword to a chessboard, spreadsheet or business plan. Sometimes there is no simple, bold solution. Other times we would prefer to untie the knot in order to retain the option of using the rope for something else. Avoiding many small, subtle decisions by taking one big one can be very tempting, but often this means burning bridges that can be left intact if we are willing to take more care and do more work.

Errors on both sides

Had I not battled against Karpov for 119 games I would have been incapable of surviving the all-important 120th. The loss of game 23 itself had the potential to be crushing, and I had less than twenty-four hours to prepare what could be my last game as world chess champion. The 'secret' of my preparation? Playing cards with my team and getting a good five or six hours of sleep.

The aggregate score of our world championship marathon was sixteen wins apiece and eighty-seven draws. Victory in this 120th game would mean not only winning this match but taking the lead in our overall score. So why cards and sleep instead of opening preparation? After 119 games with Karpov there was nothing my team and I were going to uncover in a few hours of anxious analysis. We decided on a basic strategy, nothing more than that. The rest of the time was better spent recovering my nervous and physical energy for the battle ahead. This might sound strange given my typically obsessive preparation, but it was a simple matter of allocation of resources. The strategy I had chosen would require not explosive energy but a slow burn.

The magnificent Teatro Lope de Vega was packed for game 24. The entire game was shown live on Spanish television. The usual pre-game murmur of the audience had been replaced by a low roar. I was later told that the excited Spanish radio and television commentators sounded as if they were covering the final round of a heavyweight boxing match, which in effect they were.

The arbiter started my clock and I pushed my c-pawn forward two squares, just as I had done eight times previously in the match. The difference would come in the next few moves as I kept my centre pawns back and instead developed on the flanks. My choice was to avoid a do-or-die battle from the start. I opened slowly, even a little passively, in order to keep as many pieces as possible on the board. This technique would put psychological pressure on Karpov, despite his expertise in such manoeuvrings. With no clear, forcing continuations he would be constantly tempted to simplify and exchange pieces even at the cost of a slightly inferior position. Obviously with fewer pieces on the board the level of complexity would drop, overall reducing the chances of a decisive result, but as long as I could put a sufficiently high 'quality price tag' on these exchanges I felt I was getting good value.

My slow-cook method proved to have the additional advantage of getting Karpov into serious time trouble. With the stakes so high he was being extra cautious, taking valuable minutes to double-check moves he would normally make quickly. As the game progressed Karpov managed to exchange half the pieces but his position was still under uncomfortable pressure. He was so close to equalizing on every move but he couldn't quite get his head above water; in the meantime his clock was becoming a factor.

Seeing a chance to play for an attack I moved my knight to the central e5 square, offering a pawn. Karpov took the bait and grabbed the pawn, a temptation that could have led to disaster. And he had to play quickly now, as it was still a long way to move 40 when, by the rules then in force, the game would be adjourned and more time added before continuation the next day. (Today, mostly due to the players using computers to help them analyse, such adjournments are obsolete.)

I exchanged rooks, leaving me with queen, knight, and bishop against his queen and two knights. He had an extra pawn but I had seen a tactical possibility that would give me a powerful attack. His pieces were dangerously uncoordinated and his king was vulnerable. If I could penetrate into his position with my queen I could exploit both these factors at the same time. The question was where to move my queen on move 33. Karpov could only wait, knowing he would have to reply almost immediately or he wouldn't have enough time to make the next eight moves without losing on time.

Lost in thought, I was startled by a tap on my shoulder. The Dutch arbiter leaned over and said, 'Mr Kasparov, you have to write the moves.' I had become so wrapped up in the game that I had forgotten to make a note of the last two moves on my scoresheet as required by the rules. The arbiter was of course correct to remind me of the regulations, but what a moment to be strict! Such a tap could have become the hand of destiny had things turned out differently.

I played my queen to the wrong square. I missed a subtlety and failed to see why a different move with the same idea would have been stronger. My move gave Karpov the opportunity for a clever defence and suddenly he was one move from reclaiming his title. But his hurried response also proved second best, although our mutual exchange of errors would not be discovered until well after the game.

Karpov's best opportunity to defend had passed and my forces surrounded the black king. I regained my sacrificed pawn with interest and by the time we reached move 40, ending the time scramble, my position was clearly superior. The game was adjourned until the next day with the title still up in the air. It was going to be a long night.

Learning from a crisis

Crises are when we are tested and develop our skills and our senses. It is not pure bravado that leads some individuals to constantly push themselves and those around them to the breaking point in pursuit of conflict. Chateaubriand wrote that 'moments of crisis produce a redoubling of life in man'. We should take such moments as a challenge to carry out our own performance review and to look back on our last crisis and how we handled it. If you cannot recall a recent crisis in your life, even one successfully averted, you are either very lucky, very bored or both.

Provoking a crisis requires perfect timing if we plan to survive the consequences. You can have every other factor on your side – material, time, quality – and still be run to ruin if you misjudge the prevailing environment.

Simón Bolívar was the great liberator of South America. He succeeded in ousting the Spanish colonial regime from his native Venezuela, Colombia, Peru, and from the subsequently eponymous Bolivia. His successes, soon joined by Argentine general San Martín in the south of the continent, took direct advantage of events round the globe. By 1808 Napoleon had invaded Spain and imprisoned King Charles and his son Ferdinand, disrupting Spanish control of its far-flung colonies. Seizing the opportunity, Bolívar and his supporters moved against the Spanish in the New World, launching a war of independence that would soon involve the entire continent. In only fifteen years' time Spain would be out of South America, despite having dispatched the largest military expedition ever to cross the Atlantic up to that point.

The big picture dominoes continue to fall if we look at the effects the French invasion of Spain had back in France. Spain turned into a very weak flank for Napoleon, largely due to a Spanish guerrilla war backed by the Duke of Wellington and the British army. Napoleon had failed to properly evaluate the consequences of invading Spain, which turned a weak and unstable French ally into a territory open to his British opponent. The British regiments who successfully confronted the French armies in Spain went on to lead Wellington's army at Waterloo.

It is easy to look back and talk about the tide of history and the inevitable end of colonialism. But a historical tide is not a product of fate but of real people making risky decisions and navigating crisis after crisis. Barring natural disasters, nothing happens out of the blue. In an unbalanced position the first side to take decisive action is the side that will end up writing the history books. Losing but being on the right side of history is only a consolation for your descendants, assuming you get to leave any. The timing factor is doubly critical because you can be both too early or too late. You cannot simply complete your preparations and wait for opportunity to come to you. The window of opportunity can close as quickly as it opens, so we must always be ready to force the issue.

We learn in these situations because a crisis requires atypical decisions. We find that our usual patterns don't apply very well, that easy answers aren't available. The situation can become so complicated and move so quickly that we are reduced to guesswork. In such a state more abstract and subjective factors of evaluation are forced into play. We don't have time for much concrete analysis and hard data is hard to come by. This is when the great general distinguishes himself from the merely good one and where a political leader can achieve immortality.

Of all the numerous causes of the First World War, perhaps the most significant was the participants' underestimation of the costs. By then a distant memory, the Russo-Turkish War of 1877–8 had led to the Congress of Berlin and an attempt by the great powers to establish a lasting peace. The huge number of casualties, around 200,000 on the Russian side alone by some estimates, led many of the day's statesmen to believe that war between the great powers would be impossible in the future. Modern weapons were too powerful, the loss of life too great.

And yet the harsh lessons of 1878 had been forgotten, as they would be again when the First World War ended with the ruinous Treaty of Versailles. Few imagined that the war would last for so long, let alone that it would lead to the collapse of four great empires. If the Ottomans had already looked set to topple, there had been no obvious signs of imminent ruin about the empires of Russia, Germany and Austro-Hungary. But instead of the quick resolution most expected, the war became a catalyst for almost every crisis and near-crisis on the continent.

The inability of Europe's leaders to see the potential for devastation combined with several other factors. The complex web of European treaties had grown so convoluted that an act of aggression just about anywhere could set off a chain reaction to general war. Britain, for instance, entered the war due to a treaty obligating it to come to the defence not of its powerful ally France but of tiny Belgium.

We may like to believe that such confusion and lack of perspective are things of the past. Today instantaneous international communications provide us with live information from around the world. And yet improved mediums of communication cannot in themselves neither create nor prevent a crisis. As we all know, an even bloodier war was fought twenty years after the 'war to end all wars' ended in 1918. The great powers redrew many borders in an attempt to create a long-term peace, but look at the results. Virtually every decision that followed the First World War eventually erupted into conflict and chaos. Germany and Poland, Iraq and Kuwait, the Balkans, much of Africa – the Versailles treaties laid the groundwork for crises all over the globe. The Balkans erupted yet again seventy-five years later. More recently, the American occupation of post-invasion Iraq is a case study in how looking only at the crisis in front of us can obscure our vision of an even larger one coming up behind it.

So what, then, do we learn? Every crisis has as many solutions as there are individuals who approach it. We produce custom-made solutions that suit our skills. (Unfortunately, the number of ways to do something wrong always exceeds the number of ways to do it right.) If a crisis is a moment at which questions cannot be easily answered we cannot expect generic patterns to guide us through.

Polish writer Stanislav Ezhi Letz observed that to reach the source we must swim against the current. With courage and experience we can come to accept each crisis and even seek them out in order to tackle them on our own terms. Instead of fearing these moments of maximum pressure and risk, we must accept them as inevitable and focus on improving our ability to predict them and to cope with their consequences.

Keeping a grip on the title

Getting a good night's sleep before the game had been essential, but now there was work to do. There were still thirteen pieces on the board, including queens, too much material for definitive endgame analysis. I had an extra pawn, but with such limited material Karpov had definite chances of a draw. There was still a lot of chess ahead. We spent the night investigating possible defensives and how to break them down. Before the game I gave my chances as 50–50: 50 per cent chance of a win, 50 per cent chance of a draw.

The best news was that I could play this position forever, manoeuvring around to provoke a mistake by my opponent. Black would be tied down on defence the entire time and Karpov knew it. The prospect of such prolonged torture took its toll; I could see it in his eyes when he walked on to the stage a few minutes after I did. His fatalistic expression told me that he had already lost the game psychologically, which boosted my confidence.

The manoeuvring began. I remember being very surprised when early on Karpov made a pawn push that my team and I had established was bad for black's defensive chances. His structure was now fixed, presenting me with clearer targets. Apparently Karpov and his team disagreed with us, or perhaps it was a psychological error. Karpov's move made the position more concrete, reducing the level of uncertainty. Sometimes the hardest thing to do in a pressure situation is allow the tension to persist. The temptation is to make a decision, any decision, even if it is an inferior choice. Convinced of the quality of our analysis, I took Karpov's significant deviation from it as a mistake, not a potential improvement, further increasing my confidence.

It took another ten moves of steady squeezing before I began to feel the win was in the bag. Karpov's pieces were pinned up against the wall and a little more manoeuvring would lead to decisive material gain. Later I heard that FIDE president Florencio Campomanes was busy calling a special meeting to decide how to handle the closing ceremony, which was scheduled to be held on the same day. But it still looked as if this game could last forever; what was to be done? Two crises were averted at once when someone ran into the meeting-room to announce 'Karpov resigned!'

It was without question the loudest and longest standing ovation I had ever received outside my native country. The theatre thundered as Spanish television cut from fútbol to broadcast the conclusion of the match. I had done what Karpov had failed to do in 1985. I had won the final game and drawn the match to retain my title. This time I would have three years to enjoy it.

I left the Seville stage and jumped into the arms of one of my team members, shouting 'Three years! I have three years!' Sadly, time does not stop at these moments, no matter how much we might wish it to. Those three years passed faster than I could have imagined until we were there again, Karpov and I, face to face in our fifth straight world championship match. Our epic duels have formed a part of the chess history that most of today's top players grew up watching.

By the end of that last match in 1990 – yet another narrow

win – our career scores against each other were very close. And yet in every encounter, in each match – Moscow, St Petersburg, Seville, Lyon – at each decisive moment, I had won. This means more to me than any statistic about wins and losses. It means I performed my best when it mattered most.

EPILOGUE

Your life is your preparation

What we make of the future is defined not only by our past but by how well we understand and make use of that past. I look back over the first half of my life as if at the globe my parents gave me as a child. In what we value, in where we find success and failure, our pasts create a map not only of where we have come from, but of where we are going. But the most wondrous thing about this map of the future is that it is not engraved in stone. With insight and effort we can shape it to our will.

The second half of my life will contain many new challenges. I have new goals, new people in my life, and I have left behind the only vocation I have ever known. And yet as foreign as it has seemed at first, my life in chess has left me well prepared for this new course. I ask myself, how can I be afraid of a mere KGB lieutenant-colonel after overcoming an Olympus of chess champions! Why should my nerves fail me in front of heads of state or CEOs of multinational corporations when I have spent my entire life on stage?

After a lifetime of preparation and self-examination I believe I have the tools I need to adapt to this new struggle. There are new strategies, new tactics, and I don't expect the transition always to be a smooth one. My personal map is full of grey areas and its outer borders are never entirely complete. Most importantly of all, I have learned not to fear those unknown territories.

My nine-year-old son Vadim is reaching the age where my own childhood memories are vivid. While his life will of course be very different from mine, I dearly hope to provide him the guidance I know my father would have continued to provide me. I have been fortunate to meet Daria, now my friend, supporter and wife. Above all, I'm infinitely grateful that the same person who guided me through my first career, my mother Klara, is again with me at the start of my second. Whenever I'm faced with a difficult path her words inspire me: 'If not you, who else?'

No more secrets

The purpose of this book is to inspire fellow explorers. We can all look at our own personal maps and cast off for unknown domains where we will encounter new challenges. We can accept that failure is a necessary part of success. The faith that led Magellan to attempt to circumnavigate the globe in 1519 is why we remember him. But few remember that he was not among the eighteen survivors who completed the journey.

Like any explorer we must first plan our route, our strategy. Then we must marshal our resources, allocating them carefully while obtaining what we need and discarding any excess. Once under way, we need to maintain a sharp tactical eye by never backing away from conflict unless we are certain it best suits our needs to do so. Remaining alert for dangers and opportunities should not be allowed to distract us from our course. We must be aware of changes in our environment at all times, looking for chances to make positive exchanges that will take advantage of new conditions.

Above all, we must be conscious of every decision we make. Not only in evaluating each future course of action but in looking back to analyse our past choices and the effectiveness of the process by which we made them.

Instead of making us weary, our explorations should energize us, suffusing us with new confidence and inspiration. Our senses are sharpened and unknown challenges soon become a sight more welcome than a familiar routine. New stimuli develop our intuition. We see the trends forming, the big picture and the details stay in focus at the same time, the dots become easier to connect. When a crisis comes our instincts serve as an early-warning system. If we are caught by surprise our reflexes give us the chance to take the offensive instead of playing defence.

Nearly twenty years ago I concluded a precocious auto-biography with the words 'Time after time, as I've outgrown another problem or defeated another opponent, I have seen that the main battles are yet to come ... My fight is open-ended.' Now

I know this fight wasn't only with the Soviet Sports Committee or FIDE or the Kremlin, but also with my own abilities and limitations. Our energies can be directed towards taking responsibility for our fates, towards creating change and making a difference. How success is measured is different for each of us. The first and most important step is realizing that the secret of success is inside.

ADDITIONAL EPILOGUE

A Strategy for Democracy

At the end of 2006, as this book was headed to the printer in several countries, the internal political chaos in Russia spilled out into the world's headlines. A British national, KGB agent defector and harsh critic of the Kremlin, Alexander Litvinenko, was assassinated with the rare radioactive substance polonium 210. The investigation into his death is currently taking place in at least three countries.

Litvinenko's murder came on the heels of the well-known investigative journalist Anna Politkovskaya – on Russian president Vladimir Putin's birthday, no less. The killings have turned a spotlight on what the West had assumed was the autocratic-but-stable Putin regime. Suddenly the foreign media is realizing what we in the Russian opposition have been saying for years – the Kremlin is ever closer to dictatorship than democracy and is not stable at all.

This interest has led to a corresponding increase in attention about my own role in the opposition movement, and to questions about how my former career as a chess champion has aided my mission. With that in mind, my publisher wondered if it wouldn't be appropriate to include some last-minute comments about how I have applied the lessons presented in this book to my political fight in Russia.

But this epilogue more than a topical convenience. While writing this book and preparing my business lectures, I have discovered a great deal about synthesizing these lessons and using them in practice. It is quite accurate to say that I have been learning from my own book, confirming the old adage that the best way to learn a topic is to teach it.

The most important, and most difficult, element on my new

political agenda was developing a strategy that would pump life into the anti-Putin forces. It was like sitting down to a chess game already in progress and discovering my side was close to checkmate in every variation. I could immediately draw a parallel to my first world championship match, the 1984–85 marathon against Anatoly Karpov. There I spent months a step away from total disaster, a situation that required an entirely new strategy, one based more on survival than triumph. I did it; I survived to fight another day, and the next time we met I was victorious.

The anti-Kremlin forces were in a similarly dire state in 2004. Unfortunately, in this game our opponents change the rules regularly and always to their advantage. But even in this unpredictable and unfair contest a good strategy gives us a fighting chance. I started with the fundamentals of planning: a thorough evaluation of the position and the determination of its most vital elements. Finding the outlines of the big picture came first. It was necessary to sort allies from enemies, an easy enough task in the black and white world of the chessboard but far more complex in the grey realm of politics.

Two things eventually became clear to me. First, that the continued existence of organized opposition to Putin's crackdown was in no way guaranteed. We needed to dig in to survive or risk being pushed completely off the board. There is no losing with grace or reaching a peaceful accord with such an opponent. When facing an authoritarian regime bent on total control, every day you endure sends out a message of hope: "we're still here." With no access to television and other state-controlled media, it was essential for us to find other ways to get out those vital words.

Second was the need to form a coalition. The opposition was in disarray, small political and non-governmental groups each with their own issues with the government. Despite the numerous causes and ideologies represented, I became convinced that we needed to unite, to find common cause again the repression. The one thing we all had in common was the knowledge that democracy was our only salvation. Liberals, Communists, human rights activists – we all believed, and continue to believe, that given a choice in a fair election the Russian people will reject Putin's attempt to turn our country back into a police state.

This move did not arise spontaneously. My first steps were as the co-founder and chairman of the *Committee 2008 – Free Choice* in January 2004. This was a coalition of like-minded liberals and members of the media – that is, not just politicians – dedicated to ensuring free and fair elections in 2008, when Putin's second, and constitutionally final, term of office ends. My work there convinced me that Russia's problems were too big to solve from any internal or ideological stance.

In the book I discuss the tendency to discover problems that cannot be solved from within the available framework, and here was such a problem. Negotiations were used to gain political capital that was traded for superficial concessions by the Kremlin, a process that only perpetuated the corrupt system and made us a part of it. To have a real impact it was necessary to focus on the core issue: you were either working with the Kremlin or dedicated to dismantling the regime.

Similar ideas about uniting were already in the air and they led to the formation of the *All-Russia Civil Congress* in December 2004, and I was elected co-chair. I had been observing the dissatisfaction of the activists on every side. They were tired of dancing to Putin's tune while watching their party leaders cut deals for paltry handouts. The Civil Congress was conceived as a unifying platform but it fell short when forces from both sides of the political spectrum were unable to leave behind the Yeltsin-era civil war mentality and to work alongside their traditional adversaries. It turned out that my greatest contribution would be helping to bridge this gap.

In March 2005 I retired from professional chess and could plan my next tactical manouevre on the political front. A major obstacle was that no one had access to televised media unless it was allowed by the ruling administration. Without this access the political grassroots were dying out all over the country. We needed to find a way to reach out beyond the Garden Ring, the wealthy center of Moscow. We needed an organization that would unify the opposition groups across the ideological divide as well as develop our nationwide network of activists. This new organiza-tion was the *United Civil Front* and it was under this banner I traveled Russia from Vladivostok to Kaliningrad to spread our message, to talk about why the countryside was so poor and the elites so rich. And, most importantly, to say that it was not too late to come together and fight for our civil liberties and democracy, because only those things would improve the deteriorating standard of living.

This mixing of opposition groups has also had several

positive side-effects. The leftists and those still mourning the Soviet Union have come to recognize the importance of liberal democracy and political freedom. The liberals have learned to accept the need for the social programs touted by the left. Unity has not only stiffened the opposition to the Putin government, but it has also clarified and advanced the specific goals of our member groups.

Each of these entities contributed to my education. I was learning quickly and we were making progress, but we still needed to reach a larger audience both inside and outside of Russia. It was time to go on the offensive. The Group of Eight (seven by my count!) held a summit in St. Petersburg in the summer of 2006 when the leaders and media of the free world would be in Russia. It provided a golden opportunity to unite and also to get our message out.

We organized a convention in Moscow, an international conference that brought activists from all over Russia to share ideas and support. We also invited the international media and speakers from all over the world who were not afraid to speak strongly for democracy in the shadow of the Kremlin. My All-Russia Civil Congress co-chairs and I wrote countless letters of invitation, calling in favors and twisting arms where necessary. Eventually many prominent figures contributed statements of support, although few G-8 administrations had the courage to openly endorse us. We titled our event *The Other Russia Conference*, so named to tell the world that the stable, democratic Russia Putin presented was not reality.

We knew we had achieved significant progress when the administration made efforts to harass us at every turn. (If this is truly a measure of success I should be proud that the humble UCF offices were raided by security forces this month, a few days prior to our December 16th march in Moscow.) The Other Russia movement has united the Russian opposition and although our situation is still precarious we have succeeded in forcibly promoting ourselves into an important piece on the political chessboard.

The development of the Russian opposition has occurred in parallel with my own evolution as a political thinker. The United Civil Front added political clout to the concept of the All-Russia Civil Congress. It all finally came together, literally and figuratively, in The Other Russia.

As unfavorable as our position may still be, my evaluation of our opponents' forces discovered that they are not without their own weaknesses. Unlike the old Soviet regime, this ruling elite has a great deal at stake outside of Russia. Their fortunes are in banks, stock markets, real estate, and football teams, predominantly foreign. This means they are vulnerable to external pressure. They literally cannot afford the cutting of ties that would come with open hostility between an increasingly dictatorial Russia and the West.

So far, however, it has been difficult to convince the so-called leaders of the free world and the free press to bring such pressure to bear. Putin uses Russia's energy wealth as a cudgel and Europe's leaders meekly fall into line. Thus the third element of my strategy has been to expose this hypocrisy in as many editorial pages as I can reach.

This plan is not so short-sighted as to not keep in mind the potential consequences. It is essential to maintain our coalition because if the increasingly shaky Putin regime collapses due to internal conflict it could lead to total chaos. It is worth remembering that just 15 years ago the mighty Soviet regime disintegrated, much to the surprise of Western intelligence agencies. We have to always look ahead enough moves to be well prepared, even for victory!

December 2006

GLOSSARY

This glossary is intended as a concise guide to some of the chess terminology used in the text. Many of the terms represent concepts explained in detail in the book.

Below is a chess diagram of the starting position. The chessboard has 64 squares. Each player begins with eight pieces and eight pawns.

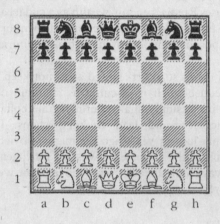

The coordinates on the edge of the board are the basis of algebraic chess notation, the symbolic language for transcribing the moves of a game. For example, '1.e4' represents a pawn moving to the e4 square on the first move. The opening moves '1.e4 e5 2.Bc4' puts a white pawn on e4, then a black pawn on e5, and then a white bishop on c4. In similar fashion games have been preserved for hundreds of years. Modern computer databases contain millions of games.

• Blitz chess – Games with very little time given to each player, usually five minutes.
• Center – The four central squares of the chessboard (d4, e4, d5, e5 in algebraic notation.) Controlling the center is one of the primary strategic goals. The player with control of the middle of the board has advantage in piece mobility and therefore, attacking potential. The positional value of various squares typically correlates to their proximity to the center.

• Check – When a player's king is under attack. The player in check must do one of three things: move the king, capture the attacking piece, or interpose a piece to block the line of attack.

• Checkmate – A position in which the king cannot avoid capture. (The king is never actually captured.) The decisive end of the game.

• Chess clock – A dual-action timepiece that records the amount of time each player has remaining. A player makes his move and presses the clock. This stops his clock's movement and simultaneously starts his opponent's clock. Clock time is measured for the entire game, not per move. A player loses when his time expires.

• Classical chess – Games with a large amount of clock time for each player. At least 90 minutes, often over two hours.

• Color – The pieces are referred to as white or black regardless of the actual color of the chessmen. White always moves first, which confers a substantial advantage at the professional level.

• Combination – A forcing sequence of moves, often sacrificial, with a specific goal.

• Draw – The end of a game without a decisive result. Usually this occurs by offer and acceptance between the players. It can also come about by rule in the cases of stalemate, lack of progress (50 move rule), or threefold repetition of the same position. In the traditional scoring system a draw is worth half a point for each player.

• Endgame – The final phase of the game, coming after the middlegame. Most of the pieces have been exchanged and play becomes technical instead of strategic.

• FIDE – The international chess federation, known by its French acronym. (Fédération Internationale des Échecs)

• Gambit – An opening in which one side offers to give up material in exchange for compensation in the form of positional advantage.

• Game – A single encounter between two players.

• Grandmaster – A player possessing the highest international title. With rare exceptions the title is awarded to a player who has achieved three qualifying tournament results and has reached a minimum 2500 rating.

• Initiative – The ability to generate threats against your opponent's position. The player with the initiative controls the course of the game through his ability to make more effective threats.

• Patch – A series of games between two players.

• Material – All of the pieces and pawns on the board, minus the kings, which never leave the board. A material advantage means having the greater total value of pieces.

• Middlegame – The phase of the game that follows the opening and precedes the endgame. The demarcation is not exact or universally agreed on. At a minimum, piece development has been completed and complex strategic and tactical play is still possible.

• Opening – The initial phase of the game. The opening moves are often composed of specific memorized sequences called openings. The opening is generally considered over when the pieces are no longer on their original squares and original play has begun.

• Pawn – The chessman of lowest value due to its limited mobility. Each side starts with eight pawns. Pawns are not usually referred to as pieces, a term used for the rest of the army. Pawns have the unique ability to promote into a piece – almost always a queen – when they reach the other side of the board.

• Piece values – The relative power of the chess pieces is typically measured by their value compared to a number of pawns. Knights and bishops are worth three pawns (or bishops a fraction more), rooks five pawns, the queen nine pawns.

• Rapid chess – Games with a short amount of clock time for each player, between blitz chess and classical chess. Typically around 30 minutes.

• Rating (or Elo rating) – A numerical representation of a player's performance based on the result of each game. The rating system developed by the American physics professor Arpad Elo was adopted by FIDE in 1970. Grandmasters are typically rated 2500–2800 plus. A strong amateur tournament player might be rated 1800. An adult beginner could be expected to reach a 1200 rating in a few months of tournament play. A range of 200 points is considered a class.

• Sacrifice – Giving up material for positional or tactical advantage. Typically a sacrifice has a specific tactical goal, such as creating attacking chances against the opponent's king.

• Space – An element of a chess position represented by greater piece mobility and the number of squares controlled. A player with an advantage in space can more freely manoeuvre his pieces.

• Tactics – The means of effecting a strategic plan. Every move in a chess game nas some tactical components. Tactics require calculation and are the foundation of combinations.

• Time control – The amount of clock time given to the players. This is decided by rules of the tournament and varies widely, from blitz games that last ten minutes to classical games that can last seven hours.

• Win – A win is worth one point and occurs when there is a checkmate or when one player resigns. Very few professional games end in checkmate as players resign as soon as loss appears inevitable.